Copyright & Registration Essentials for Visual Artists

Copyright & **Registration**
Essentials for Visual Artists

Jennifer L. Unruh

Passeri • New York

Printed in the United States of America
First Edition

Passeri · PasseriBooks.com

Library of Congress Control Number: 2021903717

ISBN: 978-1-7367303-0-0

CONTENTS

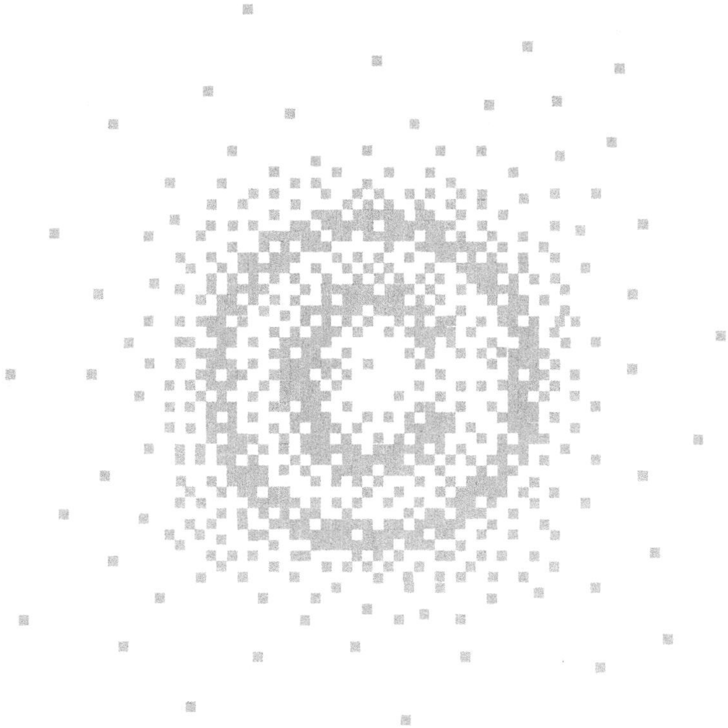

INTRODUCTION

Art has existed since humankind's earliest expressions, at least since the first ancient human stenciled the outline of a hand on a cave wall. Visual art arises from society and culture, as a product of the environment and the individual artist. It is a natural confluence that still exists in contemporary art practice.

Over time the concept of property ownership expanded. It came to be associated not only with physical objects, but with creative endeavor as an integral element of an object. For visual art, the development of copyrights, a form of property rights, is a recognition of the value in creating something new and original. In most countries of the world today, the creator of a work of visual art owns a copyright in the work that is the product of his, her, or their creativity.

Copyrights are important for contemporary artists as a means to control how their art is perceived and used. Copyrights are, in essence, the legal ability to determine how or whether a work is reproduced, how it is displayed in some instances, and whether new works based on the original can be made. These rights may seem to be fundamentally attached to the artist, but they are actually a function of copyright law. These rights are valuable instruments for contemporary artists, especially in connection with online uses of artworks, promotional activities, publishing, and licensing.

In a visually intense society, the management of an artist's copyrights is a necessary task. It is part of the practical side of an artist's career. Traditionally, a work of art is publically viewed in an exhibition space, a gallery or a museum, or through the medium of physical publications. Now, images of an artwork are easily and broadly disseminated instantaneously. Artists must be more vigilant to protect their artworks from unauthorized copying and other misuses. Registering a copyright with the U.S. Copyright Office can be an important tool for this purpose and it establishes a public record of the artwork in association with the artist that created it.

•

Copyright and Registration Essentials for Artists represents a slice of my experience working with and on behalf of artists, including the practical (legal) work of copyright management and my own personal interest in art. I have seen the gaps between the worlds of art and law, and observed significant points overlooked by one side or the other.

In a legal context, copyrights are typically discussed in technical language. Laws and regulations that govern copyrights and registrations can seem alternately obtuse or rigorous. The technical jargon tends to be repeated verbatim rather than explained in a context that is specific to art.

For artists, the legal perspective can contradict the reality of contemporary art practice. Conversely, when copyrights are discussed with *art words*, the real requirements of the copyright law, including those of the registration process, can be misperceived. Sometimes the law is not what we want it to be or what should be, but it is important to know the facts of it and its limitations. A misperception about the scope of a particular copyright for instance, can lead to an underestimation of the rights that one may be entitled to.

With these issues in mind, a goal of this book is to bridge the gap in terminology and the facts about copyrights, to enable artists to take advantage of the copyright registration system on their own and in a way that will benefit their practice the most. As a means to do this, technical legal terminology is broken down to the extent that it is possible, but with an effort towards retaining the most essential meaning. The practical target is to make both copyright concepts and the process of registration clearer and by extension, to encourage artists to register the copyrights in their artworks.

As you will learn, copyright registration requires submitting a copy of the work to the U.S. Copyright Office, and that copy becomes part of a public record of the registration. Copies of works submitted over time have become the basis of the Library of Congress' collection. I trace my interest in copyrights to a visit to the Library of Congress' Prints & Photographs Division's archives in Washington D.C. A year or two after completing my graduate studies in art in New York I assisted another artist with a photography research project that involved searching for certain types of images within the collection.

The Prints & Photographs division's reading room houses thousands of photographs, representing printed images that were acquired as a part of the copyright registration process and archived by the Library of Congress. Not many images had been digitized at that time. The only means of concisely searching for a specific subject was through a painstaking textual computerized search at on-sight workstations. It was also possible then to browse through the physical files of photographic prints for a serendipitous approach.

Looking through the file cabinets, I ran across prints of all sorts of random images, and I realized how the collection deeply represented American culture, history and the practice of image making—but without a filter. The subject of the photographic prints ranged from the extraordinary to the absolutely mundane. Each was submitted there as a part of the registration process.

At the time, I was also struck by a sense of incompleteness. I thought that if more photographs and other artwork were registered, the collection could more fully record our contemporary world and its art and artists. As a public record there is the potential for it to be a fairer history of art than the one that exists in books, museums, and other selected and curated sources. The Library of Congress collection can be one that is created even more democratically, by the contributions of the artists that made the work. It is not just a record of the privileged or conventionally successful artist. The public record and the archive can include artwork by any artist, at any point in their career. But, to create this fuller historical record, more artists would have to register their works and expand the public record. Along with sharing practical information, this is part of my interest in creating this book. I hope that it will encourage you to take that step to adding your work to the public record, and in turn, the particular benefits of registering your copyright will be available to you.

•

Registering a copyright in a work of visual art with the U.S. Copyright Office is a central subject of *Copyright & Registration Essentials for Visual Artists*. Registration is an aspect of copyright management. With a basic understanding of copyrights and a guide to the registration process, you can register your own copyright. This book approaches the material from the perspective of art practice and identifies some of the unique considerations that can arise when registering a copyright in a work of contemporary art.

The material was designed for visual artists and other individuals, anywhere in the world, who are interested in registering the copyright in their artwork in the United States of America. The first chapter discusses the benefits of registration and Chapter 2 introduces essential copyright concepts, particularly as they relate to contemporary visual artwork. The central section of the book, Chapter 4, contains detailed steps for completing each of the most common types of copyright registration applications for visual art. Chapter 5 discusses technical issues and terminology that may arise in connection with registration. Chapter 5 can be read independently or it can be used as a reference for a registration application.

The information in this book is geared primarily towards practicing artists, but the guide can be used by anyone who seeks to register a work of art that they have created, whether it is a painting, a drawing, a sculptural work, a photograph, or some other 2-D or 3-D work. Special considerations for some non-traditional forms of art are also discussed.

Chapter 1 begins by considering the decision to register the copyright in a particular work. Copyrights are an important tool for protecting the right to decide how or if your artwork can be shared or experienced by others. Managing your copyrights is important for licensing–such as authorizing copies or other uses of your work by others, including for publication purposes. Registering the copyright of some works in advance of distribution can be a good art business practice. In the United States, registering a copyright is also an indirect supplement to an artist's distinct legal right to be identified as the creator of an artwork—the process of registration establishes a public record of the artwork and the associated artist.

•

Copyright & Registration Essentials for Visual Artists is meant to be more than practical information. Because contemporary art is so diverse and complex, art that challenges the boundaries of copyrightability, and works that require a thoughtful contextualization to fit into the copyright box, are inevitable. Copyright law is immense and it is impossible to cover all the aspects in a useable and readable form, but this book is intended to elucidate a particular issue, the formal registration of a copyright in a work of visual art. Registration is, I believe, a beneficial tool for artists in today's world, one that is often overlooked or just misunderstood. By becoming engaged with managing and registering your own copyrights, perhaps you will be encouraged to explore your legal rights as an artist further and, maybe, efforts to expand the rights of artists in the United States will be encouraged to grow as well.

CHAPTER ONE

BENEFITS OF REGISTRATION

There is a distinction between *having* a copyright and *registering* the copyright in your artwork. When you have made a work of art, you have a copyright in your original work. You are the owner of the copyright. In the United States, the right arises automatically when the qualifying original work is completed.

On the other hand, the *registration* of a copyright results in an official record that identifies the work and its creator. Registration is a process of the U.S. Copyright Office, a subdivision of the Library of Congress. Records of registered works are maintained by the Copyright Office. Registration is sometimes required, such as in the event of certain lawsuits, but it is generally optional. It can be useful to have a preexisting registered copyright when, for instance, an unauthorized copy has been made of the pertinent artwork.

In practical terms, registering a copyright involves completing an application form, paying a fee, and sending a copy of the artwork to the U.S. Copyright Office.

Copyrights do not attach to a person in a general way, like personal rights do. Rather, a copyright is associated with an individual work, such as single artwork. The artist that created the original work of art is usually the owner of the copyright in that specific work. As the copyright owner, the artist can exercise the rights attached to the work. For example, the artist has the right to control whether or not a reproduction (a copy) of the work can be made.

When a registration application is granted, the Copyright Office issues a certificate of registration to the copyright owner. A certificate of registration for the copyright in a work of visual art typically shows the title of the specific work of visual art, the name of the author (artist) of the work, along with other information that is submitted with a registration application. A registration number associated with the work is assigned by the U.S. Copyright Office and printed on the certificate that is issued. For works of visual art, the copyright registration number begins with *VA*.

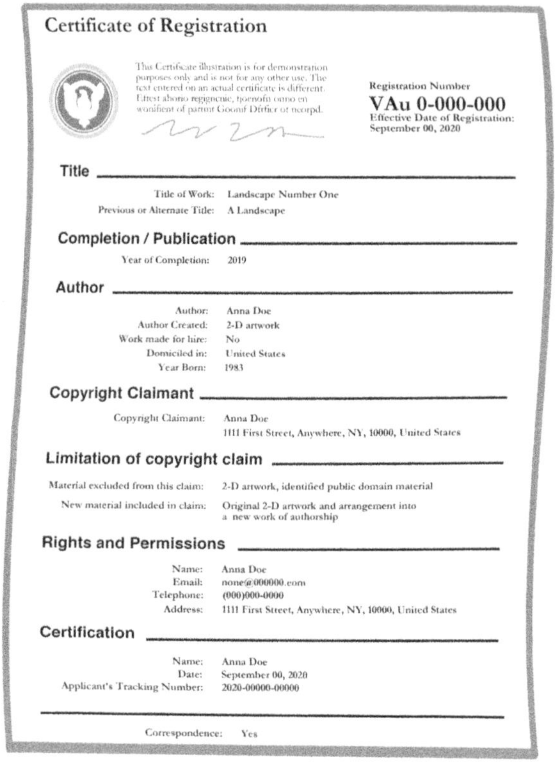

Certificate of Registration

This Certificate illustration is for demonstration purposes only and is not for any other use. The text entered on an actual certificate is different. Ettest ahorio regignenie, tjoenofn onno en wonifient of partnt Goonf Dfrfier ot neorpd.

Registration Number
VAu 0-000-000
Effective Date of Registration:
September 00, 2020

Title

Title of Work: Landscape Number One
Previous or Alternate Title: A Landscape

Completion / Publication

Year of Completion: 2019

Author

Author: Anna Doe
Author Created: 2-D artwork
Work made for hire: No
Domiciled in: United States
Year Born: 1983

Copyright Claimant

Copyright Claimant: Anna Doe
1111 First Street, Anywhere, NY, 10000, United States

Limitation of copyright claim

Material excluded from this claim: 2-D artwork, identified public domain material
New material included in claim: Original 2-D artwork and arrangement into a new work of authorship

Rights and Permissions

Name: Anna Doe
Email: none@000000.com
Telephone: (000)000-0000
Address: 1111 First Street, Anywhere, NY, 10000, United States

Certification

Name: Anna Doe
Date: September 00, 2020
Applicant's Tracking Number: 2020-00000-00000

Correspondence: Yes

When an application for a registration is submitted, it is made for the copyright in a specific individual work. In some cases it is possible to register several works with one application and each of those works will retain its individual copyright status. (Choosing an application form that fits your artwork and situation is covered in Chapter 3).

In the past, registration was required to establish a copyright. That is no longer the case in the United States—you are not required to register just to have and use the rights—but there are certain benefits and advantages for doing so. Registering the copyright can be an important decision for visual artists, especially when a specific artwork may be publically displayed, published, or accessible online.

•

There are at least two main reasons for registering the copyright in a work of art. One is to create a public record of the work and the second relates to the basis copyrights in general, the right to control if, when and how images of your work are reproduced, displayed, or distributed. The later reason for registering can be important for discouraging, preventing, stopping, or when seeking compensation for an improper infringement of the copyright.

Infringement

A violation of a copyright is an *infringement*—the work has been copied, reproduced, or distributed without permission. The owner of the copyright—perhaps the artist of an original work—can demand that the infringement stop. In serious cases, a copyright owner may seek compensation or another remedy for an infringement.

Registration on its own cannot stop an infringement from happening, but it gives weight to a complaint of infringement. An infringement could be, for example, an unauthorized copy posted online, or another situation were the artwork was reproduced without permission. Registration can be an important consideration when the artwork is to be distributed publically, such as in a publication, an unprotected online context, or if the work has features that may make it vulnerable to copying.

There are a number of ways that an artist can prevent, stop, or remedy an infringement. This could be a formal legal action, a lawsuit for infringement. But stopping infringement can often be accomplished by less drastic measures–such as by filing a complaint with an internet service provider (referred to as a takedown notice) when an unauthorized copy of your work has been put on a website without your permission. Or, alternatively, by directly notifying the infringer that you are the owner of the copyright and that they must stop the unauthorized use. These less intensive approaches often resolve the problem.

Sometimes when infringement disputes cannot be otherwise resolved, a lawsuit may be initiated by the copyright owner. It is a serious step. This process is relatively not so common for artists, but in that event, the copyright of the work *must* be registered before a lawsuit is filed. Processing a registration typically takes at least a few months. If the copyright of an infringed work is already registered, a legal action can begin promptly, with the aim of resolving the infringement sooner.

Early registration of copyrights in artworks that are likely to be targets of unauthorized copying may be a prudent decision. Registration before a later infringement has occurred has an important advantage. Statutory damages, a monetary award specified in the Copyright Law, may be available to the copyright owner. Aside from the potential monetary benefit to the copyright holder in a lawsuit, an infringer may be more likely to comply with a request to stop the unauthorized use when there is a clearer risk of financial loss to them. Registration will not necessarily prevent infringements from being committed in the first place, but when it happens, there may be stronger options for enforcing your rights.

History and The Public Record

Copyright registration may also be desirable in the context of an artist's business or career history. Registration of a copyright creates a permanent public record of that particular work of art. The record created by the registration system maintains essential facts of the artwork itself, such as the year it was made and the identity of the artist who made it.

In my view, the historical record established by registering a copyright in a work of visual art is a significant benefit to artists and their legacies. The registration process memorializes the existence of the work and the identity of those who created it. In the case of collective or joint works, registration can identify the contributions of each artist involved. If there is a dispute later, it can potentially serve as a reference to clarify those facts.

For some artists, copyright registration is a means of preserving the existence of their works in the public record. Registration of a work of visual art requires a submission of a copy of the work. The record created by registration, and the copy of the work submitted, are maintained by the U.S. Copyright Office. The Library of Congress also maintains a permanent archive of various types of works. The diverse Library of Congress collection reflects the social and cultural history of this country. Copies of works may be added to the archive after their copyright terms expire and those images are then also preserved for future generations.

The U.S. Copyright office has been updating its processes to more modern technology. As you will learn in Chapter 3, in most registration cases the required submission of a copy of the artwork can be accomplished by uploading a digital file of the work. With the ongoing movement into a fuller digital environment, it is likely the archives will become quite a bit more substantial in size, but also more inclusive in scope and media.

At the present time, images of contemporary copyrighted work are not displayed in the Copyright Office's online database. Images of works still within their copyright terms are not displayed online in any case without permission of the owner.

The existence of a public record can also minimize the possibility of the artwork becoming an *orphan work*. An artwork becomes an orphan work when it has somehow become disassociated from the artist's name. In other words, the artist of the work has become unknown. A copyright registration is a *de facto* record of the work and the artist's identity, lessening the possibility of a future orphan work.

Economics of Selective Registration

Another factor to consider is the balance of the cost of registration with your situation and your expectations. For most artists it is not financially feasible to register every single artwork that they have produced. Registering a large number of works can get expensive, but there are some options in the process that can make it more cost effective.

Some works may qualify for a group registration—several related works are registered on one special application. For qualifying works, group applications are often the most economical choice and results in a lower registration cost per artwork. For comparison, registration fees at the time of publication are listed in Appendix B.

Other choices can keep the expenses as low as possible. For example, by using the online application system rather than the printed paper forms, which have a higher fee, and by using the group registration applications. It is also important to submit an error free application, a correct fee, and a proper deposit (the submitted copy of the artwork) to avoid any penalties. Chapter 3 will help you select an application from those that are available for visual art works.

While prudent choices can help keep registration costs lower, fees can still add up quickly and it is not financially feasible for most artists to register every thing they make. A decision about which work to select for registration may need to be made.

When infringement is the main concern, one method for narrowing down the number of works to a manageable selection is to consider which pieces are most likely to be copied without permission. You can ask yourself how likely the risk of infringement is for this particular artwork. The answer could be based upon the potential appeal of a particular image or how easily it might be accessed. For instance, works posted on social media or upon an artist's website are vulnerable to being copied by downloading, sharing, and by screenshots. A work that is not going to be publically displayed, or which may be shown in a physical exhibit only, would tend to be at a lesser risk of unauthorized copying. Making this kind of assessment is obviously not a guarantee of protection from infringers, but it is a method for selective registration when funds are limited, as they are for most artists.

Whether the reason for registering is to create a public record, or because of infringement concerns, or for personal reasons, the process is the same. To complete a registration application accurately, it helps to have an understanding of basic copyright concepts. The next section covers the essentials with an emphasis on how these concepts relate to visual art and artists.

CHAPTER TWO

ESSENTIAL COPYRIGHT CONCEPTS

A copyright is a legal right to control the reproduction of a certain work, such as a specific work of visual art. Copyrights in the United States include the right of reproduction, distribution, public display of copies, the right to create derivative works from the original, and the right to perform certain types of works publically. These are known as the exclusive rights or the bundle of rights. Each of the rights is distinctive, and collectively they are known as copyrights.

The copyright holder—the owner of the copyright—decides if the work can be reproduced and how copies are treated. In other words, the copyright owner possesses the exclusive rights.

When an artist makes an original work of art, generally, that artist is the owner of the copyright in that particular work. The copyright in the original work ensures that the artist has authority to permit or restrict the making of copies of the original creation.

When you create an original painting or photograph or sculpture for example, you have the right to make your own copies and to make your own derivative works, i.e., new versions or adaptations, and you have the right to publish and distribute your work. At the same time, you have the right to prevent or permit someone else from making copies, creating derivative works, or publishing images or copies of your work. There are nuances and some limitations to these rights, which are discussed further in the chapter, but in essence, the original creator typically controls all forms of reproduction of the original work.

In the United States, a copyright is created automatically when a qualifying work is created. When an original work is made by a person, a copyright comes into existence. The copyright automatically exists when the work is physically created and complete.

> ...To promote the Progress of Science and useful Arts, by securing for limited Times to Authors and Inventors the exclusive Right to their respective Writings and Discoveries...
>
> **United States Constitution**
> Article 1, Section 8

Most countries in the world have copyrights laws in some form. In the United States the fundamental basis for the existence of copyrights is contained in the text of the Constitution, which granted Congress the power to establish certain rights for creators. Congress created the first U.S. copyright law in 1790. The current version in effect is primarily based upon the Copyright Act of 1976 (enacted in 1978) and it has been modified periodically since then.

The Copyright Law defines what categories of works are eligible for copyright protection, such as works of visual art. It specifies the type of rights that are created, identifies exceptions to the rights, sets the duration of time for copyright protection, and it also includes some of the basic rules for registering a copyright.

The registration of copyrights is administered by the U.S. Copyright Office, a division of the Library of Congress. The Copyright Office plays an active role in the ongoing modifications to the Copyright Law, for instance, by developing proposals for regulations that reflect the evolution of technology and other factors that affect rights.

Physical versus Intellectual Property

Copyrights fall under a branch of law known as intellectual property. Just as the phrase suggests, copyrights are a non-physical form of property ownership. For this reason, an actual work of art and its copyright are two distinct entities—there are two different forms of property involved. In a legal context, the copyright is completely separate from the physical work and each of the exclusive rights (reproduction, public display, derivative works, etc.) are distinct from each other.

The artwork, in this context, is a physical object that can be possessed or owned—a physical property. The copyrights are a legally created property right—an intellectual property. The physical artwork and the copyright are fully separable from each other and can be owned by different persons.

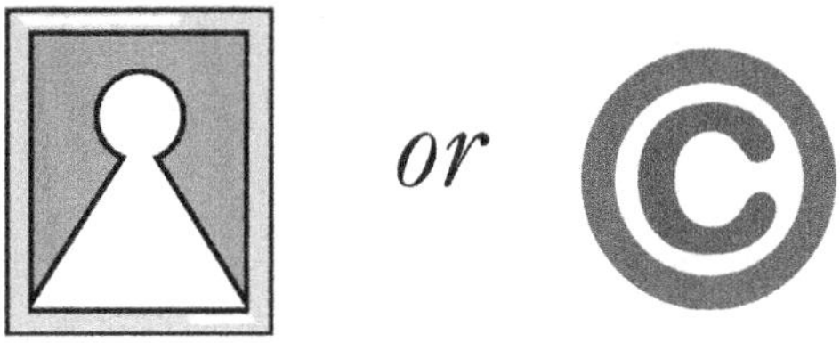

Copyrights are legally distinct from the object that they arise from, but in some cases, there may be the appearance of an overlap. For instance, a buyer who purchases a contemporary photographic print does not have the right to copy or publish it without specific permission from the creator. Buying a physical work of art, or receiving a gift of a physical work, does not transfer any copyright to the receiver or buyer, unless copyrights were expressly made to be a part of the purchase or gift.

Rights and Licenses

A creator of an original work can authorize copies or the publication of the original work. This is referred to as licensing or sometimes it is simply called "permissions" or "rights."

When an artist independently makes a work of art, and the work of art is original—meaning that it is not a copy of something else and it is the product of the artist's creativity—the artist owns the copyright in that work. There is a narrow exception known as "work made for hire" that is discussed in the *Authorship & Ownership* section later in this chapter.

Normally, when a physical artwork is sold, the copyrights are not sold or transferred along with it. Unless they are expressly transferred by the original artist, usually in written document like a contract, the copyrights are typically retained by the artist. The artist continues to hold the power of the rights.

Significantly, the retention of the copyrights also means that the artist has the continuing right to freely reproduce the work, to sell copies, and make new versions based on the original—even if the physical artwork is no longer owned by the artist. The default retention of copyrights is obviously important for artists.

A copyright can be sold, in whole or in part. Or, individual rights can be licensed—rented or loaned for free or for compensation—for a limited purpose or quantity, or for a set period of time. When a copyright owner authorizes someone else to use the rights, it should be done in writing, like a contract or other such agreement. This type of document would specifically describes the right or rights that are being transferred, whether the transaction is a sale or a license, and the type of license involved.

One example of a license is where an artist authorizes a publisher to reproduce an image of an artwork in a book or magazine article. This is not a sale of the copyright. A license is usually for a set limited use, for a specific number of reproductions or for a set period of time, and in most cases like this it should be a *non-exclusive* license. A non-exclusive license in one where the owner-artist typically continues to have the right to create copies, make derivative works, grant other licenses, and such. A non-exclusive licenses does not usually interfere with the artist's own use of the copyright.

The Exclusive Rights

A copyright means that you and only you have the "exclusive" legal right to "do and to authorize" certain uses of your original work, by law. Each of these rights is individual and distinct. Collectively they are known as the exclusive rights of copyright, and they can be used together or separately.

- **Reproduction** – to make copies of the work.
- **Distribution** – to disseminate copies of the work to the public by sales or other transfers, or by rental, lease, or lending.
- **Derivative works** – to create new versions or adaptations based upon the preexisting original work.
- **Display** – to show a copy of the work publically. The display can be direct or indirect, or through a device or process.
- **Public performance** – to perform the work (when applicable) and determine whether others can publically perform the work.

Together these distinct means of controlling forms of reproduction are referred to as the *bundle of rights*. As the owner of a copyright, you can exercise and enforce these rights for a specific work.

As you can see, each of the exclusive rights relates to some form of copying or copying process, like reproduction (duplication), or the making of a derivative work, such as a drawing made from a photograph. A display of a copy is also a form of reproduction of the work, like the transmission of a broadcast image or an online posting of an image of the work. In essence, the individual rights all concern some form of reproduction of the original work and the copyright owner's right to control the use of the protected creation.

Each of the exclusive rights includes its inverse. For instance, the copyright owner has the right to display copies of the work publically, but also has the right to keep the copies private. Or, the copyright owner has the sole right to create derivative works of the original, but can also prevent others from making derivative works of the original. Only the copyright owner can authorize others to use the rights, to make copies, derivatives, distribute, display or perform the work.

The exclusive rights of copyright owners are defined within the U.S. Copyright Law as follows:

... [T]he owner of copyright under this title has the exclusive rights to do and to authorize any of the following:

(1) to **reproduce** the copyrighted work in copies or phonorecords;

(2) to prepare **derivative works** based upon the copyrighted work;

(3) to **distribute** copies or phonorecords of the copyrighted work to the public by sale or other transfer of ownership, or by rental, lease, or lending;

(4) in the case of literary, musical, dramatic, and choreographic works, pantomimes, and motion pictures and other audiovisual works, to **perform** the copyrighted work publicly;

(5) in the case of literary, musical, dramatic, and choreographic works, pantomimes, and pictorial, graphic, or sculptural works, including the individual images of a motion picture or other audiovisual work, to **display** the copyrighted work publicly; and

(6) in the case of sound recordings, to perform the copyrighted work publicly by means of a digital audio **transmission**.

(U.S. Copyright Law, 17 U.S.C. § 106, excerpt)

Infringement & Fair Use

Infringement is an act of using a copyright protected work without the permission of the copyright owner. If a copy of your work is made without your authorization, that is said to be an *infringement* of the copyright. An infringement can involve any one of the six exclusive rights of copyright ownership listed above.

The owner of the copyright can demand a stop to the unauthorized use. The owner may send a "cease and desist" letter to the infringer. For web-based infringements, a copyright owner may file a formal demand (known as a DMCA takedown notice) with the internet service provider that is hosting the infringing web page. In the most serious infringement situations, the copyright owner could sue the infringer and seek compensation for the unauthorized use of the copyright protected work.

There is an important exception to infringement, a principle referred to as fair-use. Fair-use of a copyright protected work is considered to be a form of free-speech. For example, a news article critiquing an art exhibition might show photographic images of the artwork hanging on the gallery walls. A different type of fair-use is a parody or some other such commentary on the original work. Some other transformational uses of a copyrighted work *might* be considered to be fair-use.

Because fair-use is considered to be an exception to infringement, the doctrine presupposes that an infringement has occurred. To assert fair-use as a defense to an accusation of infringement, there is—or there is alleged to be—a legally accepted basis for the use of the copyright protected material. In essence, a person asserting fair-use as a defense is tacitly admitting an infringement of the copyright involved.

There is no bright line test for the existence of a fair-use. Whether fair-use exists in a particular circumstance is typically decided by a court or by other authorities on a case-by-case basis. There are a number of factors that are considered in each case, depending upon the circumstances.

There can be a fine line between a wrongful infringement and fair-use in some cases. It's not a straightforward position that can be taken—to be for or against fair-use as a general approach. Artists can easily find themselves on both sides of the fair-use versus infringement dilemma. They want to protect their own work from copying, but they may also compose works out of source material for which the rights are owned by someone else.

Infringement and fair-use can be complex in relationship to art traditions and the artistic process. The perspectives of art and law can conflict. Much of the history of art reflects the practice of artists copying the work of other artists and building upon it. In this way art progresses or advances over time with the modifications of generations of artists. The fundamental premise of copyrights can sometimes conflict with this tradition by inserting the notion of property rights upon the products of creativity.

Regardless of how artists may perceive their process, when a work is copyright protected, an unauthorized copy is often an infringement of that copyright. In any case where copyright material has been used without permission, there is the possibility that the use is an infringement that carries the potential for liability. This risk exists so long as the copyright term has not expired.

Duration of Copyright Protection

Copyrights are limited by time. The period of copyright protection is fairly substantial, reaching beyond the original artist's lifetime. The term of copyright for a work of visual art by a single artist generally lasts for the life of the artist plus an additional 70 years after the death of the artist.

For the purpose of calculating the copyright expiration of most post-1978 works, it does not matter when the work was made—the expiration is calculated from the year of the artist's death (usually by adding 70 years).

Copyright terms for joint or collaborative works are typically calculated from the death of the last surviving artist. There are some exceptions and different terms, for example, for pseudonymous works (where an artist does not use his or her real name).

Also, because different rules were in place at the time, for works that predate 1978, the copyright term may be different or expired, depending on a number of factors, such as whether the work was registered or not, whether it was published, and if it complied with a number of formalities that were existing at the pertinent time. The patchwork of legacy rules for pre-1978 works can make calculating a copyright term challenging. The following chart shows the current term of years for copyright protection.

Term of Copyright Protection for Works of Visual Art

Works created on or after January 1, 1978

Authorship Status	Term of Copyright	Other Factors
An original work made by 1 artist (author)	Life of the artist plus 70 years	
Joint work (made by 2 or more persons)	Life of the artist plus 70 years after the death of the last surviving artist	
Anonymous work (a work without an attribution to a named artist or author)	If published, 95 years from the year of first publication, *OR* if not published, 120 years from the year the work was created, whichever term is *shortest*	If the identity of the artist is revealed in a registration record before the copyright expires, then the usual term, life of the artist + 70 years, applies
Pseudonymous work (a work attributed to a pseudonym of the author or artist)	If published, 95 years from the year of first publication, *OR* if not published, 120 years from the year the work was created, whichever term is *shortest*	If the identity of the artist is revealed in a registration record before the copyright expires, then the usual term, life of the artist + 70 years, applies
Works made for hire	If published, 95 years from the year of first publication, *OR* if not published, 120 years from the year the work was created, whichever term is *shortest*	

After the copyright term expires, the work becomes part of the public domain. When a work is in the public domain due to the expiration of its copyright, anyone can make copies and other reproductions, derivative works based upon it, and public displays of copies can be done without restriction.

Copyrightability

To have a copyright, a work must be eligible for copyright protection in the first instance. Whether a work can qualify for copyright protection is sometimes referred to as *copyrightability*. Copyrights are created by law and the specific criteria for determining what works are eligible for protection is contained in the written law. The text of the Copyright Law identifies what types of works are covered.

Understanding the elements that make a work eligible for copyright protection may help you later in the process of registering your claim. This section is also intended to reflect a simplified version of an analysis that a Copyright Office agent might consider when reviewing a copyright registration application.

For your own copyright registration purposes, it is usually unnecessary to do a detailed analysis. If the artwork was originally made by you, and it is a work of visual art (as defined by the Copyright Law) then it most likely qualifies for registration as well. But, if the work, or an element of the work, is atypical, a copyrightability analysis may be a useful tool for identifying the protectable elements of your work for registration purposes.

The eligibility criteria is defined within the text of the Copyright Law, and these are the three basic qualifications for copyright protection of a specific work:

1. The work is a **subject matter** covered by copyright. It is a category or type of work that the copyright law specifies is protectable.

2. The work is an **original work of authorship**. It is not a copy itself and the work is the result of some minimal degree of human creativity.

3. The work is **fixed in a tangible medium of expression** that is **perceivable**. The work exists physically and it can be seen, felt, heard, or otherwise perceived.

To be copyrightable–and by extension, to be registered–the work must meet all three of the criteria.

Copyrightable Subject Matter

In copyright terminology, types of work or categories of work are referred to as *subject matter*. The initial eligibility requirement is that the work must consist of a proper **subject matter** type. Eight broad categories of protectable works are specified in the Copyright Law.

Works of visual art are part of a larger category of subject matter that is covered under the Copyright Law. A wide range of creative works, including literature, music, drama, choreography, motion pictures, audiovisual works, sound recordings, and architecture are also covered as protectable subject matter by the Copyright Law.

> Copyright protection subsists, in accordance with this title, in original works of authorship fixed in any tangible medium of expression, now known or later developed, from which they can be perceived, reproduced, or otherwise communicated, either directly or with the aid of a machine or device...
>
> Works of authorship include the following categories:
>
> (1) literary works;
>
> (2) musical works, including any accompanying words;
>
> (3) dramatic works, including any accompanying music;
>
> (4) pantomimes and choreographic works;
>
> (5) **pictorial, graphic, and sculptural works**;
>
> (6) motion pictures and other audiovisual works;
>
> (7) sound recordings; and
>
> (8) architectural works.
>
> U.S. Copyright Law, 17 U.S.C. § 102 (a) (excerpt)

The subject matter category we are primary concerned with here is **pictorial, graphic, and sculptural works**. This expansive category includes fine art and it encompasses the creative elements of commercial-type visual art works as well.

Many forms of visual artwork fit into this broad category. An artwork that is some type of pictorial work, graphic work or sculptural object would usually qualify for copyright protection (so long as it meets the other basic qualifications).

> "Pictorial, graphic, and sculptural works" include **two-dimensional** and **three-dimensional works of fine, graphic, and applied art, photographs, prints** and **art reproductions**, maps, globes, charts, diagrams, models, and technical drawings, including architectural plans...
>
> U.S. Copyright Law, 17 U.S.C. § 101 (excerpt)

Some forms of contemporary artworks do not fit into the "pictorial, graphic, and sculptural works" category, but they may still be covered under a different subject matter type. For instance, video-based works can be categorized under the motion picture provision. Or, artworks that consist primarily of a computer program may qualify as a literary work. Some artworks, such as multi-media or installation works that have several elements, can qualify as proper subject matter under multiple categories.

When a work is a type that fits within any of the broad categories of the Copyright Law it is then said to be a proper *subject matter* — it meets the threshold requirement for copyrightability.

An Original Work of Authorship

The second prong of the copyrightability criteria is originality. To be eligible for copyright protection, a work must be an original creation, not a copy. In the words of the Copyright Law, the work must be an "original work of authorship." Let's unpack that a little.

First, there is an *author*. The author is the originator, the creator of the work. The artist that created an original work of art is the author of that work. *Authorship* is essentially the author's act of creating. A *work of authorship* is the product of creativity–the artwork, the writing, the music, and so on, that was made by the author.

Copyrights are available for original works of authorship. The issue of originality—or of original*ness*—is a key concept for determining if a work, or an element of a work, is eligible for copyright protection. In the context of registering a copyright, the elements of a work that are original are also the copyrightable content. This is often fairly clear with traditional artworks. For instance, a landscape painting made from the imagination of the artist, or *en plein air*, so to speak, would tend to be entirely original. The whole painting is original in the context of copyrights. Some works present a more complex question of originality.

> Copyright protection subsists...in original works of authorship...
>
> U.S. Copyright Law, 17 U.S.C. § 102 (a) (excerpt)

To be copyrightable, the work—or an element of the work—must itself must be *original*. This does not mean that the work must be novel, special, or unique. Original or originality in this context means the work was independently created. It is not a copy or an imitation. It is the product of the author/artist and was made with some degree of creativity. Establishing original authorship is not a large burden. Rather, the work must just have a *minimal* amount of sufficient creativity to meet it.

As part of the registration review process, an agent of the Copyright Office will consider whether the work submitted for registration contains the minimal amount of original authorship. The Copyright Office has said that whether a work is novel, distinctive, innovative, or unique is irrelevant to its determination of originality. Aesthetic value, artistic merit, and intrinsic quality of the artwork, symbolic meaning, impression of an artwork, the artist's inspiration, intent, the intended meaning, visual appeal, look and feel, time to create, effort, expense of the creation, and the skill of the execution of the work are *not* considered in that review.

The Conflict of Originality and Art

There are conceptual differences between the art world perspective and copyright requirements on the point of originality. For instance, some works that consist solely of common shapes, symbols, or designs may not meet the Copyright Law's minimum criteria for originality on the surface.

A work that consists only of a common geometric shape may not be eligible for copyright protection unless the use of the shape or shapes results in a work that is sufficiently creative. Seemingly ordinary shapes may be considered sufficiently original when they have been transformed in some way, perhaps through arrangement, the manner of physical construction, or some other mode that involves creativity. The amount of creativity required to meet this standard is considered to be fairly minimal, but there must be some degree of originality for a work to be eligible for copyright protection. For artists registering these types of works, the ability to articulate the creative aspect of a work that consists of common elements is important.

The Copyright Office gives an example of a work that it considers to be ineligible for registration on this basis, a painting that consists of a solid color background with evenly spaced identical geometric shapes, such as circles.

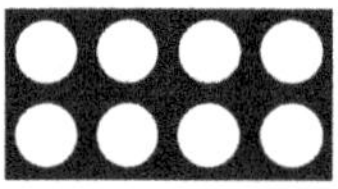

Some other familiar symbols or designs that are alone considered unoriginal by the Copyright Office include a standard fleur de lys, typographical symbols like an ampersand, numbers, currency symbols, arrows, a heart, diamond, star, spade, yin yang, gender symbols, simple emoticons, the peace symbol, and common patterns like polka dots or a checkerboard.

Variation in coloring or coloration in itself is not eligible for copyright protection. For instance, if there is a pre-existing work in black & white, changing its color alone does not necessarily make the new version an original in a copyright context. (Whether the first was eligible or not). In other similar contexts, copyright protection does not generally extend to short word phrases, including names, titles, and slogans, and typically not to variations on typographic elements, but there are some exceptions as well, such as those that have distinct ornamentation.

Again, while common shapes, patterns, and such are not considered sufficiently original, there are countless ways that that they can be used in an original way, as an element in a work that is in itself sufficiently original for copyright protection. Only a small amount of creativity is required, and for most artworks, it probably will not be a significant concern.

The rectangle with eight circles is a particular example of the limitations of copyright eligibility. The conflict reflects one of the challenges that visual artists can face when presenting non-traditional, minimalistic, or conceptual artwork for registration. Some rules for copyright eligibility are not accommodating to all types of art. Most works can find a path for completing a copyright registration, and in the process, establish that the work or elements of the work are copyright protectable. The key to identifying or registering a copyright for this type of art and within the constraints, in my view, is to focus on the creativity that exists in the work. Then, identify the physical expression of that creativity that is contained in the work—that will often be the copyrightable element if there is one. For most artworks, especially those made in more traditional media, the originality of the work is evident from a copyright standpoint and identifying it is very straightforward.

Fixation in a Tangible Medium of Expression

The final eligibility requirement for copyrightability is concerned with physicality and perception–the work must be fixed in a tangible form and be perceivable in some way. The Copyright Law specifies that the work must be fixed in a "tangible medium of expression" and that the work can be perceived, either directly or indirectly. So long as the work has some type of persistent physical existence or is embodied in some type of media, and it can be seen or heard or otherwise perceived, it should meet this requirement.

For instance, a drawing is a pictorial work that is *fixed* upon a piece of paper with ink or graphite, and it is perceivable by the eye of a viewer. An oil painting is fixed on canvas. A sculpture is fixed in the metal, wood, plaster, or another substance that composes it. A photograph might be fixed in silver particles or dyes upon paper, or by color inks on paper. Or, a digital photographic image is fixed in a digital file on a hard drive, a flash drive, or disk and the work is perceived through a computer screen or some other device. A sound recording is fixed in a digital file on a device, or on an audiotape, and is perceivable by means of an audio player, computer, or by another device.

> Copyright protection subsists...in original works of authorship fixed in any tangible medium of expression, now known or later developed, from which they can be perceived, reproduced, or otherwise communicated, either directly or with the aid of a machine or device...
>
> U.S. Copyright Law, 17 U.S.C. § 102 (a) (excerpt)

A work that exists only ephemerally or which is not fixed in tangible media does not meet the criteria for copyright protection. A work that is not perceivable or which is not fixed in a tangible medium is essentially not copyrightable. Of course, an ephemeral work can still exist as art, and might be legally protectable under other laws or through other means.

Limitations on Copyrightability

To understand what a copyright is, it is important to also know what it is not. The earlier section on the originality requirement discussed how some simple shapes and common forms are considered to be uncopyrightable by the Copyright Office. This section instead discusses the main types of works that are specifically excluded from copyright protection by the Copyright Law.

Copyrights are one type of intellectual property. Other types of intellectual property include patents and trademarks. Some works can be protected by multiple forms of intellectual property law, and each type of law has distinct requirements and procedures. Most patents and trademarks involve commercial products, inventions, or branding, respectively.

Patents primarily protect inventions, including new or unique processes or methods, and useful or functional items. Examples of works that may be covered by patents include pharmaceutical products, technology hardware, and machine processes. The distinct category of design patents can include objects of industrial design, such as the ornamental element of a functional item. This could include a computer icon, a distinctive bottle design, jewelry or furniture, for example.

Trademarks are another type of intellectual property that is intended to indicate the source of a service or product. Familiar brand names, logos, branded packaging, and sometimes, certain phrases associated with a product or service are typically protected as trademarks. Trademarks are intended to provide reliability in the marketplace, to ensure that consumers can properly identify a product with its manufacturer.

Intellectual property can also sometimes include publicity rights, such as those involving the right to use a person's image in an advertisement, and trade secrets, such as a secret formula for a soft drink.

× Ideas, Methods, Concepts and More

Copyright protection is available for many types of creative works, but there are specific exclusions. Concepts, ideas, methods, and systems and other modes are defined as unprotected by the Copyright Law. These exclusions are absolute.

> Exclusions from copyright protection:
>
> In no case does copyright protection for an original work of authorship extend to any idea, procedure, process, system, method of operation, concept, principle, or discovery, regardless of the form in which it is described, explained, illustrated, or embodied in such work.
>
> U.S. Copyright Law, 17 U.S.C. § 102 (b)

A method for creating an artwork or the concept underlying it cannot be copyrighted. On the other hand, the physical artwork resulting from a method of creation or an artwork developed from a concept and physically executed, could potentially be copyright protected.

Further consider that the creation of a work of art typically starts with a thought. The pure thought or the idea in the mind is ephemeral and intangible; it cannot be copyrighted because the law excludes it as "any idea" and also because an idea does not in itself have a physical form. Yet the artwork embodies that originating thought, and a tangible physical artwork is an expression that can meet the standard for copyright protection, so long as it meets the other basic requirements.

In the context of registering a copyright for artwork, it is important to consider this distinction. In an application it may seem natural to describe the work as a concept, but this will run afoul of the specific exclusion of concepts from copyright protection. Instead, when describing a copyright claim, it is better to focus upon the physical expression of the concept that composes the work.

× Useful Articles

Copyright protection does not extend to useful articles—such as objects that are purely utilitarian or functional. For an artwork that incorporates functional or mechanical aspects, those *elements* are not copyright protected on that basis, although other creative expressive features of the artwork may be covered. When pre-existing utilitarian objects are incorporated within an artwork, those objects are not copyright protected. However, the arrangement of the objects as a creative expression, may be copyrightable.

> A "useful article" is an article having an intrinsic utilitarian function that is not merely to portray the appearance of the article or to convey information. An article that is normally a part of a useful article is considered a "useful article".
>
> (U.S. Copyright Law, 17 U.S.C. § 101, excerpt)

Copyright protection can cover elements of artistic features incorporated within a useful article, so long as those artistic features can be separately identified. For example, a lamp—purely as a utilitarian object—would not be copyrightable. However, an original design painted on the lamp could be copyrightable and registered, so long as it meets the other regular criteria for a copyright. A sculpture that happens to function as a lamp, could also potentially be copyright protected as a sculptural object, but the functional element would be excluded.

> ...Such works shall include works of artistic craftsmanship insofar as their form but not their mechanical or utilitarian aspects are concerned; the design of a useful article, as defined in this section, shall be considered a pictorial, graphic, or sculptural work only if, and only to the extent that, such design **incorporates pictorial, graphic, or sculptural features that can be identified separately from, and are capable of existing independently of, the utilitarian aspects of the article.**
>
> U.S. Copyright Law, 17 U.S.C. § 101 (excerpt defining pictorial, graphic and sculptural works that are embodied in a "useful" or utilitarian object)

In some cases an artwork might be composed of objects that are essentially functional, for example, picture a sculpture created from a number of hammers and other functional tools. The arrangement of the objects *could* encompass creative expression. For copyright protection, it would be necessary to be able to identify the creative aspect separately or distinctly from any utilitarian function. If the artwork meets the threshold criteria, including originality on such a basis, then it could potentially be copyright protected to that extent and eligible for registration.

× Nature and Mechanical Processes

Natural objects or phenomena are not copyright protectable in their own right. These objects were not created by a human and lack the required creative expression and originality. Alone, natural objects also fail to meet the threshold subject matter test; they are not identified in the Copyright Law as eligible for protection. A piece of driftwood, shaped only by natural action of the sea, for example, is not eligible for copyright protection. The creative element that is necessary is generally minimal, but simple acts may not fulfill this requirement. For example, a found stone that is polished and mounted is also not copyrightable according to the Copyright Office.

Naturally occurring phenomenon does not have *original authorship*. The object must be a work of original creation by a real human, whether directly or indirectly. This also means that there is no copyright protection for an artwork allegedly made by a cat or a chimpanzee or by any other non-human.

A work made purely by a random or automatic mechanical process, without human creative input or intervention, would not meet the requirements. This does not necessarily exclude the potential protection of works made in mechanical process that do involve human input or some other form of human creativity.

Similarly, a work that is composed of natural elements may be copyrightable based upon the creative expression of the composition. If such a work meets the other threshold criteria (subject matter, originality, tangible media) then it could potentially be copyright protected as a whole.

•

It is possible, and actually somewhat common, for a contemporary work of art to include elements that are copyrightable and some elements that are not copyrightable. There are a number of reasons why some discrete elements may not be copyright protected, while the work as a whole may still be eligible for copyright protection, including those discussed earlier.

In the context of a copyright registration application for these types of mixed works, it is important to recognize which elements are new and original as well as those elements that are pre-existing or ineligible for copyright protection. The former are said to be included in the copyright claim and the later are excluded from the claim. When completing the registration application, a general identification of the included and excluded material is made. Works that contain public domain material, which is covered in the next section, have a similar issue in the context of registration.

The Public Domain

Copyright protection does not extend to works that are now in the public domain. Public domain means that the work is not protected by copyright for some reason, such as the expiration of the term of its copyright. When a copyright term has expired, it is said to enter the public domain and the work can be reproduced in any manner by anyone.

Some works are in the public domain because they were never protected in the first instance. Works created by the U.S. government are not copyrightable and are in the public domain.[1] Works that are not eligible for copyright protection may be in the public domain

[1] There are some very limited exceptions. For instance, works created by the U.S. Postal Service, the Corporation for Public Broadcasting, PBS, National Public Radio, and the Smithsonian Institution are not considered works of the U.S. government and may be copyright protected.

(though they may be covered by other property laws). Works that predate applicable copyright laws are also in the public domain. For example, Leonardo da Vinci's *Mona Lisa* is in the public domain because copyrights did not exist when it was created over five hundred years ago.

For other works, their public domain status depends upon when they were created, if they were published, or when they were published, depending upon the version of the law in effect at the pertinent time. At a point in the future, the date when the creator of a work dies will ultimately affect the date upon which the work eventually enters the public domain. Contemporary terms of copyright are shown earlier in this chapter for reference.

Calculating copyright terms for the purpose of determining when an existing work enters the public domain can be complex because of the numerous changes to the Copyright Law over the past several decades. For older works there are some general guidelines. For instance, works *published* between 1923 and 1977 do not fall under the contemporary rule based upon the creator's lifespan, but instead the copyright term is a fixed period of 95 years.

Derivative works, those that incorporate preexisting material, including those that contain public domain material, can be copyrightable, so long as the derivative work contains new original authorship to a sufficient degree. A copyright would protected the part of the work that is new or original, but not the part that consists of public domain matter or other preexisting material.

Derivative Works

A derivative work is a new work that is based upon or incorporates one or more preexisting works. Derivative works may be new versions of an earlier work, adaptations, modifications, or another transformation of a preexisting work. The right to make derivative works is one of the exclusive rights of a copyright owner.

The Copyright Law defines a derivative work as:

> ...a work based upon one or more preexisting works... in which a work may be recast, transformed, or adapted. A work consisting of editorial revisions, annotations, elaborations, or other modifications, which, as a whole, represent an original work of authorship, is a "derivative work".

U.S. Copyright Law, 17 U.S.C. § 101 (excerpt)

"Derivative" can sometimes be a negative word in the art world. To say that a work is *derivative* can be a harsh criticism, meaning that a work has taken too much inspiration from an earlier work. In a copyright context, this is not the case at all. The word has a different meaning and no negative connotation. It is simply a signifier of preexisting material that has been incorporated into a new work and it also refers to the related exclusive right to create them. Many copyrights registrations are made for derivative works.

In copyright terms, a derivative work of visual art is one that typically builds upon or is based upon preexisting art or other preexisting creative material. It incorporates some form of creative, physical expression (authorship) that was already in existence. The new work incorporating or modifying the preexisting material is said to be a derivative work of the original earlier work. A derivative work contains, in essence, two distinct forms of authorship: the preexisting material and the new creative expression.

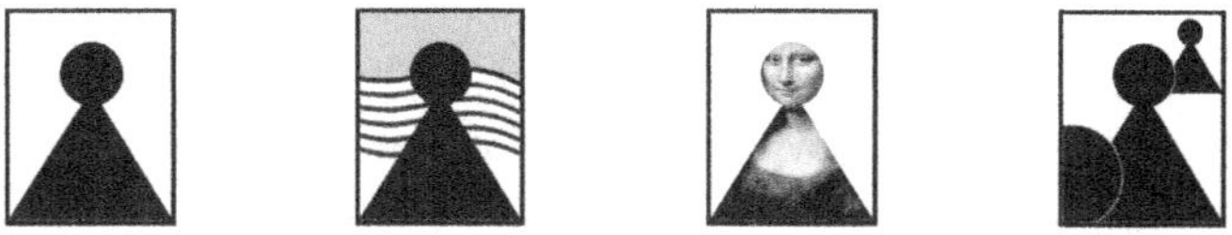

The preexisting material can be almost any form of work. It could incorporate a copy of the artist's own earlier artwork—a fairly common art practice. It could be public domain material. The preexisting material could potentially be a work made by someone else, to which the artist has made alterations, an adaptation, or some other transformation. A new work based upon an earlier work, re-created in a different media, such as a drawing made from an existing photograph, is a derivative work.

An artwork that is only conceptually derived from another work, but does not contain a copy of that physical expression, may not be considered to be an actual derivative work from a copyright perspective. For example, a series of sculptures that appear to be different, but which are all based upon the idea of *light*, are not necessary derivative works for copyright purposes. Ideas alone are not copyrightable. Derivative works tend to build upon or modify the physical aspect, the creative expression, of a preexisting work.

A derivative work can be based upon earlier artwork, or it could be created from or incorporate a work in the public domain. In either case, an element of the new work is something that already existed. One somewhat provocative example of a derivative work incorporating public domain material is Marcel Duchamp's *L.H.O.O.Q.* Duchamp made a number of versions. The first version, made in 1919, consists of a postcard type reproduction of Leonardo Da Vinci's *Mona Lisa* upon which Duchamp drew a mustache and goatee and added the text "L.H.O.O.Q." When Duchamp added writing and drawing to the *Mona Lisa* image, he created a new work, a derivative work of the *Mona Lisa*.

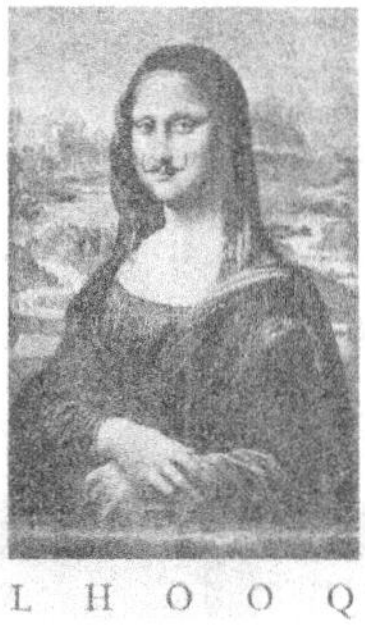

Marcel Duchamp, L.H.O.O.Q., 1919, as published in *391*, n. 12, March 1920

The original source work, *Mona Lisa*, was in the public domain when the first *L.H.O.O.Q.* was made. (Copyrights did not exist in the sixteenth century). The inexpensive postcard of the *Mona Lisa* used in the 1919 *L.H.O.O.Q.* work is itself a reproduction of the public domain image of the painting.

The addition of the mustache, goatee, and text transformed the original source image of Leonardo's *Mona Lisa* into a new work.

Duchamp labeled the new work *L.H.O.O.Q.*, an amorous pun in French. In this case, Duchamp's new work can be viewed as a commentary upon the original and its status in society. *L.H.O.O.Q.* can also be seen as a transformative work. The new elements, the text and drawing, are Duchamp's original authorship and were potentially copyrightable by him. The portion of the work that is the *Mona Lisa* was not copyrightable by Duchamp because it was (1) already in the public domain and (2) was not Duchamp's original creation.

After Duchamp's first version of L.H.O.O.Q., the many versions made by him are derivative works of both the earlier L.H.O.O.Q. and of Leonardo's *Mona Lisa*. Duchamp later made "shaved" versions of L.H.O.O.Q., appearing to return to an unmarked image of Mona Lisa. The variations are like a play on the concepts of derivative works and originality, though it probably cannot be said that a comment on copyright law was Duchamp's actual intent.

There are a number of ways that a derivative work is created. A new work can build upon an artist's own preexisting work. Or, a new work incorporates a work created by someone else (the result of which may or may not be infringing or copyrightable). Or, the new work can build upon or incorporate a public domain work. In all such cases though, some element of a derivative work is preexisting and is not original to the new work.

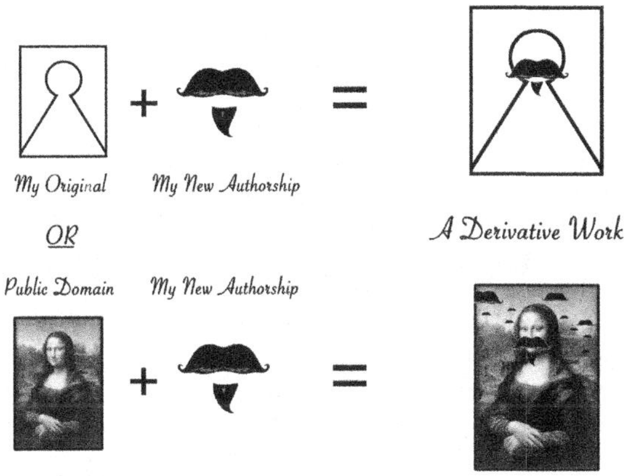

The scope of the copyright in a derivative work is limited to the new authorship—the new material or creativity that the artist combined with the preexisting material to create a new work. The creation of a derivative work does not extend the copyright term on the underlying source material or recreate a copyright on existing public domain material.

> A copyright in a derivative work is independent from that of the preexisting source material it incorporates:
>
> > The copyright in a compilation or derivative work extends only to the material contributed by the author of such work, as distinguished from the preexisting material employed in the work, and does not imply any exclusive right in the preexisting material. The copyright in such work is independent of, and does not affect or enlarge the scope, duration, ownership, or subsistence of, any copyright protection in the preexisting material...
>
> U.S. Copyright Law, 17 U.S.C. § 103 (b) (excerpt)

When registering a copyright in a derivative work, the *new* elements are the heart of the claim. Chapter 5 discusses derivative works and identifying the scope of your copyright claim for registration purposes in further detail.

Authorship & Ownership

For artists, authorship and copyright ownership often go together, but each status is distinct. Authorship points to the origin of the work itself; the author is the creator. An artist that independently makes a work of visual art is the author of that particular work and the independent artist is also the owner of the copyright.

The U.S. Supreme Court has said that, "As a general rule, the author is the party who actually creates the work, that is, the person who translates an idea into a fixed, tangible expression entitled to copyright protection." Community for Creative Non-Violence v. Reid,

490 U.S. 730 (1989). The primary exception to this general rule is work that has been made for hire.

To create a work independently means that the work was not made as part of employment duties or in certain specific conditions. Independent creation means, in essence, that the work was made freely by the artist. The artist made the creative decisions and was ultimately responsible for the resulting work of art.

An artist who independently creates an original work is the owner of the copyright and the rights that flow from that. In the past other steps were required to establish a copyright, but in the United States today the copyright comes into being automatically.

Independent Creation
↙↗ ↘
Authorship ⟶ **© Ownership** ⟶ **Exclusive Rights**

What does it mean to own a copyright? To own a copyright ultimately means being able to control if a specific work is reproduced, the way it is reproduced, and limitations or conditions on the reproductions. This includes nearly any type of copy of the work, as well as distribution, display or performance of the copies, and the authority to create derivative works. The rights are positive—giving the copyright owner the right to do those things. The rights are also inverse—the copyright owner can restrict someone else from doing those acts. Or, if someone else copies the work without permission, infringing the copyright, the owner can enforce the exclusive rights and potentially seek a legal remedy for the unauthorized act.

There are a few situations where authorship and ownership are not held by the artist who made the work, or where the artist shares authorship and ownership with another person. The primary examples related to visual art and some related issues are discussed in the next sections.

Collaborative or Joint Works

When an artist has independently made a work of art, the artist is the original owner of the copyright in that artwork. The artist is both the author of the work and the rights owner. Consider the case of an artwork that was made by two or more people.

> A "joint work" is a work prepared by two or more authors with the *intention* that their contributions be merged into inseparable or independent parts of a unitary whole.
>
> U.S. Copyright Law, 17 USC § 101 (excerpt)

If a work of visual art was made independently, but jointly, such as a collaborative work, each of the artists is an author and owner of the rights. A joint work was created. For purposes of registering a copyright, each such contributing artist is also a copyright co-claimant. A claimant is a person that can officially assert the existence of the copyright and ownership of the rights in the context of the registration of the copyright. Each claimant should be identified in an application to register a copyright.

Licensing

A license is an authorization that is given by the copyright owner to another party, granting permission to use part or all of a copyright protected work. Strictly speaking, a license is not a sale of a copyright, but rather, it is a specific authorization to use the rights that belongs to the copyright owner. Licenses are commonly used by artists in formal and more casual circumstances. They are often granted for promoting art exhibitions, publications, and other activities. Licensing agreements should be considered carefully.

A licensing agreement can be made to cover a number of situations. They may be complex or simple and can involve virtually any aspect of the exclusive rights. A license to reproduce a work might be limited in the number of copies it permits, or for the period of time that copies can be made, or it could specify conditions for selling or displaying copies. An owner can grant a license free of charge or for monetary compensation.

An artist could decide to allow another person or organization to reproduce copies of the artist's work. For example, an artist might grant a specific license to a publisher to reproduce an image of his or her artwork in a book that will be sold worldwide. In that case, the terms within the license agreement would probably be designed to permit the publisher to reproduce the image and to distribute it in the form of the published book. In that example, the artist is the licensor and the publisher is the licensee.

Exhibition promotional materials are another common example of licensing for fine artists. For instance, an artist might agree to allow an art gallery to produce exhibition announcement cards featuring the artwork or to use an image of the artwork in an advertisement. This type of license is often arranged fairly casually in the contemporary art world, but there may also be a written license agreement spelling out the terms.

A copyright owner can potentially sell or permanently transfer a copyright or specific rights, but strictly speaking, licenses are not an actual sale of rights. When a copyright owner grants a license, this does not affect the property ownership in the copyright. However, depending upon the terms of a license, an owner could voluntarily limit his or her own rights too, but this depends upon the specific agreement and the type of license involved.

An *exclusive* license typically means that only the licensee can use or control the rights and the artist/copyright owner has relinquished their own rights in whole or in part. If the license is exclusive, then the artist may not be able to continue to freely use his or her own copyright, or some aspect of the copyright, as long as the license is in effect. Exclusive licenses are not commonly granted by artists in the fine art area. Exclusive licenses, or even permanent sales of the copyrights, may be more commonly made for commercial or advertising related purposes.

A *nonexclusive* license is the more typical arrangement when artists license their works. *Nonexclusive* means that the artist/copyright owner has granted permission to reproduce the work, but the artist also retains the ability to use those same rights. A *nonexclusive* license is a particularly useful because the artist can continue to use the copyright, or even grant additional licenses, without limitation. With a *nonexclusive* license, the artist continues to have control over the copyright, including quite significantly, the right to make derivative works, and to use the other exclusive rights.

Works Made For Hire

When an the artist is employed or commissioned to make a work of art, in the context of the copyright, it may be said to be a work made *for hire*. This terminology is specific to copyrights and it has important implications for artists.

An artist is considered to be the author of the original work that he or she independently created and the owner of the copyright, but there is an exception for certain works that are made *for hire*. When a work is made for hire, and when it meets certain specific conditions, the artist is not the owner of the copyright. This obviously has an impact upon an artist's rights. For copyright registration purposes, it is important to understand the criteria that defines a work as one that was made for hire.

"Work made for hire" is a narrow principle that is defined in the Copyright Law. When the work is made *for hire*, the authorship is attributed to the hiring party, such as the employer or the person who commissioned the work, rather than to the artist. Normally the artist is the initial owner of the copyright of an original work. But, when a work is truly made *for hire* within the meaning of the Copyright Law, the artist does *not* own the copyright to the work. It is owned instead by the hiring party. However, the criteria for qualifying a work as one made for hire is fairly specific.

There are *only* two primary situations where a work is made for hire: (1) job duties in employment and (2) certain types of commissions or orders. If the work was not made in those situations or if it doesn't fit the required criteria, it is not a work made for hire, and the artist is the author of the work and retains the copyright ownership.

> A "work made for hire" is–
>
> (1) a work prepared by an employee within the scope of his or her employment; or
>
> (2) a work specially ordered or commissioned for use as a contribution to a collective work, as a part of a motion picture or other audiovisual work, as a translation, as a supplementary work, as a compilation, as an instructional text, as a test, as answer material for a test, or as an atlas, if the parties expressly agree in a written instrument signed by them that the work shall be considered a work made for hire.
>
> U.S. Copyright Law, 17 USC § 101 (excerpt)

The flow chart on the next page illustrates a method for determining whether or not a work was made for hire. To use it, focus upon the specific artwork that is at issue. Answer the path of the questions. If and when you are directed to a box on the chart that indicates the work is *not* made for hire, then that is as far as you need to go. The artwork was not made for hire in that case and the principle does not apply.

Where the factual circumstances are clear, the flow chart should result in an accurate answer. However, where the factual conditions are unclear or a legal interpretation is needed, the status of the work may not be evident. These ambiguities mostly arise when the work was created in an employment situation. For instance, if it's not clear whether making the artwork was a part of official job duties or if there is a question of whether the artist was a qualifying employee at the time, more information may be needed.

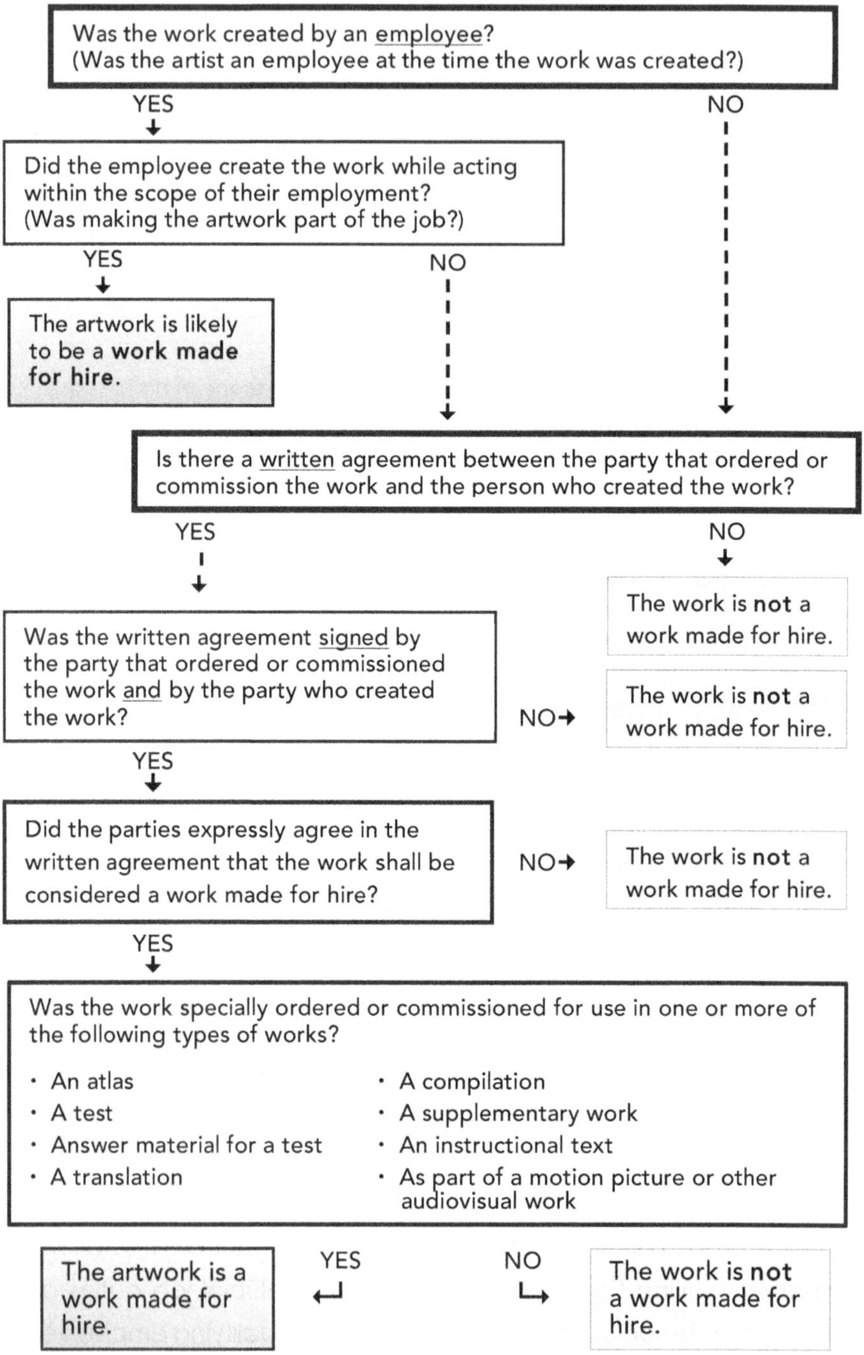
Was the work created by an employee?
(Was the artist an employee at the time the work was created?)
YES
NO
Did the employee create the work while acting within the scope of their employment?
(Was making the artwork part of the job?)
YES
NO
The artwork is likely to be a **work made for hire.**
Is there a written agreement between the party that ordered or commission the work and the person who created the work?
YES
NO
The work is **not** a work made for hire.
Was the written agreement signed by the party that ordered or commissioned the work and by the party who created the work?
NO
The work is **not** a work made for hire.
YES
Did the parties expressly agree in the written agreement that the work shall be considered a work made for hire?
NO
The work is **not** a work made for hire.
YES
Was the work specially ordered or commissioned for use in one or more of the following types of works?
• An atlas
• A test
• Answer material for a test
• A translation
• A compilation
• A supplementary work
• An instructional text
• As part of a motion picture or other audiovisual work
The artwork is a work made for hire.
YES
NO
The work is **not** a work made for hire.

The flowchart reflects that there are just two paths whereby a work may be considered to have been made for hire. In the context of copyrights, any other arrangement does not qualify.

The first category to consider is work that was made in an **employment** situation as part of the duties for a regular job. Generally speaking, work made on the job, at the direction of the employer, as part of the employment responsibilities, could be considered as work made for hire. Conversely, an independent contractor is not an employee and does not meet the criteria for defining a work as one made for hire. The difference in these two situations can involve several factors, such as whether the artist used his or her own tools, the location, or which party controlled decisions about the work.

The second category to consider is work that was ordered or **commissioned** specifically for a use *within* some other project. To be considered as a work for hire on this basis there must be an express agreement in writing that specifies that the work is to be made for hire. Yet, even in that case, if the incorporating project is not one of eight types specified in the Copyright Law, then the work would not be considered to have been made for hire on this point.

If a commissioned work is not one of the types of work listed (see the last question box in the flowchart) or if the work was not made in the course of employment, then the work *cannot* be considered to be a work made for hire on either basis.

Most of the works that can qualify as commissions are fairly straightforward in their descriptions (an atlas, a part of a motion picture, etc.), but among the commissioned works listed is a type of work described with the broad term of "supplementary" work. This has a specific definition in the Copyright Law. In terms of visual art, a supplementary work could include, for example, commissioned illustrations within a book written by someone else, or visual materials used for instructional purposes.

> [A] "supplementary work" is a work prepared for publication as a **secondary adjunct to a work by another author** for the purpose of introducing, concluding, illustrating, explaining, revising, commenting upon, or assisting in the use of the other work, such as forewords, afterwords, pictorial illustrations, maps, charts, tables, editorial notes, musical arrangements, answer material for tests, bibliographies, appendixes, and indexes, and an "instructional text" is a literary, pictorial, or graphic work prepared for publication and with the purpose of use in systematic instructional activities.
>
> U.S. Copyright Law, 17 USC § 101 (excerpt)

For copyright registration purposes, the applicant makes the determination of whether the work was made for hire or not, and the determination should be based on the facts that existed at the time that the work was created. The Copyright Office does not make the determination and will generally accept the applicant's representation unless it is contradicted by other information.

If the artwork was indeed made for hire, the artist can still register the copyright, but the copyright will belong to the hiring party. There may be reasons why an artist would choose to register a work for hire despite not owning the copyright. For instance, an artist still has an interest in being associated with the work and may want to establish a public record showing that he or she was the actual creator of that work.

Art, Media, and Terminology

The Copyright Law contains words and phrases that have particular contextual meanings. As you can see from the examples on the next page, these words and phrases may have different a meaning, broader or narrower, than you might expect.

You may encounter these words in a registration application or if you communicate directly with the Copyright Office. Be aware that the copyright contextual meaning of words can be quite specific. The list that follows was adapted from the official definitions, but with additional descriptive information.

Pictorial, graphic, and sculptural work includes 2-D and 3-D works of fine art, graphic and applied art, photographs, prints, and also includes art reproductions, maps, globes, charts, diagrams, models, technical drawings and architectural plans.

Visual Art Works collectively include pictorial, graphic, and sculptural works, as well as architectural works.

In reference to the Visual Artist Rights Act (VARA), a **Work of Visual Art** is a subset of works, specifically a painting, drawing, print, sculpture, or photograph that is either a single copy or consists of a numbered limited edition of 200, signed or marked by the artist. (For more, refer to Chapter 6).

Motion Pictures are a form of audiovisual work that consists of a series of related images that impart an impression of motion when shown in succession, sometimes with accompanying sounds. Films and video works are examples.

Audiovisual works consist of a series of related images, with or without sound, that are to be shown by using a device, machine, or other equipment. The images are not required to create an impression of motion, but the need to use a machine or device to view them is an essential to categorizing it as an audiovisual work. Audiovisual works often incorporate visual art works, specifically pictorial and graphic images. Some examples are slide presentations, webinars, videogames, and virtual reality environments. Animated graphics are also categorized as an audiovisual work.

Literary works are those that are expressed in words, numbers, verbal, numerical symbols, or other indicia, irrespective of the physical form in which the work is embodied (books, periodicals, manuscripts, phonorecords, film, tapes, disks, or cards), but does not include audiovisual works.

Performing Arts, with respect to works, refers to motion pictures, audiovisual works, musical works, sound recordings, dramatic works, pantomime, and choreography, in the terminology of the Copyright Office. Some videogames, interviews, and other works may also be classified as performing arts.

Sound recordings consist of a series of musical, spoken, or other sounds that are fixed and embodied in a disk, tape, phonorecord or other such form. They do not include those that accompany a motion picture or other audiovisual work. Sound recordings do not include soundtracks.

CHAPTER THREE

SELECTING A REGISTRATION METHOD

There are three essential parts to every copyright registration:

1) A completed application,

2) payment of the correct fee, and

3) submission of a copy of the work to the Copyright Office.

This chapter discusses the first step, choosing the specific application form that you will use to register your copyright. For comparison, these are the main application options that will be covered:

Standard Application (online)	1 work	published or unpublished
One Work By One Author / Single Application (online)	1 work	published or unpublished
Form VA (paper application submitted by mail)	1 work	published or unpublished
Group of Unpublished Works Application (online)	2-10 works	unpublished works only
Group of Photographs Application (online)	2-750	all published or all unpublished

Copyright registrations can be submitted either through an online application or by a paper form. Both of these options are covered here, but with an emphasis on the online process because it is generally preferred by the Copyright Office and it is the most common method at this time.

Paper Applications

Paper based forms that are mailed to the Copyright Office along with a fee and copy of the work are still available for some types of registrations. These forms are being increasingly phased out and availability may change. The application form is chosen according to the type of work registered, such as **Form VA** for visual art work.

Form VA is used to register a work of 2-D or 3-D visual art. Paper application forms can only be used to register a single work of visual art and they have a higher fee than online registration. Processing time can be substantially longer and if a registration is needed promptly, this is a factor to consider. Paper forms may not be the ideal choice for many registrants, but they are an option that some may prefer.

The paper form selected for registration must conform to the type of work registered. Sample images of paper registration applications are found in Appendix D, including Form VA for visual art and Form PA for motion picture and audio-visual works. If you decide to use this method of registration, original forms can be printed from the Copyright Office website.

Electronic Applications

Most copyright registrants will find that an electronic application is the easiest way to register their copyright. The electronic applications are accessed directly through the Copyright Office's website. There are currently four primary applications for registering a copyright in visual art.

Rather than being tied to the type of work being registered, the primary criteria for selecting a particular electronic application is the number of works to be registered and whether or not the work or works have been published. However, there is one option that is specifically for registering photographs only.

The online registration process is beneficial for several reasons. The fee for an electronic application is typically less than the corresponding paper form and there are more options. For instance, the group applications permit the registration of multiple qualifying works in a single application, and this option is only available in the online system. When a group of artworks is eligible for registration on a group application, a single fee covers all of the works submitted for registration—often a significant savings compared to other options.

At the end of the online application process you can upload an electronic copy of the work and immediately confirm that it has been received by the Copyright Office. This copy is known as the deposit and the timely submission of it is a critical requirement for completing a copyright registration. The online system also allows you to check on the status of the application while it is processed.

The online applications are recommended for most registrations of visual art. Descriptions of the primary electronic applications available for visual art are covered in the following section.

The online registration system is known as the Electronic Copyright Office, or **eCO**, at www.copyright.gov. The main online applications available for visual art are:

- Standard Application
- One Work By One Author or the "Single" application
- Group Registration of Unpublished Works
- Group of Photographs

Each of these forms can be used to register works of visual art that are 2-D or 3-D (and other types of work). The last option in the list is specifically for registering multiple photographic works. Choose the application that best fits your work and circumstances. When you choose one of these application types, you will be directed to enter information in accordance with the requirements for that particular application.

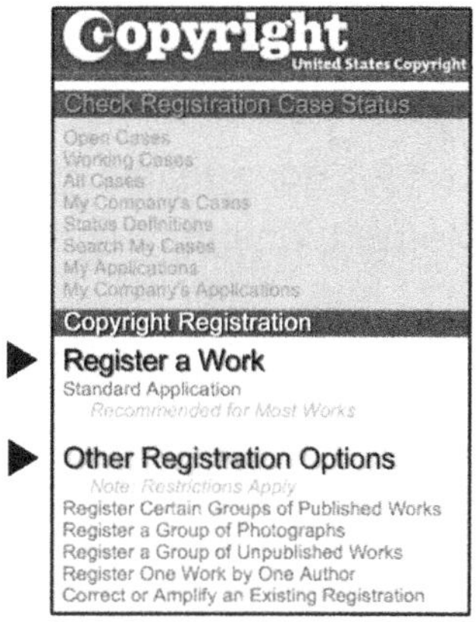

The first screen of each online application is a confirmation that the work to be registered meets the criteria for using that particular application. Chapter 4

covers this in more detail for each of the online application options.

To register a single work only, choose either the Standard Application or the One Work By One Author application. The Copyright Office suggests the online Standard Application for "most" registrations. However, when registering only one work, the One Work By One Author application (also known as a Single Application) has a lower fee and requires less information. So long as the work matches the criteria, the Single Application may be a preferable option for most artists that are registering only one work.

To register multiples works in one application, use one of the group registration applications if your works fit the requirements. The main group application can be used only for works that are unpublished, but the group of photographs application can be used for published or unpublished, so long as the group is not mixed. The group applications are the most economical choice for registering two or more qualifying works. Group registration is only available through the online registration process.

The next section covers the eligibility requirements and some other considerations for the online applications. After confirming that your work meets the criteria for a particular application method, the steps for completing the process are covered in Chapter 4. Fee comparisons for the different applications and options are shown in Appendix B. A chart of common application form options based on media is included at Appendix C. If your work is not 2-D or 3-D or is an non-traditional art form, or does not seem fit into the usual applications, consider the options discussed in the Alternative Registration Method section near the end of this chapter.

■ The Standard Application

The Standard Application is used for registering a single work that is either published or unpublished and it is the basic option available in the online registration system. Specifically, the Standard Application can be used to register **a single work of visual art**, or a single work of some other type. It can also be used to register a collective work or a unit of publication.

First, it is appropriate to use the Standard Application to register the copyright in **one work** of visual art, a painting, print, sculpture, or a single photograph, for instance. (The One Author One Work application, described in the next section, is another option for registering one work, and at a lower cost).

The Standard Application can also be used to register a single **collective work**. In this context a collective work is a type of compilation, an assemblage of independent works that make up a single, whole, collective work. A collective work is *not* a collection and it is not a collaborative work. A typical example of a collective work is an anthology. An issue of a periodical, a magazine, or newspaper could also be a collective work. When the components are made by different authors the registration would not cover those individual contributions, but it may cover the selection, coordination, or arrangement of those elements in the larger work.

> A "compilation" is a work formed by the collection and assembling of **preexisting materials...selected, coordinated, or arranged** in such a way that the resulting work as a whole constitutes an original work of authorship. The term 'compilation' includes collective works...
>
> A "collective work" is a work, such as a periodical issue, anthology, or encyclopedia, in which a number of contributions, constituting separate and independent works in themselves, are **assembled into a collective whole**.
>
> U.S. Copyright Law, 17 USC § 101 (excerpts)

However, individual works within a collective work may only be covered by the copyright (and by the registration) if the individual registering the collective work owns *all* of the copyrights in the individual works as well as the whole, and if the works were not previously published or registered and are not in the public domain. In this particular instance, an artist could potentially use the Standard Application to register a collective work that consisted solely of that artist's contributions. To register a group of individual works that are not a collective work, consider one of the group application options that are discussed later in this section.

The Standard Application can also be used to register a **unit of publication**, an assemblage of multiple works physically *bundled together* as a single unit and distributed publically, generally, for sale. Some examples include a package of greeting cards, a book published with a CD or DVD, or a board game packaged with instructions and playing pieces. A unit of publication has additional eligibility requirements that must be met to use the Standard Application. In some cases, when the individual pieces are made by the same artist, and especially if they have not been published yet, it may be more feasible to register the components together using one of the group-based applications.

■ The One Work By One Author Application

The One Work By One Author application, also known as the Single Application, is a good registration option when there is only one work to be registered. It can be used for either published or unpublished work. The application is simplified and the fee is less than the Standard Application.

The application has specific eligibility requirements and because it is an abbreviated form, it has fewer options for adding detailed information about the copyright claim. For example, the Standard Application permits multiple titles for one work, but the One Work application permits only one title. This does not affect the scope of the copyright in the work.

Some examples of works that could be registered with this application include one photograph, a single drawing, an illustration, a painting, a logo, one piece of jewelry, a sculpture, or another type of eligible work, so long as it was created by one person.

All of the requirements must be met to use the One Work By One Author application:

1. One work to be registered.
2. The work was created by one individual only and all of the material or elements in the work were created by the same individual.
3. The person submitting the registration is the creator of the work and owns the copyright in the work.
4. The work is not a work made for hire.

To use the One Work application, you must be the person who created the work, and you must own all of the copyrights in it. For most fine artists, unless they have expressly transferred the copyright permanently, the condition is usually met.

Works that were made for hire are not eligible for registration with this application. Works that have more than one creator—a joint work or a collaborative work—are also not eligible for this application. Even if you intend to exclude the other author's contribution from the registration claim, it would not be eligible for One Work By One Author registration. The Standard Application does not have these restrictions and may be used in these cases instead.

For the registration of a single work, the One Work By One Author application is the most economical and easiest option for many artists. However, if you have multiple works to register, and the works meet the qualifications, the group applications are often the most efficient and least expensive registration option.

Registering Multiple Works with Group Applications

Group applications are a good option for registering copyrights in multiple works. There is one application to complete and one fee covers all of the works on the application. This is referred to as a group registration and there are two main options for visual artwork.

One application is solely for registering either a group of published photographs or a group of unpublished photographs. The other application can be used for any type of unpublished works. There is no group registration application for non-photographic published visual artworks at this time, but compilations may be registered on the Standard Application, discussed earlier in this chapter.

Group registration applications are only available through the online system and each has specific qualifications and limitations. Some applications require the submission of additional materials, along with copies of the works that are being registered. Before selecting a group application, read through the requirements and confirm that your works fit within the rules.

■ Group Registration of Unpublished Works

The application for a Group Registration of Unpublished Works (abbreviated as "GRUW") is for registering 2 to 10 related visual artworks, or other types of work, with a single filing fee. For many artists this application is the most economical registration method.

To qualify for group registration, the artwork must meet certain criteria. All of the works must be unpublished and must be the same type of work. For example, a group of drawings or a group of ceramic sculptures. Each individual element of a group registration consists of a single artwork that is part of the larger whole group. A logical group registration might be a series of related works, an artist's series of paintings on a related subject, or a group of works that are considered to be a body of work.

Nearly any type of copyrightable matter can be registered with this application, so long as it meets the requirements. Along with traditional 2-D or 3-D art, a group of video works could potentially be registered (as a group of motion pictures), or a group of poems (as a group of literary works). In theory, a group of multi-media works can also be registered with this application, but in that case, each individual work in the group must be clearly recognizable as one complete cohesive work when it is submitted to the Copyright Office. The group form of registration can be adapted so long as the essential criteria is met.

All of the requirements must be met to use the Group Registration of Unpublished Works application:

1. All of the works in the group must be unpublished.
2. Maximum of 10 works in the group.
3. Each of the works must be the same type of work.
4. All of the works must have been created by the same author (artist) or by the same co-authors. The person or persons who are claiming the copyright must be the same for all of the works in the group.
5. The works are not websites, architectural works, compilations, or collective works.
6. Copies of the work must be capable of being deposited electronically, in individual digital files, and each file must not exceed 500MB.

Each of the works must not have been published prior to registration. "Publication" has a different meaning in a copyright context than in daily language, and the word can encompass not only distributed printed matter, but also products that have been offered for sale in some instances. For reference, Chapter 5 includes a detailed discussion on the meaning of publication for the purpose of copyright registration.

The GRUW application can be used to register the copyrights in joint (collaborative) works, so long as each of the contributors was involved in every one of the works contained in the group. In other words, the authorship must be the same for each work in the group.

Unpublished photographic works can also be registered using the GRUW application, but are limited to 10 works. The photo-specific registration is a preferred option in most cases.

■ Group Registration of Photographs

The Group of Photographs option is certainly the most economical choice to register multiple photographs at the same time. Up to 750 photographs can be registered in one application with a single filing fee. When registered as a group, each of the photographs is effectively registered as a separate work and is not considered to be a compilation or a collective work. This option is only available through the online system.

The Group of Photographs application has specific eligibility requirements and in addition to the completed application, payment of the filing fee, and submission of a digital copy of each photo, a list of the individual photographs is also required. This application can be used for either a Group Registration of Published Photographs ("GRPPH") or a Group Registration of Unpublished Photographs ("GRUPH"). For reference, Chapter 5 includes a discussion on publication in a copyright registration context.

To use this application option, the work can consist only of photographs. There can be no other media in the work and no other type of authorship in the work. **Only** works that are perceptible as photographs can be registered as a group of photographs. If another type of work is included in this application, it will be rejected by the Copyright Office.

The Copyright Office defines photographic works as a category that "**includes photographs that are created with a camera and captured in a digital file or other visual medium such as film. Examples include color photos, black and white photos, and similar types of images.**"

In general, photographs that have been retouched or which have been similarly altered in the original digital source file can still be registered in this group category. However, new works or derivative works that simply incorporate photographs or photographic images are not eligible for registration in the group of photographs categories.

Each of these requirements must be met to register photographs as a group:

- The group must consist only of photographs.
- The group must include at least 2 and no more than 750 photographs.
- The group must consist solely of published or solely of unpublished photographs. Unpublished and published works cannot be mixed in the same application.
- An application to register a group of published photographs (GRPPH) must contain only photos that have been published within the same calendar year. The *earliest* date of publication and the *latest* date of publication must be indicated in the application.
- All of the photographs in the group must have been created by the same individual photographer.
- The claimant(s) for the registration must be the same person or persons or organization for all works in the group.

There is additional information that must also be submitted to complete the application.

- The group of photographs must be given a title as a whole. (Individual photographs in the group can be titled as well).
- A numbered list of the individual photographs, with titles and matching digital file names, must also be submitted. If published, the publication date information is also required.
- If any of the photos in the group were made as works made for hire, the name of the photographer and the photographer's employer must be included in the appropriate section of the application

The photographs in a group registration must have been created by the same *author*. This is a technical term, and in many cases it simply means the same photographer created all of the photographs in the group. As with any independently made work, the individual photographer or artist can register the copyrights of the group of photographs–assuming that the minimal requirements for copyrightability are met.

If the photos were made for hire they must be identified as such in the application and the photographer must also be identified. An individual photographer can register photographs made for hire as a group if they were made for the same employer. If the work was made for hire, the employer is considered to be the author, but in that case also, a group application submitted by the employer should involve only one photographer's work. Chapter 2 includes a discussion on works made for hire and how to determine if a work fits this category.

The required deposit of copies of the photographs must be made in digital form only. At this time, the copies can be uploaded at the end of the application process or mailed to the Copyright Office on a flash drive, CD, DVD, or similar device. Only JPG, GIF, or TIFF files are accepted for the upload option and individual file size is limited to 500MB. If you are registering film-based photographs, the deposit copies will need to be made in digital form to use this application.

The Group of Photographs application also requires a numbered list of the photos with titles of all of the works and the names of their digital files, along with the online application registration. If the works were published, the date of publication in the same calendar year should be included as well. Information about creating the list is included in the application details in the section of Chapter 4 that describes the steps for completing this application.

Alternative Registration Methods For Certain Works

In the context of copyright registration, visual art is defined as 2-D or 3-D art. Although there is a broad range of works that fit within that parameter, others—like videos and films—may not. This classification does not greatly affect the registration process in most cases, especially when the electronic applications are used, but there are some adjustments that might need to be made.

The first three online registration applications discussed earlier in this section can be used to register other types of works besides those defined as visual art. Except for the Group of Photographs application, the online applications can be used to register nearly any type of work that is copyrightable. For instance, a single video work could potentially be registered using the Standard or One Work By One Author option. Or, a group of unpublished videos could potentially be registered using the group application, assuming the qualification criteria is met. Because a video work is usually categorized as a "motion picture," that classification would be selected at the appropriate point in the application, rather than "visual art." Print application forms are limited, but may be used for some single works—such as Form PA for a motion picture work.

The online applications can also be used to register works that consist of more than one media type, except for the Group of Photographs application, which does not permit any non-photographic works or elements. Mixed media works can be registered using one of the other online forms and should be categorized by their primary authorship. For instance, a book that contains literary work (writing) and illustrations by the same creator would likely be registered primarily as a literary work. The copyright could still cover all of the original material in the book, including the original illustrations. For a single such work, either the Standard Application or the One Work By One Author application could be used, so long as the work meets the criteria for each.

Registering Certain Groups of Published Works

Beyond the four main options, there are other methods that can potentially be used to register works of visual art. For example, some artists may elect to register a work that was published in a magazine or another periodical. There is no existing registration application for a *group* of published works, except for photographs. There is essentially a gap in the registration options for published works, as a group, but there is one alternative.

The application for contributions to a periodical (shown as a registration for *Certain Groups of Published Works* on the Copyright Office website) enables a group registration of some types of works that have been published in a periodical, including photographs, illustrations, cartoons, and other visual art works or text. Periodicals typically include newspapers, newsletters, journals, and magazines. A book is usually not considered to be a periodical and works published in that form would not be eligible for this application.

The individual works that are to be registered are referred to as *contributions*. The application can be used to register published contributions that consist of work that is either primarily visual art ("VA") or primarily text ("TX").

The *Certain Groups of Published Works* online option is a relatively simple application and it can be used to register qualifying works of visual art by selecting *Contribution to Periodicals VA* from the menu in the first full screen of the application. *The Certain Groups of Published Works* application mainly requires information about the publications in which the works were published, such as the date, issue number, and so on. This online application is presently the only means of registering published non-photographic works together, though single published works can be registered individually on the Standard or Single applications. There is currently no option for registering groups of non-photographic visual art works published in a non-periodical format.

- All of the contributions must have been created by the same person.
- The copyright claimant must be the same person or same organization for all of the contributions.
- All of the works must have been published in a periodical, and the first publication of each contribution must be within a twelve-month period.
- Each work must not have been published before its inclusion in the periodical, and the contribution to the periodical involved in the registration must be the first publication of the work.
- Each contribution must be individually identified in the application, including the date and the periodical in which it was first published.
- The individual contributions to be registered cannot be works made for hire.
- Works made before March 1, 1989 have additional requirements. Contributions published before March 1, 1989 must each bear a separate copyright notice with the owner's name (or abbreviation), and the notice on each contribution must be the same.
- One copy of each contribution, either the entire issue of the periodical or the entire section of a newspaper, or the specific page(s) where the contribution was first published, must be submitted as the deposit.

The publication containing the work must qualify as a periodical to use this application option. Regulations describe a periodical as..."a collective work that is issued or intended to be issued on an established schedule in successive issues that are intended to be continued indefinitely" and "In most cases, each issue will bear the same title, as well as numerical or chronological designations." (37 C.F.R. § 202.4(b)(3)). The Copyright Office recommends that registrations for contributions to periodicals be submitted within 3 months after the date of publication to the extent it is possible.

Works that were contributed to qualifying digital or electronic periodicals may be eligible to use this application as well. The Copyright Office refers to certain electronically printed matter as "ePrint" publications. An ePrint publication is defined as one that has been distributed online or by email, is self-contained, and does not change once it has been distributed. Examples are digital versions of newspapers, magazines, and newsletters.

Articles, blog entries, artwork, photographs, or other contributions that were *first* published in the form of an ePrint publication may be registered with this application option if that publication fits within the definition of a periodical. In other words, if the ePrint publication has an established schedule of issues and other such indicators that it is a periodical in the view of the Copyright Office.

A website is generally not considered to be a periodical for the purposes of registration. If a website appears to qualify as a periodical, then the *Group Registration For Contributions to Periodicals* option could potentially be used to register the contributed works, so long as the other criteria is met. However, the Copyright Office has expressed doubts about this and has indicated that most websites typically do not meet the requirements because they tend to be updated continually rather than on an established schedule and are not discrete self-contained works in themselves. Therefore, there is a risk to using this form of registration for a website contribution. An application will be rejected by the Copyright Office if the website does not meet the periodical criteria.

In 2020 the Copyright Office introduced a new electronic application that is designed solely for short literary works that are online, such as blog entries, social media posts and short online articles. The copyright claim is limited to the text only and this new application option *cannot* be used to register visual work. The *Group Registration of Short Online Works* (also known as "GRTX") can be used to register 2 to 50 qualifying online text works, with at least 50 but not more than

17,500 words, published within a 3 month period. Additional information can be found on the Copyright Office's website.

•

For most artists, it is most practical, economical, and safest to simply register works in one of the primary applications methods—the Standard Application or the One Work By One Author application. Or, as a group of unpublished works, or a group of photographs, when the works are eligible.

Ultimately, registration is designed to protect your interests in the event that your copyright is infringed. For that reason it is important to follow the rules and be particularly mindful of the eligibility criteria for the application you plan to use. Some mistakes may be simply administerial, but others could cause a delay in processing or have an impact on the registration itself. Contemporary art, particularly non-traditional works, can sometimes be hard to categorize. If in doubt about what form to use in an unusual situation, or for any other question, it never hurts to call or email the Copyright Office. The agents cannot give legal advice, but they can provide guidance to the Office's policies and procedures.

CHAPTER FOUR

COMPLETING THE APPLICATION

This chapter takes you through each step in the process of registering your copyright with the Copyright Office using one of the four electronic applications covered in the previous chapter or the paper-based form for visual art.

Registering your copyright online involves logging in to the Copyright Office's online registration system (eCO), completing the appropriate electronic application, paying the fee, and submitting the deposit copy of the work. The copy is uploaded as a digital file, or in some cases, a copy of the work may be mailed to the Copyright Office. Some applications have additional requirements.

If you choose to use a paper-based form instead, the completed application should be mailed to the Copyright Office with the fee and the deposit copy of the work.

Getting Started With the eCO System

The Electronic Copyright Office (eCO) is the online copyright registration system. If you haven't registered a copyright before, the first thing you need to do is create an account at **www.copyright.gov**.

On the home page, go to the log-in page by selecting the **Register Your Work** or Register a Copyright link in the Registration menu.

Find the button or link to ***Log in** to the Electronic Copyright Office (eCO) Registration System* and click. If you do not have one, create an account by selecting the "new user" link under the log in fields.

Set up an account (name, email, a selected user ID, password, challenge questions, address, telephone, and preferred contact method). Setting up a user account is free. Payment information is not entered until a registration application is to be filed. Each time you return to register a copyright, to complete an application that is in progress, or to check on a pending application, you will need to log in to the system.

After setting up an account you can log in to the registration system. If necessary, return to the log in page to do that. Logging in will direct you to the registration services portal page.

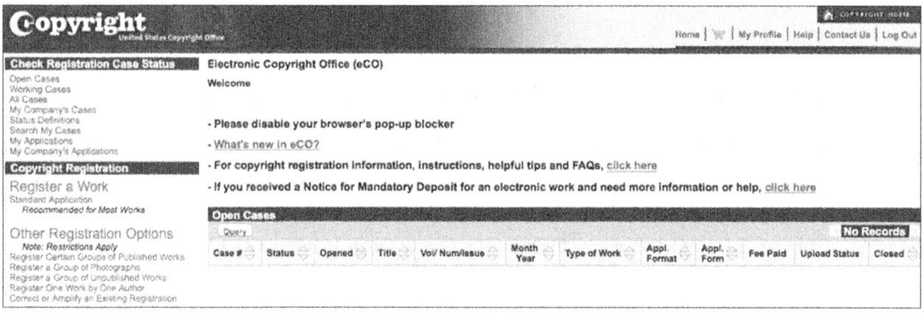

Copyright.gov > Register a Copyright > Log-in > *Registration Portal*

Overview and Navigation

The registration portal page is where a registration application begins. Electronic applications in progress can be saved and resumed later through the Working Cases link. Once an application is complete, and the fee and deposit have been made, it is called an Open Case. The processing status of an Open Case review can be checked on this page as well.

Select an application.

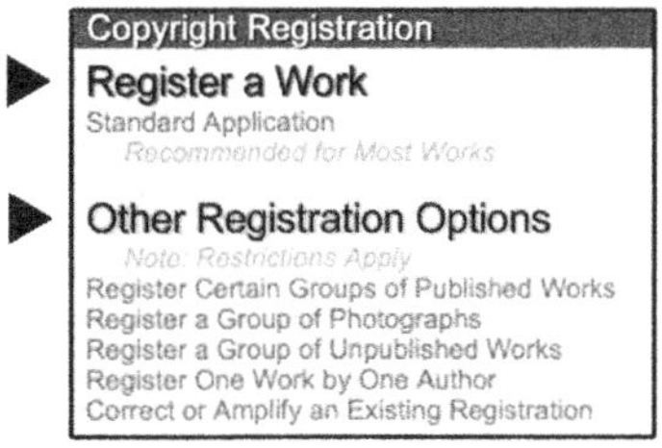

The option under the **Register a Work** heading on the left side menu includes:

- The **Standard Application**

Or, under **Other Registration Options** select one of the following:

- Register Certain Groups of Published Works
- Register a **Group of Photographs**
- Register a **Group of Unpublished Works**
- Register **One Work by One Author**

Each application will take you through a similar pattern of steps with specific information to be entered in each section.

First, choose the application type and on the first screen you can confirm that the work meets the eligibility requirements for that form. Next, information about the work is entered, such as the type of work, the title(s), and publication information. The author(s) and the claimant are identified. The limitation of the claim information is entered (which identifies the copyright protected material in the work). Contact and mailing information is entered.

The final parts in an application involve reviewing and verifying the accuracy of the application, entering the payment, and in most cases, uploading the deposit copy or copies of the work.

Application & Navigation Tips

- The assigned **case number** will appears near the top of the screen once an application has been started. Make a note of the number for future use.

- Use the contextual left side menu navigation links to review or make **changes** to any specific section of the application.

- To pause an application and return later, select the **Save For Later** button near the top of the page. This option only appears when an application form is open.

- To resume working on an application, login and select **Working Cases** from the Check Registration Case Status menu. Choose the application from the list of case numbers that appears in the main window frame.

- Navigate to sections of a resumed application by using the contextual menu that appears on the left when an application is open.

- Fee and deposit information cannot be entered until the application data is fully completed.

- Incomplete applications will be deleted by the Copyright Office after one year.

The Standard Application

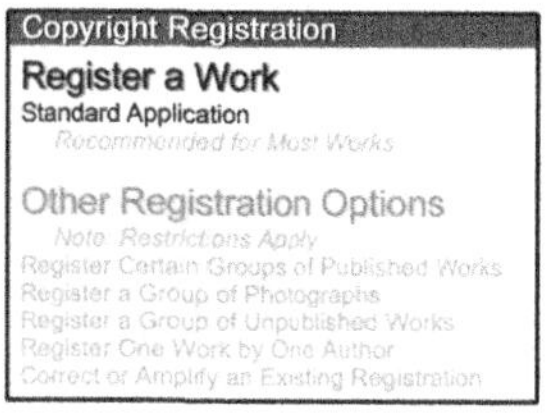

The Standard Application, as you may guess, is the all-purpose form for registering a single work. It can be used to register either a published or an unpublished work. This section covers the steps required to complete the Standard Application for a work of visual art.

START ▶ On Copyright.gov, go to Registration menu and the Register Your Work or Register a Copyright link.
Login to the eCO system.
Under Register A Work, select **Standard Application**

The first screen of the Standard Application shows eligibility requirements that should be reviewed. Confirm that the work fits the requirements and pay particular attention to works that cannot be registered on this form. (For instance, this application cannot be used for group registrations). If the work is not eligible for the Standard Application, return to the registration home screen and choose one of the other forms. Otherwise, you can begin the registration with this application.

1 Select **Start Registration**.
This will take you to the next screen.

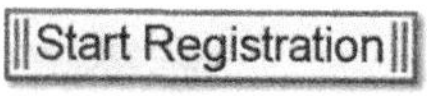

↓

Select the **Type of Work** from the drop-down list:

Literary Work
→ **Work of the Visual Arts**
Sound Recording
Work of the Performing Arts
Motion Picture/AV Work
Single Serial Issue

- Choose **Work of the Visual Arts** (or other appropriate selection) from the pull-down list.

- Review text describing the type of work and click the **checkbox** to indicate your understanding and agreement.

- Select **Continue** or save the application to finish later.

> Once you click Continue, the type of work cannot be changed. If there is a mistake, select the Save For Later button, return to the registration home page, delete the application, and start over.

2 TITLES

Entering the Titles for the work

- Click **New** to enter the title of the work you are registering. You will be directed to another screen to enter that information.

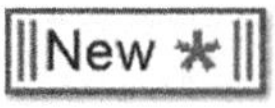

- Select **Title of work being registered** from the drop down list and enter the text of the work's title in the box. Enter the title in *plain* letters or numbers, *without* diacritical marks (such as ç, à, ñ, or ü). If there is no title for the work, enter a description or identifying phrase of your choice.

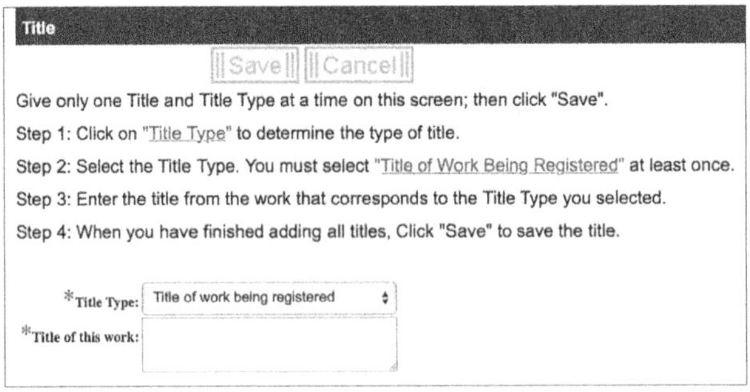

- Select **Save**. This will return you to the prior screen where you can choose to enter additional titles for the work.

Adding Optional Titles

Enter any additional titles for the work. A **series** title reflects an individual work that is akin to an episode or installment. A **larger work** is one that contains the individual work being registered. Adding a larger work title will display optional fields for volume, number, issue date and page information that can be completed if it applies. A **content** title typically refers one work in a larger work, such as one story in a book of short stories, when the larger work is the one being registered (e.g., the whole book). A **previous or alternative** title could include an earlier title, a working title, or a title in another language. To add a title:

- ▶ Click **New** again on the main title page.
- ▶ Select the title type, such as Previous or Alternative Title or Title of Larger Work or Series Title or Contents Title from the list.
- ▶ Enter the text for the additional title and any other appropriate information.
- ▶ Select **Save** to return to the previous screen—which should now show the additional title information.

To add further titles, repeat the process.

- When you have completed entering titles, select the **Continue** button.

3 PUBLICATION / COMPLETION

Entering Completion Date & Publication Information

- **Has the work been published?**

  Select **Yes** or **No** from the pull-down list option. Then enter the information requested:

- If **NO**, enter the **year** that the work was **completed** on the new screen. If you do not know the year the work was completed, you can enter an approximate year and later in step 11, add a note about the date with a qualifying statement, such as "on or about" "on or before" or "approximately."

  - Select **Continue**.

- If **YES**, enter the information:

  1) Year of **Completion** (the year in which the work was finished),

  2) Date the work was **first published** (month, day, year), and

  3) **Nation** where the work was first published.

Publication Note: Do not enter a future publication date. If the work was published on the same date in the U.S. and another country, identify the U.S. as the nation of first publication. If there were first publications in multiple countries on the same date, an explanatory statement should be provided in the Note to Copyright Office box in step 11.

Optional

For print published works, you may also enter information for an international standard number, such as an **ISBN** number for a published book, if it is applicable. Additional information concerning preregistration (not common) can also be entered in this screen.

- Select **Continue** when done.

4 AUTHORS

Entering the Author/Artist Information

- Select the **Add Me** button to automatically enter yourself and the contact information from your eCO login account.

OR

- Select **New**.
  Enter the **name of the artist** (author).
  Or, if the author is an organization, such as in the case of a work made for hire situation, enter the organization's name here.

Next, enter additional information about this author:

- The artist's **citizenship country** or **domicile** (country of permanent residence).
- The **artist's year of birth** (optional). If entered, this information will become public.
- Is this an **anonymous** or **pseudonymous** work?
  If yes, check the appropriate box. Enter the pseudonym in the text box.

- Indicate if this author's contribution is a **work made for hire**. Enter yes or no.
- Click **Save**. A new screen will open for entering information about this author's creative contribution.

Entering this Author's contributions:

- Select each checkbox that describes the author's contribution to the artwork that is being registered. In other words, indicate what this artist originally created. Multiple items can be selected if appropriate.

☐ Photograph	☐ Map
☐ 2-D artwork	☐ Architectural work
☐ Jewelry design	☐ Technical drawing
☐ Sculpture	☐ Other

If the type of contribution is not otherwise listed here, check the "other" box and enter a description. This could include some type of non-visual artwork contained in the work, such as a literary or audio-visual element. If you are registering a work that is not categorized as visual art, you will see different contribution options here.

- Select **Save**.

> For **joint work** (such as collaborative works), repeat the process for each of the authors of the work, click **new**, enter the information, and save. Select **Save** when the contribution section is complete.

- On the main Author's page select **Continue** when all author/artist information has been entered.

5 CLAIMANTS

Entering information about the person or persons claiming the copyright

The author or artist is the original copyright claimant. A claimant is also a person or organization that own the whole copyright in the work, and who owns the authorship in the work being registered. If you made the work and own the copyright, you are the claimant. The steps illustrated below are based upon an artist registering their own independently made, original artwork.

First, review the text on the Claimants screen. Then enter the individual claimant information:

- Select the **Add Me** button to automatically enter yourself and your contact information from your eCO login account if you are the artist/author.

OR

- Select **New**.
  Then enter the **name of the claimant** and the address information. The claimant entered must be either an individual or an organization, but not both.

- If any copyright claimant is not an author of the work, enter information about the ownership transfer. See the following note on Transfer Statements.

- Select **Save**. This will return you to the main Claimants page.
  - ▶ If there are **additional Claimants** repeat the steps above to enter their information and select Save. If this is a **joint work**, complete the claimant information for each author.
- Back on the main Claimants page, when all the claimants are entered, select **Continue**.

About Transfer Statements

If there has been a transfer of the copyright, this information should be entered on this screen in the area provided. A transfer means that actual ownership of the copyright has occurred. In that case, enter a transfer statement. Select how the copyright was obtained from the options: By written agreement, Inheritance, or Other. If Other is selected, enter a description of the transfer. For artists registering their independently made artwork, and who continue to own the full copyright in the work, do not enter any transfer information.

6 LIMITATION OF CLAIM

Entering information that defines the copyright

All original authorship should be "included" in the claim and generally, each element that is not original—such as public domain material—should be "excluded" from the claim. There are three parts to this section of the application: Material Excluded, Previous Registration, and New Material Included.

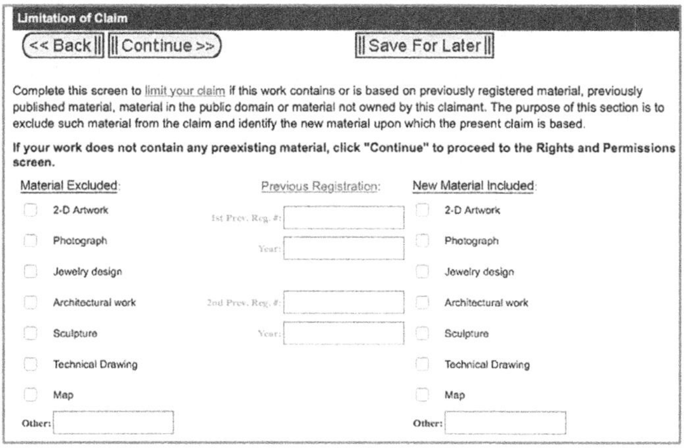
Limitation of Claim

<< Back || Continue >> || Save For Later ||

Complete this screen to limit your claim if this work contains or is based on previously registered material, previously published material, material in the public domain or material not owned by this claimant. The purpose of this section is to exclude such material from the claim and identify the new material upon which the present claim is based.

If your work does not contain any preexisting material, click "Continue" to proceed to the Rights and Permissions screen.

Material Excluded:	Previous Registration:	New Material Included:
☐ 2-D Artwork	1st Prev. Reg. #:	☐ 2-D Artwork
☐ Photograph	Year:	☐ Photograph
☐ Jewelry design		☐ Jewelry design
☐ Architectural work	2nd Prev. Reg. #:	☐ Architectural work
☐ Sculpture	Year:	☐ Sculpture
☐ Technical Drawing		☐ Technical Drawing
☐ Map		☐ Map
Other:		Other:

Identifying the Excluded Material:

- Select the checkbox or boxes that identify the type of material that is to be **excluded** from your copyright claim. This is material that will **not** be included in your copyright claim, such as public domain matter. Multiple boxes can be checked as needed.

☐ 2-D Artwork	☐ Sculpture
☐ Photograph	☐ Technical drawing
☐ Jewelry design	☐ Map
☐ Architecture work	☐ Other

Other Excluded Material: The Other box can be used to provide more specific or detailed description information, or to exclude a form of material that is not listed.

- Enter any **Prior Registration** information if it is applicable. This is not common, but if you have previously registered *this* artwork or a version of it, enter the prior registration information for the two most recent registrations. Leave the spaces blank if you have not previously registered the work you are registering now.

Identifying the Included Material:

- Identify the type of material is that is to be included in your copyright claim.

This section is essentially the heart of your copyright and of the registration process. It should be completed carefully. Be sure to select each type of material that is part of the original authorship of the work. Multiple boxes can be checked as needed.

☐ 2-D Artwork
☐ Photograph
☐ Jewelry design
☐ Architecture work
☐ Sculpture
☐ Technical drawing
☐ Map
☐ Other

Other Included Material: The Other box can be used to include a material that is not listed or which is not 2-D or 3-D artwork, such as literary or audio-visual elements. The Other box can be especially important for including all elements of an original multiple media work within the claim.

> Derivative Works
>
> If you are registering a derivative work all of the new material should be **included** in the claim. When a derivative work contains an appreciable amount of unclaimable material, previously published or registered material, public domain matter, or other material that is not owned by the claimant, these should be identified in the **excluded** section of the screen. Generally, if the preexisting material in the derivative work was created by you and has not been previously registered or published, it does not need to be specifically excluded.

- Select **Continue** when completed with the claim limitation screen.

7 RIGHTS & PERMISSIONS

This section is for entering contact information related to the **management** of the copyright. Enter yourself here or another person or organization who should be contacted for copyright management issues and any request for permission to use the work. Information entered here will be publically viewable in the Copyright Office's online catalog. If you do not want this information to be public, do not complete this section and select Continue to skip to the next screen.

- Select **Add Me** to automatically enter yourself and your login account information,

OR

- Select **New** and enter contact information manually or for another person or organization,

OR

- Opt to skip this section and not enter any information.

- Select **Continue**.

8 CORRESPONDENT

This section requires **contact information** for a person that can communicate with the Copyright Office if there are any questions about the registration. Enter your own information here or that of someone else of your choosing.

- Select **Add Me** to automatically enter yourself and your login account information,

OR

- Select **New** and enter contact information manually or for another person or organization.

- Select **Continue** when done.

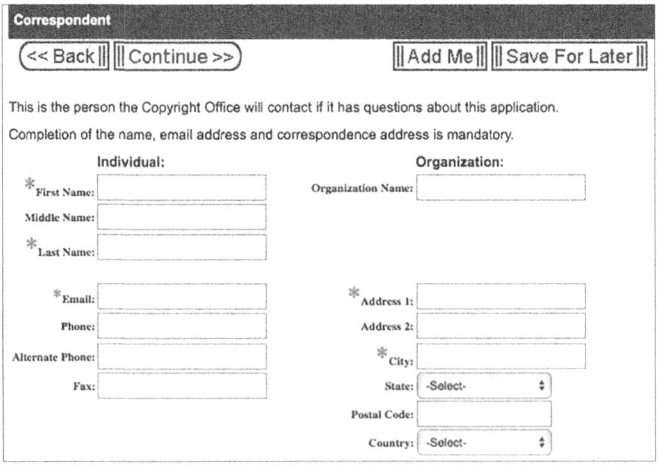

9 MAIL CERTIFICATE

The **mailing** information for the copyright registration certificate is entered in this screen. Enter your own name and mailing address information here or for the person to whom you want the copyright registration certificate to be sent.

If lost, a replacement certificate has an additional fee. If you change addresses in the interim be sure to continue mail forwarding or contact the Copyright Office instructions.

- Select **Add Me** to automatically enter yourself and your login account information,

OR

- Select **New** and enter contact information manually or for another person or organization.

- Select **Continue** when done.

10 SPECIAL HANDLING

This section of the application concerns expedited processing. The service is **restricted** to expected or pending litigation, customs issues, and publication deadlines. There is a **significant additional fee** and a request for expedited handling may be rejected by the Copyright Office–without a refund–if the criteria is not satisfied. The special handling surcharge is a minimum of $800 per claim at publication time, and additional fees may also apply. If you believe you want and qualify for expedited handling, review the requirements on the screen carefully.

- If you are **not** seeking special handling, do not enter anything and **skip this section** entirely by clicking **Continue**.

OR

- If you want and qualify for special handling, then you must indicate the **compelling reason** for the request: (1) Pending or prospective litigation, (2) customs matters, or (3) contract or publication deadlines that necessitate the expedited issuance of a certificate.

  - A certification is required, indicating that you are the author, claimant, or authorized agent. If this is the correct, **check** the appropriate box.

  - Enter an **explanation** for the Special Handling request in the text box as indicated.

  - Select **continue** when complete

11 CERTIFICATION

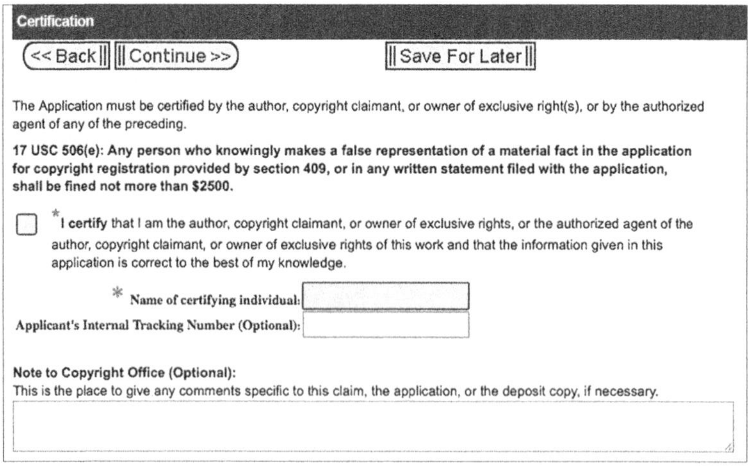

Certification

<< Back | Continue >> | Save For Later

The Application must be certified by the author, copyright claimant, or owner of exclusive right(s), or by the authorized agent of any of the preceding.

17 USC 506(e): Any person who knowingly makes a false representation of a material fact in the application for copyright registration provided by section 409, or in any written statement filed with the application, shall be fined not more than $2500.

☐ * **I certify** that I am the author, copyright claimant, or owner of exclusive rights, or the authorized agent of the author, copyright claimant, or owner of exclusive rights of this work and that the information given in this application is correct to the best of my knowledge.

* **Name of certifying individual:**

Applicant's Internal Tracking Number (Optional):

Note to Copyright Office (Optional):
This is the place to give any comments specific to this claim, the application, or the deposit copy, if necessary.

The required certification statement affirms that the application information is true and correct to the best of your knowledge and that the person making the registration is the proper person to do it. The text refers to penalties for improper representations. Review the text on this screen carefully before proceeding.

- To certify the application, **check the box**. When doing so, you are affirming facts, as shown on the screen:

> **I certify** that I am the author, copyright claimant, or owner of exclusive rights, or the authorized agent of the author, copyright claimant, or owner of exclusive rights and that the information given in this application is correct to the best of my knowledge.

- To complete the certification, **enter your name** in the box provided and, if desired, a personal tracking number can be entered as well. (The tracking number will appear on the registration certificate).

  ▸ **Optional**: **Add a comment** for the Copyright Office. At the bottom of the screen is a box for providing further information concerning the registration. Enter any pertinent comments concerning the claim, the application, the deposit copy, or other related issues, such as clarifying publication details.

- Select **Continue**.

12 Review Submission

This screen shows the entries that you have made in the application. This point in the application is the last opportunity to make any changes to the information that you entered. Review your entries carefully and correct any errors or omissions.

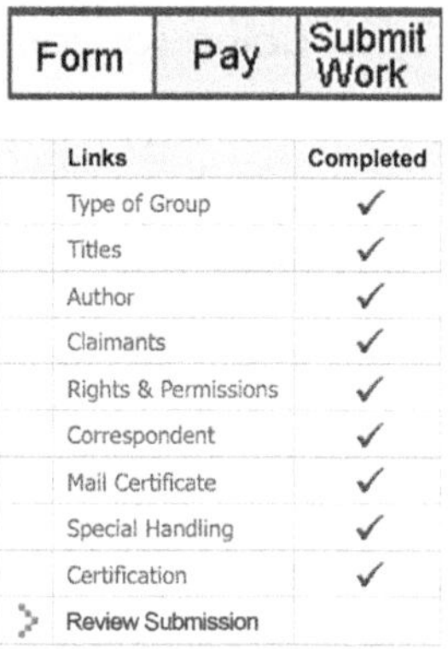

- **To make any changes** use the links on the left side of the screen to navigate to the step that you want to change. Save the entries on each screen that you change.

- **Return** to the Review Submission screen by clicking the link.

  All sections of the application should have a checkmark by their link, showing that they have been completed. If not, return to that section and complete any missing information required, saving the changes by selecting either the save or continue button, as necessary. Return to the Review Submission screen.

- Review the final application entries.

The process is not yet complete. Continue with the steps below to complete the application submission, payment processes, and to deposit a copy of the work.

13 Submit the Application & Pay the Fee

- On the Review Submission screen, select **Add to Cart.**

  Note: Changes cannot be made to the application once it is added to the cart.

On the **My Cart** screen, you should see your application in the **Cases in Cart** list with the **Fee Due** indicated.

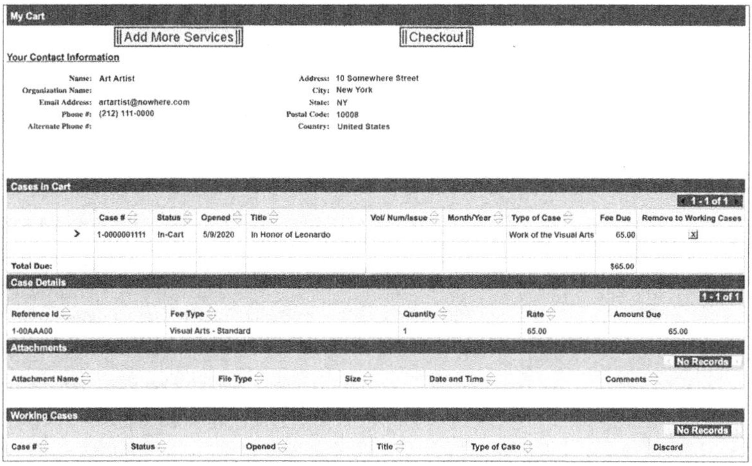

- Select the **Checkout** button.
  (Alternatively, the Add More Services button takes you out of the pay system to add more items from the registration home page).

To enter payment information:

- Select **Pay - Credit Card/ACH** to pay with a credit or debit card, or to pay from a checking or savings account. (Or, users with a pre-paid Copyright Office account can select the Pay-Deposit Account option instead).

Do you wish to proceed with the payment?

- Select **OK.** Alternatively, Cancel to discontinue, but note that the registration is not complete without payment.

↓

The system will automatically redirect you to a Pay.gov screen for **Copyright Fee Services**.

Choose your method of payment:

○ A withdrawal from a checking or savings account (ACH)

OR

○ A debit or credit card. Accepted types are shown on the screen.

- Select **Continue**.

- Enter your payment details and review the information.

> Registrations filed fully via the eCO system become effective for the date the application materials are submitted online (along with the fee and an uploaded deposit copy).

- To submit the payment, select **Continue**. This will return to the eCO application system. (To discontinue the payment process at this stage, select Cancel or Previous instead).

- When you see the **payment successful** screen, select **Continue.** This will take you to the deposit section of the registration process.

14 Upload A Copy of the Artwork

The final step is uploading a copy of the artwork that is the subject of the application. This is called the deposit and to use the online system, it must be in digital form. Each digital file uploaded is limited to 500 MB, preferably in .jpg (.jpeg), .tif (.tiff) or .gif format. Generally, upload a single digital image file for a 2-D work. 3-D works may be deposited as multiple digital files to show other sides of the work, for instance. Once uploaded, the digital files cannot be deleted or changed. Alternatively, the deposit can be made by mail. **Choose either the upload or mail-in method, but not both.**

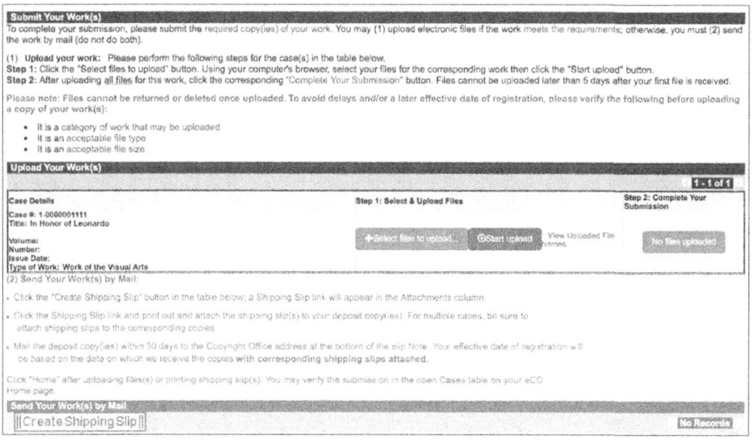

To Upload the Deposit:

- **Review** the text on the page and confirm that your files match the requirements, the **file types** are acceptable, and each file to be uploaded is 500 MB or less.

- Select the **+Files to Upload** Button. A new window will open.

- Navigate to the files on your computer. **Select each file** to be uploaded.

- Select the **Start Upload** button. When each file is fully uploaded, the phrase *Successfully Uploaded* will be automatically added to the file name shown on the screen.

> → Confirm that you have selected the correct image file or files for uploading. To delete a file, select the Remove button shown to the right of the item listing.
>
> → Do not leave the page or close the application until all of the files have been successfully uploaded.
>
> → No more files may be uploaded after the "Click Here to Complete Your Submission After Uploading All Files" link has been activated.

- When ALL files are successfully uploaded, click the green **Complete Your Submission After Uploading All Files** link.

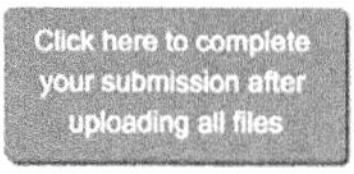

The screen should now display a message stating **Claim Submission Complete, No Further Action Required**. You should receive an e-mail from the Copyright Office confirming the receipt of your files. Do not print a shipping slip and do not mail a physical copy if you have uploaded your deposit copy through this method.

At this point **logout** of eCO. Or, select **Home** from the upper right menu on the screen to return to the main Registration page where you can confirm that the application you just completed is shown as an Open Case or to continue with other services.

To Mail In Deposit Materials:

As an alternative to the upload method, the Standard Application permits the submission of your deposit copy by mail.

The mail-in option may be used when a file exceeds the current maximum of 500 MB or to send materials that are not digital files, such as a printed photograph of the work. Do not mail your deposit copy if you have already submitted it through the upload process.

The mail-in process begins on the **Submit Your Works** screen that appears after the fee payment has been completed.

- Select the **Create Shipping Slip** button shown on the lower part of the Submit Your Works screen.

  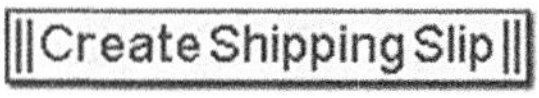

  Within a few seconds, an attachment link will appear on the lower area of the screen. Click the link to open the document and select **OK** in the pop-up window. When the document opens, print a copy.

- **Attach** the shipping slip to the physical material or to the device that you are submitting with the files–a CD or DVD, flash drive, or other storage device.

- Mail the materials **within 30 days** to the address shown on the shipping slip. Because the registration is not effective until the materials are received by the Copyright Office, prompt mailing is important.

One Work By One Author: The Single Application

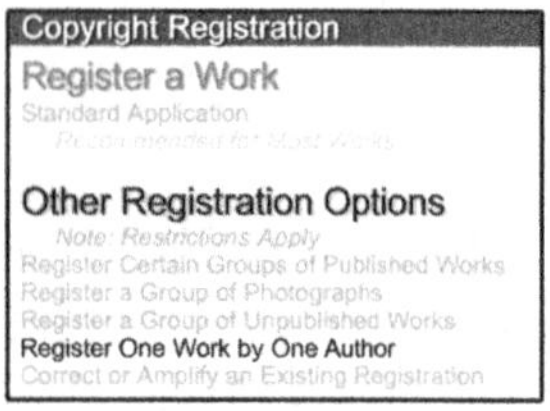

This section covers the steps required to complete the *One Work By One Author* application, also referred to as a *Single Application*, for one work categorized as a work of visual art. This is the simplest and least expensive method for registering a single work. It has some minor differences from the Standard Application and some restrictions. Be sure and read the section on this application in the prior chapter before beginning. The Single Application can be used for any type of qualifying work. This example shows the steps for registering a work categorized as visual art.

START ▶ On Copyright.gov, go to the Registration menu and the Register York Work or Register a Copyright link.
Login to the eCO system.
Under Other Registration Options, select **Register One Work by One Author**.

The first screen of this application shows eligibility requirements that should be reviewed. Confirm that the work fits all requirements:

- Only one work is to be registered with this form.
- The work was created by one individual only. Joint (or collaborative) works are not eligible.
- All of the material in the work was created by the same individual.
- The author/artist of the work, owner of all of the copyrights in the work, and the claimant are the same person.
- The work was not made for hire.

- The deposit copy or copies of the single work must be able to be uploaded in digital form. This application does not permit the deposit copy to be mailed in physical form.

When reviewing the criteria, pay particular attention to works that cannot be registered on this form. If the work is not eligible for this application, return to the registration home screen and choose one of the other forms. Otherwise, if your work meets **all** of the eligibility criteria for this application, continue with the registration.

1 Select **Start Registration**. This will take you to the next screen.

||Start Registration||

↓

Select the **Type of Work** from the drop-down list:

Literary Work
→ **Work of the Visual Arts**
Sound Recording
Work of the Performing Arts
Motion Picture/AV Work
Single Serial Issue

- Choose **Work of the Visual Arts** (or other appropriate selection) from the pull-down list.

- Review text describing the type of work and click the **checkbox** to indicate your understanding and agreement.

- Select **Continue** or save the application to finish later.

> Once you click Continue, the type of work cannot be changed. If there is a mistake, select the Save For Later button, return to the registration home page, delete the application and start over.

2 TITLE

Entering the title of the work

- Enter the **Title** of the work in the text box on the screen. If the work does not have a title, enter a description of the work instead. Only one title or one description may be entered. Use letters or numbers. If the title contains diacritical marks (ç, à, ñ, or ü) enter them as plain text.

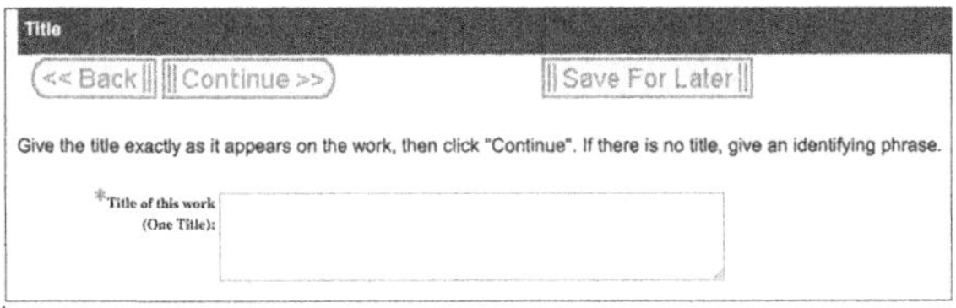

- Select the **Continue** button.

3 PUBLICATION / COMPLETION

Entering the Completion Date & Publication Information

Has the work been published?

▶ Select **Yes** or **No** from the pull-down list option. Then enter the information requested in the new screen that appears:

○ If **No**, enter the **year** that the work was **completed**.

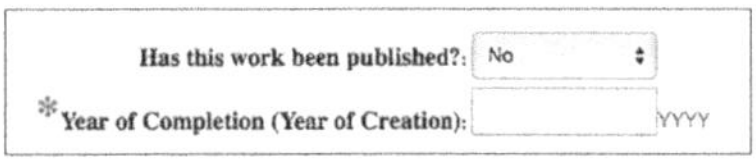

If you do not know when the work was completed, enter an approximate year. Later in step 10, add a note about the completion date with a qualifying statement, such as "on or about" "on or before" or "approximately."

- Select Continue.

- If **Yes**, enter the information:

    1) Year of **Completion** (when the work was finished),

    2) Date the work was **first published** (month, day, year), and

    3) **Nation** where the work was first published.

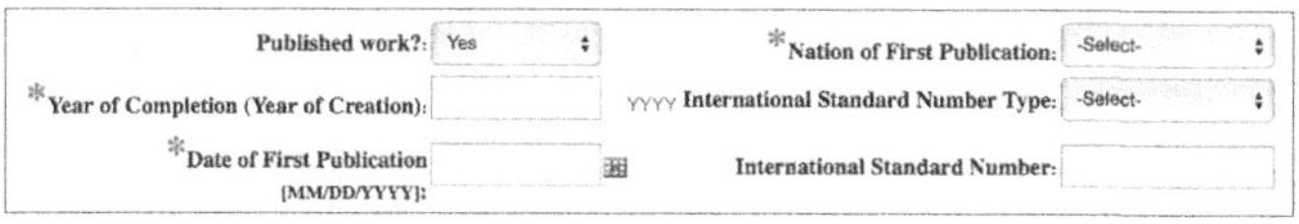

Do not enter a *future* publication date. If the work was published on the same date in the U.S. and another country, identify the U.S. as the nation of first publication. If there were first publications in multiple countries on the same date, an explanatory statement should be provided in the Note to Copyright Office box later in step 10.

Optional

For published works, you may also enter information for an international standard number, such as an **ISBN** number for a published book, if it is applicable to your work.

- Select **Continue** when done.

4 AUTHOR / CLAIMANT

Entering the Author and Claimant Information

This application requires that the author (artist) and the claimant are the same person and therefore the author and claimant's information is combined into one section.

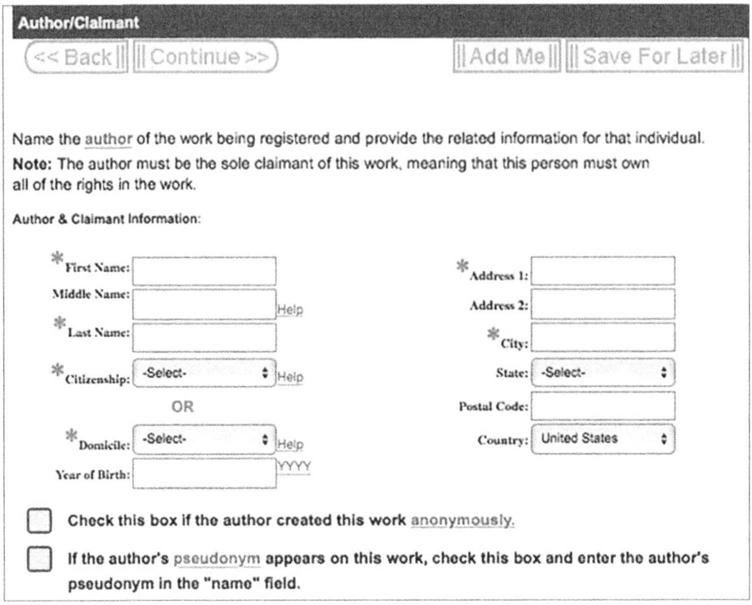

- Select the **Add Me** button to automatically enter yourself and the contact information from your eCO login account.

OR

- Select **New**.
  Then enter the **name of the author/claimant** (the artist) and address information.

Next, enter information about the artist on the same screen:

- The artist's **citizenship country** or **domicile** (country of permanent residence).
- The **artist's year of birth** (optional). If this is entered, it will be become public information.

- Is this an **anonymous** or **pseudonymous** work? If yes, check the appropriate box. Enter the pseudonym in the box.

Next, enter a basic description of what the **artist created**.

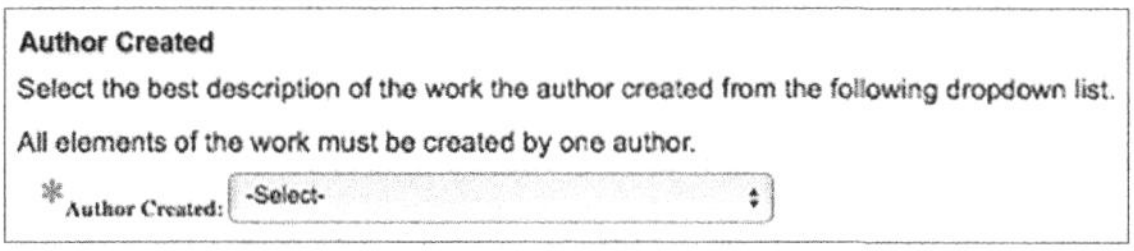

- **Select** the option in the drop-down list that **best** describes the work created:

One Photograph
One Logo
One Sculpture
One piece of Jewelry
One Painting
One Drawing
One Illustration
One Comic Strip
One Fabric Design
One Textile Design
One Wallpaper Design
One Artwork

For works of visual art that do not fit into the other choices, the last item, **one artwork**, may be selected.

- Select **Continue**.

5 LIMITATION OF CLAIM

Entering information that defines the copyright

The information entered in this screen essentially defines the copyright that is being registered. The Single Application only requires an identification of the material that is specifically excluded from the claim. Elements that are excluded are not covered by the copyright. For this application, if an element is *not excluded*, then it will be considered to be *included* in the copyright claim. *Included* material is the essence of the copyright in the work.

Only exclude elements that are not part of your copyright in the work. Typical elements that may be excluded are public domain material and other preexisting material that has been previously published or registered. If there is no public domain material in the work, nor other such preexisting material, leave all fields **blank** in this screen and continue to the next one

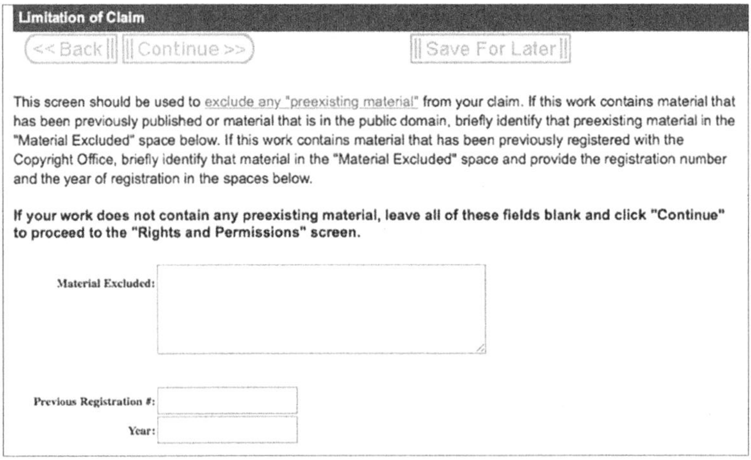
Limitation of Claim

<< Back | Continue >> | Save For Later

This screen should be used to exclude any "preexisting material" from your claim. If this work contains material that has been previously published or material that is in the public domain, briefly identify that preexisting material in the "Material Excluded" space below. If this work contains material that has been previously registered with the Copyright Office, briefly identify that material in the "Material Excluded" space and provide the registration number and the year of registration in the spaces below.

If your work does not contain any preexisting material, leave all of these fields blank and click "Continue" to proceed to the "Rights and Permissions" screen.

Material Excluded:

Previous Registration #:

Year:

- Read the text on the Limitation of Claim screen.

- If there is any material that you want to exclude from the claim, briefly describe the material in the text box labeled **Material Excluded**.

> ! Important: Do not enter any new or original material for this claim on this screen. Do not enter any element or material that forms a part or the whole of your copyright in the work.

Then, *if* the pre-existing material that is identified in the Material Excluded box has been registered before, enter the **prior registration number** and the year. If there has been multiple such registrations, enter the most recent. If there is no prior registration, leave the last two boxes on the screen blank.

OR

- If there is no preexisting material to exclude, leave all spaces on this screen **blank**.

- Select **Continue** when completed with the claim limitation screen.

6 RIGHTS & PERMISSIONS

This section is for entering contact information related to the **management** of the copyright. Enter yourself here or another person or organization who should be contacted for copyright management issues and any request for permission to use the works. Information entered here will be publically viewable in the Copyright Office's online catalog. If you do not want this information to be public, do not complete this section and select Continue to skip to the next screen.

- Select **Add Me** to automatically enter yourself and your login account information,

  OR

- Select **New** and enter contact information manually or for another person or organization,

  OR

- **Skip** this section and do not enter any information.

- Select **Continue** when done.

7 CORRESPONDENT

This section requires **contact information** for a person that can communicate with the Copyright Office if there are any questions about the registration. Enter your own information here or that of someone else of your choosing.

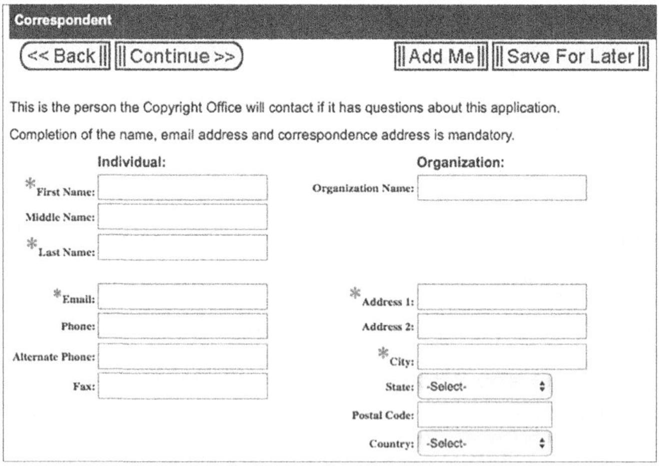

- Select **Add Me** to automatically enter yourself and your login account information.

OR

- Select **New** and enter contact information manually or for another person or organization.

- Select **Continue** when done.

8 MAIL CERTIFICATE

The **mailing** information for the copyright registration certificate is entered in this screen. Enter your own name and mailing address information here or for the person to whom you want the copyright registration certificate to be sent.

If lost, a replacement certificate has an additional fee. If you change addresses in the interim period be sure to continue mail forwarding or contact the Copyright Office for instructions.

- Select **Add Me** to automatically enter yourself and your login account information.

OR

- Select **New** and enter contact information manually or for another person or organization.

- Select **Continue** when done.

9 SPECIAL HANDLING

This section of the application concerns expedited processing. Expedited processing is **restricted** to situations where there is expected or pending litigation, customs issues, and publication deadlines. There is a **significant additional fee** and a request for expedited handling may be rejected by the Copyright Office–without a refund–if the criteria is not satisfied.

The special handling surcharge is a minimum of $800 per claim at publication time and additional fees may also apply. If you believe you want and qualify for expedited handling, review the requirements on the screen carefully.

- If you are **not** seeking special handling, do not enter anything and **skip this section** entirely by clicking **Continue**.

OR

- If you want and qualify for special handling, then you must indicate the **compelling reason** for the request: (1) Pending or prospective litigation, (2) customs matters, or (3) contract or publication deadlines that necessitate the expedited issuance of a certificate.

    - A certification is required, indicating that you are the author, claimant, or authorized agent. If this is the correct, **check** the appropriate box.
    - Enter an **explanation** for the Special Handling request in the text box as indicated.
    - Select **continue** when complete

10 CERTIFICATION

The required certification statement affirms that the application information is true and correct to the best of your knowledge and that the person making the registration is the proper person to do it. The text refers to penalties for improper representations. Review the text on this screen carefully before proceeding.

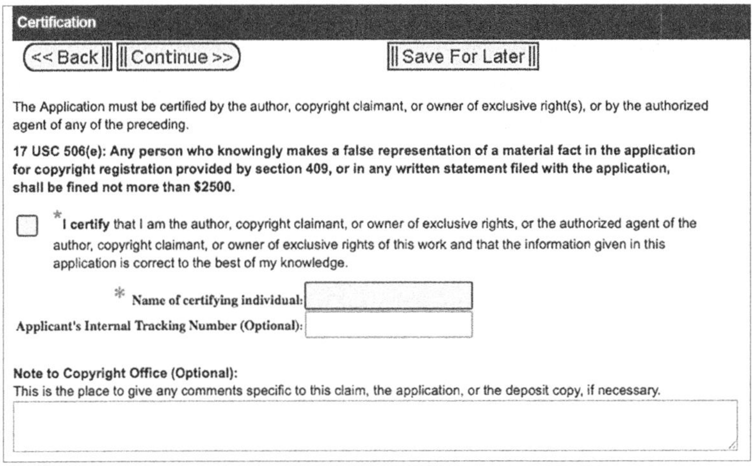

- To certify the application, **check the box**. When doing so, you are affirming the facts and information that were entered:

> **I certify** that I am the author, copyright claimant, or owner of exclusive rights, or the authorized agent of the author, copyright claimant, or owner of exclusive rights and that the information given in this application is correct to the best of my knowledge.

- To complete the certification, **enter your name** in the box provided and, if desired, a personal tracking number can be entered as well. (The tracking number will appear on the registration certificate).

    ▶ **Optional**: **Add a comment** for the Copyright Office. At the bottom of the screen is a box for providing further information concerning the registration. Enter any pertinent comments concerning the claim, the application, the deposit copy, or other related issues, such as clarifying publication details.

- Select **Continue**.

11 Review Submission

This screen shows the entries that you have made in the application. This point in the application is the last opportunity to make any changes to the information that you entered. Review your entries carefully and correct any errors or omissions.

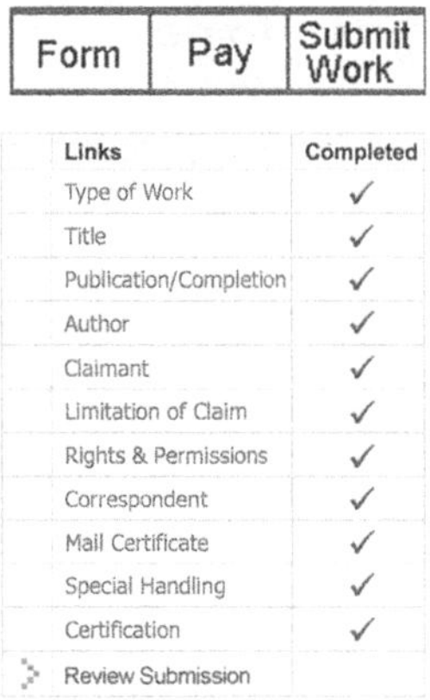

- ► **To make any changes** use the links on the left side of the screen to navigate to the step that you want to change. Save the entries on each screen that you change.

- **Return** to the Review Submission screen by clicking the link in the left menu. All sections of the application should have a checkmark, showing that each has been completed. If not, return to that section and complete any missing information required. Save your changes by selecting either the save or continue button, as necessary. Return to the Review Submission screen.

- **Review** the final application entries.

The process is not yet complete. Continue with the steps below to complete the application submission and payment processes, and to deposit a copy of the work.

12 Submit the Application & Pay the Fee

- On the Review Submission screen, select **Add to Cart.** **Note**: Changes cannot be made to the application once it is added to the cart.

On the **My Cart** screen, you should see your application in the **Cases in Cart** list with the **Fee Due** indicated.

- Select the **Checkout** button. *(The Add More Services button takes you out of the pay system to add more items from the registration home page).*

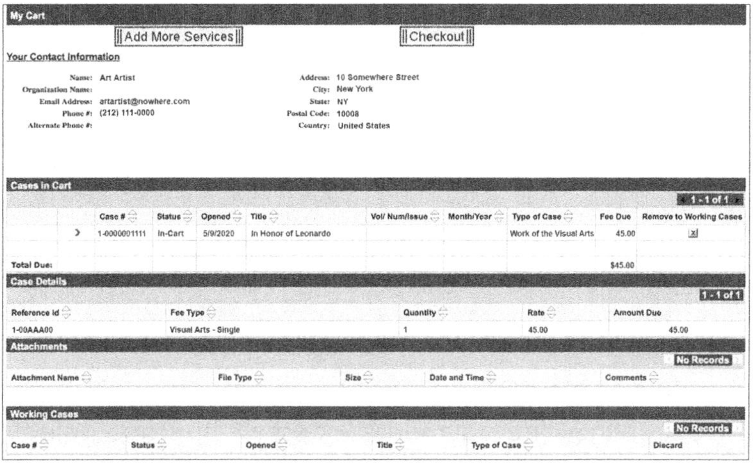

To enter payment information:

- Select **Pay - Credit Card/ACH** to pay with a credit or debit card, or to pay from a checking or savings account. Alternatively, users with a pre-paid Copyright Office account can select the Pay-Deposit Account option instead.

Do you wish to proceed with the payment?

- Select **OK.** (Alternatively, Cancel to discontinue, but note that the registration is not complete without payment).

↓

The system will automatically redirect you to a Pay.gov screen for **Copyright Fee Services**.

Choose your method of payment:

- ○ A withdrawal from a checking or savings account (ACH),

OR

- ○ A debit or credit card. Accepted types are shown on the screen.

- Select **Continue**.
- Enter your payment details and review the information.
- To submit the payment, select **Continue**. This will return to the eCO application system. (To discontinue the payment process at this stage, select Cancel or Previous instead).
- When you see the **payment successful** screen, select **Continue.** This will take you to the deposit section of the registration process.

Registrations filed entirely via the eCO system become effective for the date the application materials are submitted online (along with the fee and uploaded deposit copy).

13 Upload A Copy of the Artwork

The final step is uploading a copy of the artwork that is the subject of the application. This is called the deposit and to use the online system, it must be in digital form. Each digital file uploaded is limited to 500 MB, preferably in .jpg, .tif (.tiff) or .gif format. Generally, upload a single digital image file for a 2-D work. A copy of a 3-D work may be deposited as multiple digital files to show the back side of the work, for instance. Once uploaded, the digital files cannot be deleted or changed. Alternatively, the deposit can be made by mail. **Choose either the upload or mail-in method, but not both.**

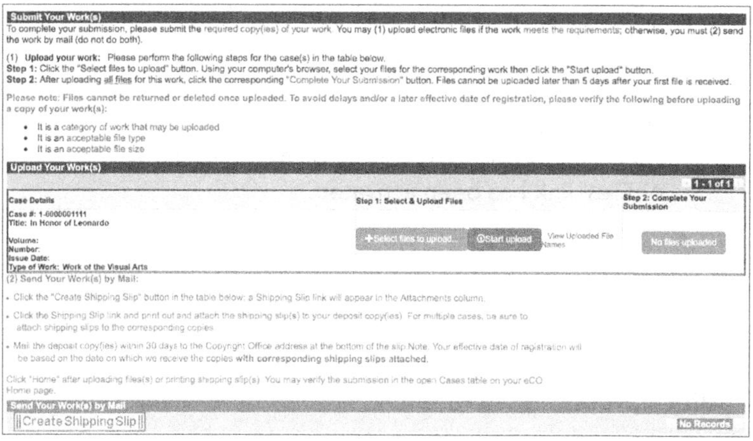

To Upload the Deposit:

- **Review** the text on the page and confirm that your files match the requirements, the **file types** are acceptable, and each file to be uploaded is 500 MB or less.
- Select the **+Files to Upload** Button. A new window will open.

- Navigate to the files on your computer. **Select each file** to be uploaded.

- Select the **Start Upload** button. When each file is successfully uploaded, the phrase *Successfully Uploaded* will be automatically added to its file name on the screen.

> → Confirm that you have selected the correct image file or files for uploading. To delete a file, select the Remove button shown to the right of the item listing.
>
> → Do not leave the page or close the application until all of the files have been successfully uploaded.
>
> → No more files may be uploaded after the "Click Here to Complete Your Submission After Uploading All Files" link has been activated.

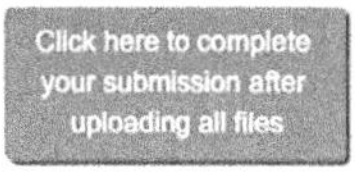

- When ALL files are successfully uploaded, click the green **Complete Your Submission After Uploading All Files** link.

The screen should now display a message stating that the **Claim Submission Complete, No Further Action Required**. You should receive an e-mail from the Copyright Office confirming the receipt of your files. Do not print a shipping slip and do not mail a physical copy if you have uploaded your deposit copy through this method.

At this point you can log out of eCO. Or, select Home from the upper right menu on the screen to return to the main Registration page where you can confirm that the application you just completed is shown as an Open Case or continue with other services.

To Mail In Deposit Materials:

As an alternative to the upload method, the One Work by One Author/Single Application permits the submission of your deposit copy by mail.

The mail-in option may be used, for example, when a file exceeds the current maximum of 500 MB or to send materials that are not digital files, such as a printed photograph of the work. Do not mail your deposit copy if you have already submitted it through the up-load process.

The mail-in process begins on the **Submit Your Works** screen that appears after the fee payment has been completed.

- Select the **Create Shipping Slip** button shown on the lower part of the Submit Your Works screen. Within a few seconds, an attachment link will appear on the lower area of the screen. Click the link to open the document and select **OK** in the pop-up window. When the document opens, print a copy of it.

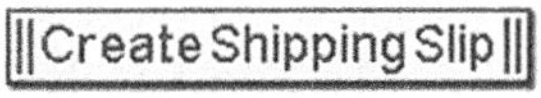

- **Attach** the shipping slip to the physical material or to the device that you are submitting with the files – a CD or DVD, a flash drive, or another storage device.

- Mail the materials **within 30 days** to the address shown on the shipping slip. Because the registration is not effective until the materials are received by the Copyright Office, prompt mailing is important.

Application for Group Registration of Unpublished Works

A group application is used to submit one application to register multiple qualifying works together for one fee. The group application is only available in the online eCO system and may be used for registering up to 10 unpublished works. The deposit copies of the works must be submitted in digital form via the eCO upload process.

Suggested Preparation

- Prepare and **collect the digital files** that will be submitted later as the deposit copies of the works. Place them into a single folder on your computer or device. The individual file size is limited to 500 MB.

- Using a text or word processing program, **create a list of the titles** of each of the works in the group. This will be useful for inserting the titles in the application and also for reviewing the information before the final submission.

START ▶ On Copyright.gov, go to the Registration menu.
Select Register Your Work or Register a Copyright.
Login to the eCO system.
Under the Register A Work heading, select **Register a Group of Unpublished Works**

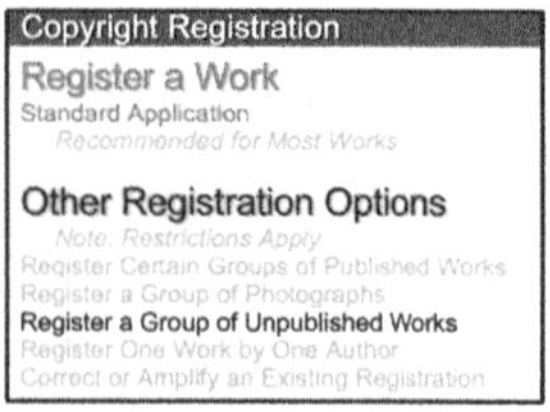

The first screen of the Unpublished Group Application shows eligibility requirements. Review these and confirm that the work fits the requirements.

- Each of the works must not have been published.
- All of the works must be the same type; the authorship (creativity) must be the same. Example: a group of drawings, a group of sculptures, or a group of paintings.
- All of the works must have been created by the same author/artist or by the same co-authors.

This application cannot be used for works made in different types of media, published works, or works that were created by different artists that were not co-authors of each and every work in the group. Some works, including websites, databases, other compilations, or collective works cannot be registered with this application. If the work is not eligible for this application, return to the registration home screen and choose one of the other forms. Otherwise, you can begin the registration with this application. The examples that follow reflect the process for registering a group of unpublished works of visual art.

1 Review the eligibility requirements on the screen, and if they are met, select the **Start Registration** button to continue. This will take you to the next screen.

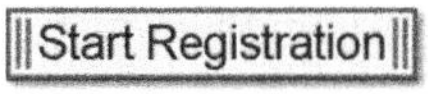

↓

Select the **Type of Work** from the drop-down list:

	Literary Work
→	**Work of the Visual Arts**
	Sound Recording
	Work of the Performing Arts
	Motion Picture/AV Work

- Choose **Work of the Visual Arts** (or other appropriate selection) from the pull-down list.

- Review the text describing the type of work and click the **checkbox** to indicate your understanding and agreement.

- Select **Continue** or save the application to finish later.

Once you click Continue, the type of work cannot be changed. If there is a mistake, select the Save For Later button, return to the registration home page, delete the application and start over.

2 TITLES

Entering Titles for the works included in the group

A title should be entered for each of the individual works in the group. Enter at least 2 titles, but not more than 10 titles total. Separately, an administrative title for the entire group will be automatically generated as part of the process. The automatic group title typically incorporates the title of the first work entered in this section and the number of additional works in the group. Such as, "Portrait of New Mona Lisa *and 9 other works*."

The system generated group name does not have a bearing on the copyrights. If you want the individual work titles to be cohesive in the Copyright Office's catalog, consider incorporating a group or series name as part of each individual title that you enter. Such as "Paintings of 2019: Portrait of New Mona Lisa." Regardless, the content of the titles entered for the works are entirely your choice.

- Click **New** to enter the title of the first work in the group and a new screen will appear.

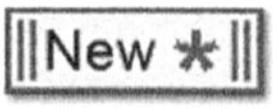

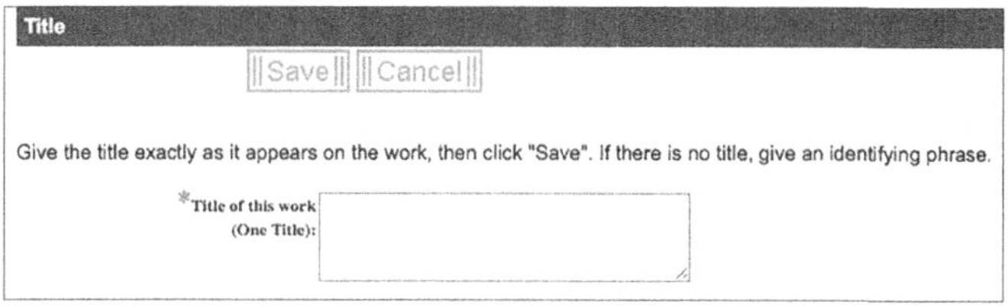

- **Enter the title** in plain letters or numbers. Avoid diacritical marks (such as ç, à, ñ, or ü) and also avoid commas and semicolons, which can confuse the eCO system. Other punctuation forms, such as dashes, colons, and periods should be fine. If there is no title for the work, enter a description or identifying phrase of your choice.

- Select **Save**. This will return you to the prior screen.

- Select **New** again and enter the title for the next work in your group.

- Click **Save**.

  ▸ **Repeat** the process for each work in the group, entering up to 10 titles maximum.

- When you have entered all of the titles, **review** the **All Titles** list on the main Titles screen. It should contain a title for each of the works being registered in the group.

  If you make a mistake, simply delete the title or edit it using the icons shown in the *All Titles* list on the main Titles screen.

- Select **Continue** when all titles are entered and correct.

- When you have completed entering titles, select the **Continue** button.

3 COMPLETION

Entering the date that all of the works were completed

- In the box, enter the four-digit **year that the group of works was completed**. If the works were completed over two or more years, enter the year that the most recent work in the group was completed.

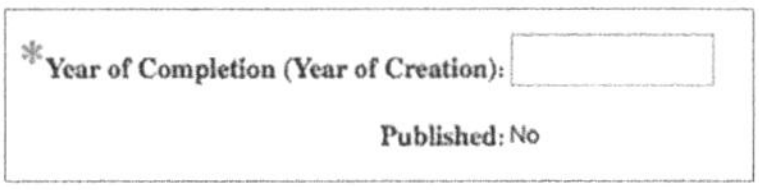

- Select **Continue** when done.

> The Completion screen contains important information about publication status. Publication is automatically entered as "No" because the Group of Unpublished Works application can be used only to register copyrights in works that have not been published. For more information about determining publication status in the context of copyright registration, refer to the section covering publication in Chapter 5.

4 AUTHORS / CLAIMANTS

Entering the author/artist information

The author and claimant must be the same person or the same organization for all of the works in the group. In the case of jointly made (or collaborative) works, all authors and claimants must be the same for all of the works as well. If you created the works in the group and own the copyrights, you are the author and the claimant.

- Select the **Add Me** button to automatically enter your information from your eCO login account.

OR

- Select **New**. Then enter the **name of the artist** (author).

  Or, if the author is an organization, such as in a work made for hire situation, enter the organization's name here.

Next, enter additional information about this author:

- The artist's **citizenship country** or **domicile** (country of permanent residence).
- The **artist's year of birth** (optional). Note that if entered, this will be become public information.
- Is this an **anonymous** or **pseudonymous** work? If yes, check the appropriate box. Enter the pseudonym in the box.
- Indicate if this author's contribution is a ***work made for hire***. Select yes or no from the pull-down list.
- Click **Save**. A new screen will open for entering information about this author's creative contribution.

On the new screen, enter information about this author's contribution to the work:

- In the **Author Created** pull-down list near the bottom

of the screen, select the *best* description of the creative contribution by the author identified above. The options are:

Unpublished Pictorial or Graphic Works
Unpublished Sculptural Works
Unpublished Jewelry Designs
Unpublished Maps
Unpublished Technical Drawings
Unpublished Illustrations
Unpublished Fabric, Textile, or Wallpaper Designs
Unpublished Flooring Designs
Other Unpublished 2-D Artwork
Other Unpublished 3-D Artwork

For the purposes of registration, pictorial or graphic works encompasses a wide range of 2-D and 3-D works (refer to page 49). Yet, 2-D Artwork and 3-D Artwork are also included in the options, as well as "Sculptural Works." There is obviously some overlap and not much guidance from the Copyright Office as to the differences. It could be deduced that, for instance, the label of "sculptural work" would tend to apply to actual sculptures. Whereas 3-D Artwork could be some other type of work that has volume, but which is not a "sculpture" per se. Choose whichever description seems most appropriate to your work. If none of the other descriptions fit, choose one of the "Other" options. For qualifying groups of multi-media works, choose the option that best matches the predominant form in the works.

- Select **Save**.

- If these are **joint works** (collaborative works), repeat the process, adding each of the authors of the works:

  Click **new**, enter the information.

  Select **Save** when the contribution section is complete.

  If you made an error, simply click the "edit" link for the particular author and make your changes.

A Note on Joint Works and Multiple Contributing Artists:

All authors must have contributed to each one of the works registered in the group, and the creative contributions of all authors must match identically. For example, if all authors entered the contribution of "Unpublished Pictorial or Graphic Works" (in the menu), this should be fine. However if one author contributed 2-D material and another author contributed 3-D material, this can be an issue. Where there is a difference between the type of creative contributions for each author, the application will not advance beyond this point because the disparate information conflicts with criteria for using it.

- On the main Author's page select **Continue** when all author/artist information has been entered.

5 LIMITATION OF CLAIM

Entering information that identifies the copyright in the works

The Group of Unpublished Works application requires identifying the material that is *excluded* from the claim. Excluded elements are not covered by the copyright. *Included* material is the essence of the copyright in the works. If an element is *not excluded* here, then it is considered to be *included* in the copyright claim.

Only exclude elements that are not part of your copyright in the works. Typical elements that may be excluded are those consisting of public domain material and other preexisting material that has been previously published or registered. If there is no public domain material in the work, nor other such preexisting material, leave all fields **blank** in this screen and continue to the next one.

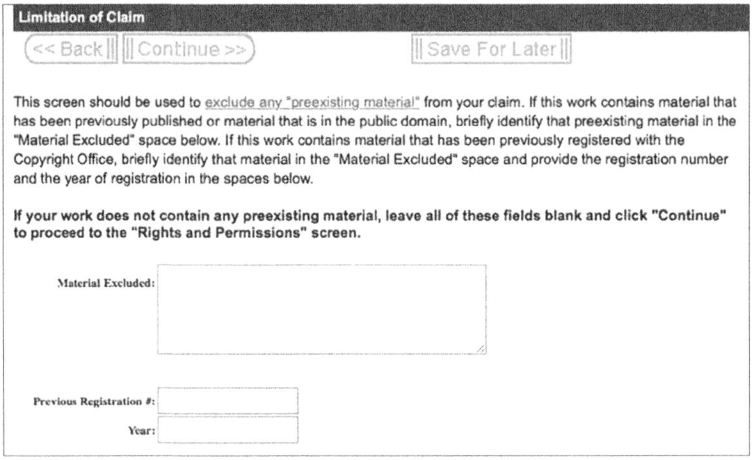
Limitation of Claim

<< Back | Continue >> | Save For Later

This screen should be used to exclude any "preexisting material" from your claim. If this work contains material that has been previously published or material that is in the public domain, briefly identify that preexisting material in the "Material Excluded" space below. If this work contains material that has been previously registered with the Copyright Office, briefly identify that material in the "Material Excluded" space and provide the registration number and the year of registration in the spaces below.

If your work does not contain any preexisting material, leave all of these fields blank and click "Continue" to proceed to the "Rights and Permissions" screen.

Material Excluded:

Previous Registration #:

Year:

- Read the text on the Limitation of Claim screen.

  - If there is any material that you want to exclude from the claim, briefly describe the material in the text box labeled **Material Excluded**.

    If you have previously registered the pre-existing material identified in the Material Excluded box, enter the **prior registration number** and the year. If there has been multiple such registrations, enter the most recent.

OR

  - If there is no preexisting material to exclude, leave all spaces on this screen **blank**.

- Select **Continue** when the claim limitation screen is completed or to bypass the section.

> ! Important: Do not enter any new or original material for this claim on the Limitation of Claim screen. Do not enter any element or material that forms a part or the whole of your copyright in the work.

6 RIGHTS & PERMISSIONS

This section of the application is for entering contact information related to the **management** of the copyright. Enter yourself here or another person or organization who should be contacted for copyright management issues and in the event there is a request for permission to use the works. Information entered here will be publically viewable in the Copyright Office's online catalog. If you do not want this information to be public, do not complete this section and select Continue to skip to the next screen.

- Select **Add Me** to automatically enter yourself and your login account information,

OR

- Select **New** and enter contact information manually or for another person or organization,

OR

- Skip this section and do not enter any information.

- Select **Continue** when done.

7 CORRESPONDENT

This section requires **contact information** for a person that can communicate with the Copyright Office if there are any questions about the registration. Enter your own information here or that of someone else of your choosing.

- Select **Add Me** to automatically enter yourself and your login account information,

OR

- Select **New** and enter contact information manually or for another person or organization.

- Select **Continue** when done.

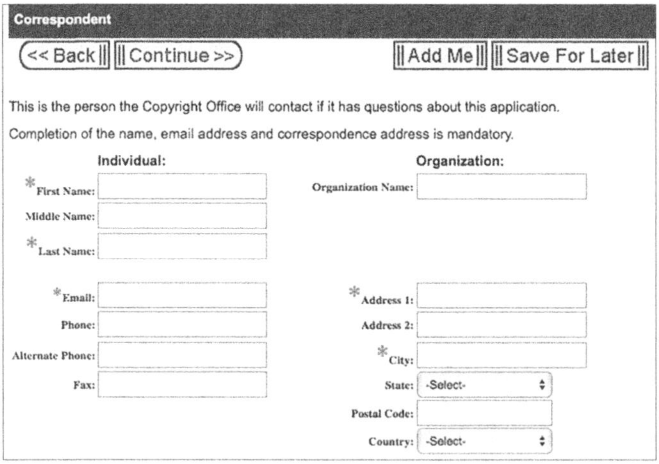

8 MAIL CERTIFICATE

The **mailing** information for the copyright registration certificate is entered in this screen. Enter your own name and mailing address information here or for the person to whom you want the copyright registration certificate to be sent.

If lost, a replacement certificate has an additional fee. If you change addresses in the interim period be sure to continue mail forwarding sufficiently or contact the Copyright Office for instructions.

- Select **Add Me** to automatically enter yourself and your login account information,

OR

- Select **New** and enter contact information manually or for another person or organization.

- Select **Continue** when done.

9 SPECIAL HANDLING

This section of the application concerns expedited processing. The service is **restricted** to expected or pending litigation, customs issues, and publication deadlines. There is a **significant additional fee** and a request for expedited handling may be rejected by the Copyright Office–without a refund–if the criteria is not satisfied. The special handling surcharge is a minimum of $800 per claim at publication time, and additional fees may also apply. If you believe you want and qualify for expedited handling, review the requirements on the screen carefully.

- If you are **not** seeking special handling do not enter anything and **skip this section** entirely by clicking **Continue**.

OR

- If you want and qualify for special handling, then you must indicate the **compelling reason** for the request: (1) Pending or prospective litigation, (2) customs matters, or (3) contract or publication deadlines that necessitate the expedited issuance of a certificate.

  - A certification is required, indicating that you are the author, claimant, or authorized agent. If this is the correct, **check** the appropriate box.
  - Enter an **explanation** for the Special Handling request in the text box as indicated.
  - Select **continue** when complete.

10 CERTIFICATION

The required certification statement affirms that the application information is true and correct to the best of your knowledge and that the person making the registration is the proper person to do it. The text refers to penalties for improper representations. Review the text on this screen carefully before proceeding.

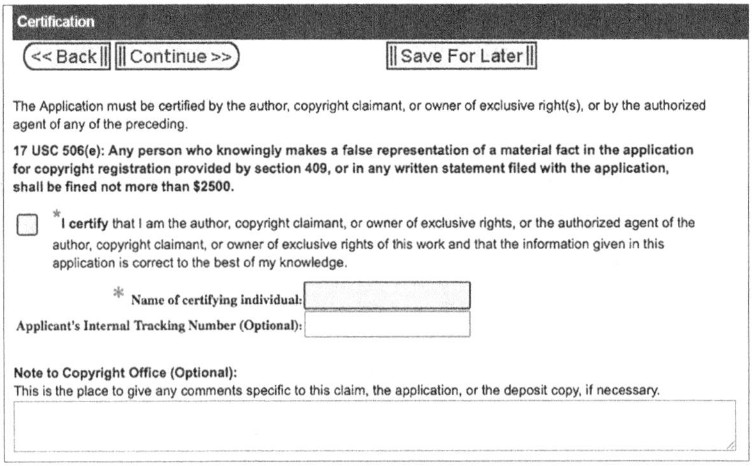

Certification

<< Back || Continue >> || Save For Later ||

The Application must be certified by the author, copyright claimant, or owner of exclusive right(s), or by the authorized agent of any of the preceding.

17 USC 506(e): Any person who knowingly makes a false representation of a material fact in the application for copyright registration provided by section 409, or in any written statement filed with the application, shall be fined not more than $2500.

* **I certify** that I am the author, copyright claimant, or owner of exclusive rights, or the authorized agent of the author, copyright claimant, or owner of exclusive rights of this work and that the information given in this application is correct to the best of my knowledge.

* Name of certifying individual:

Applicant's Internal Tracking Number (Optional):

Note to Copyright Office (Optional):
This is the place to give any comments specific to this claim, the application, or the deposit copy, if necessary.

- To certify the application, **check the box**. When doing so, you are affirming facts, as shown on the screen:

I certify that I am the author, copyright claimant, or owner of exclusive rights, or the authorized agent of the author, copyright claimant, or owner of exclusive rights and that the information given in this application is correct to the best of my knowledge.

- To complete the certification, **enter your name** in the box provided and, if desired, a personal tracking number can be entered as well. (The tracking number will appear on the registration certificate).

    ▸ **Optional**: **Add a comment** for the Copyright Office. At the bottom of the screen is a box for providing further information concerning the registration. Enter any pertinent comments concerning the claim, the application, or the deposit copies.

- Select **Continue**.

11 Review Submission

This screen shows the entries that you have made in the application. This point in the application is the last opportunity to make any changes to the information that you entered. Review each section on this screen carefully and correct any errors or omissions.

- **Confirm** that each of the works is listed in the Titles section. You should see that a group title has been generated and added to the first line in the Titles section and the title of each work in the group follows on the lines below.

- **Review** and confirm the information entered in each section shown on the Review Submission screen.

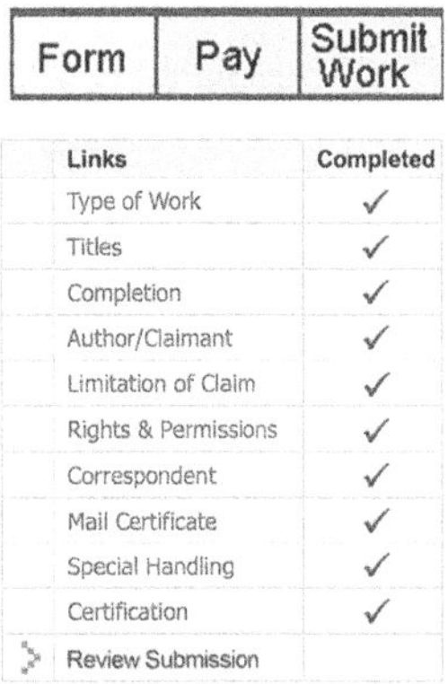

► **To make any changes** use the links on the left side of the screen to navigate to the step that you want to change. Save the entries on each screen that you change.

- **Return** to the Review Submission screen by clicking its link. All sections of the application should have a checkmark, showing that they have been completed. If not, return to that section and complete any missing information required, saving the changes by selecting either the save or continue button, as necessary. Return to the Review Submission screen.

- **Review** the final application entries.

The process is not yet complete. Continue with the steps below to complete the application submission and payment processes, and to deposit a copy of the work.

12 Submit the Application & Pay the Fee

- On the **Review Submission** screen, select **Add to Cart.**

  Note: Changes cannot be made to the application once it is added to the cart.

On the **My Cart** screen, you should see your application in the **Cases in Cart** list with the **Fee Due** indicated.

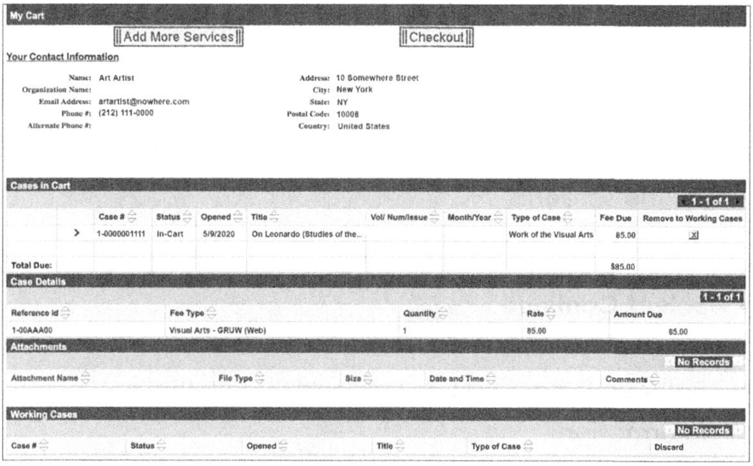

- Select the **Checkout** button.
  (The *Add More Services button* takes you out of the pay system to add more items from the registration home page).

To enter payment information:

- Select **Pay - Credit Card/ACH** to pay with a credit or debit card, or to pay from a checking or savings account. (Those with a pre-paid Copyright Office account can select the Pay-Deposit Account option instead).

Do you wish to proceed with the payment?

- Select **OK.** Alternatively, Cancel to discontinue, but note that the registration is not complete without payment.

↓

The system will automatically redirect you to a Pay.gov screen for **Copyright Fee Services**.

Choose your method of payment:

○ A withdrawal from a checking or savings account (ACH)

OR

○ A debit or credit card. Accepted types are shown on the screen.

- Select **Continue**.

- Enter your payment details and review the information.

- To submit the payment, select **Continue**. This will return to the eCO application system. (To discontinue the payment process at this stage, select Cancel or Previous instead).

- When you see the **payment successful** screen, select **Continue.** This will take you to the deposit section of the registration process.

> Registrations filed entirely via the eCO system become effective for the date all application materials are submitted online (along with the fee and uploaded deposit copies).

13 Upload Copies of the Artworks

The final step is uploading a copy of each artwork in the registration group. This is called the deposit and the copies must be in an appropriate digital file form. Each digital file uploaded is limited to 500 MB, preferably in .jpg (jpeg), .tif (.tiff) or .gif format. Generally, upload one digital image file for each 2-D work. 3-D works may be deposited as multiple digital files to show the back side, for instance. Once uploaded, the digital files cannot be deleted or changed.

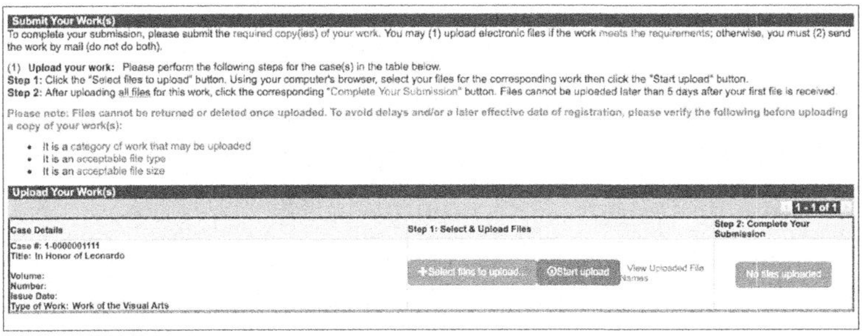

To Upload the Deposit:

- **Review** the text on the page and confirm that your files match the requirements, the **file types** are acceptable, and each file to be uploaded is 500 MB or less.

- Select the **+Files to Upload** Button. A new window will open.

- Navigate to the files on your computer. **Select each file** to be uploaded.

- Select the **Start Upload** button. When each file is successfully uploaded, the phrase *Successfully Uploaded* will be automatically added to its file name on the screen.

- → Confirm that you have selected the correct image file or files for uploading. To delete a file, select the ⊘ Remove button shown to the right of the item listing.

- → Do not leave the page or close the application until all of the files have been successfully uploaded.

- → No more files may be uploaded after the "Click Here to Complete Your Submission After Uploading All Files" link has been activated.

- Only when ALL files are successfully uploaded, click the green **Complete Your Submission After Uploading All Files** link.

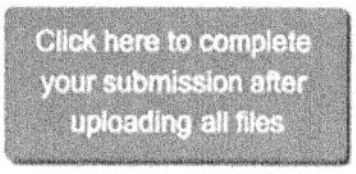

The screen should now display a message stating that the **Claim Submission Complete, No Further Action Required**. You should receive an e-mail from the Copyright Office confirming the receipt of your files. Do not print a shipping slip and do not mail a physical copy. Mail-in deposits are <u>not</u> permitted for this application.

At this point you can **logout** of eCO. Or, select **Home** from the upper right menu on the screen to return to the main Registration page where you can confirm that the application you just completed is shown as an Open Case or to continue with other services.

A Group of Photographs Application

This application is the most economical method of registering multiple photographs—up to 750—for one fee. There are distinct requirements and all of the works must be photographs with no other media incorporated (except retouching). The application can be used to register *either* a group of published photographs that were all published within the same year *or* a group of unpublished photographs completed over one or more years. To qualify, there can be only a single author for the whole group. Joint (or collaborative) works are ineligible for this application. A numbered list of the photos must be submitted in addition to the completed application, fee, and deposit requirements.

Recommended Preparation of Digital Files and the List of Photographs

Steps A through E should be completed before beginning the online application.

Step A: **Assemble the deposit files.** Collect the digital files that you will later submit as copies of the photographs and save them in one folder on your computer.

The files must be .jpg, .tif, or .gif format.

These files will later be uploaded later in the process in most cases. If individual files exceed the 500 MB limit, then instead of using the standard upload process you must mail the entire deposit, all digital files, to the Copyright Office on a storage device. If each individual image file is

500 MB or less, the standard upload submission is preferred by the Copyright Office.

Step B: **Assign conforming titles** to the digital files.
The names of the digital files must **match** those on the list of photographs, which is created in Step E.
If necessary, adjust the title of each file. Titles should not contain diacritical marks, such as ç, à, ñ, or ü, and should be represented as plain letters or numbers. Avoid using commas or semicolons, but other punctuation can be included in an individual title.

Step C: **Create a descriptive title for the entire group**. The group title can contain nearly any information that you choose. Consider including information about the subject, the artist name, project name, or other pertinent information. The group title can be a name created for a project series, or a mixture of a name and descriptive information. This descriptive title will later be added to the list and entered in the application.

Step D: **Compression.** The Copyright Office recommends submitting all of the photographs in a single compressed file. To do this, compress the folder that contains all of the digital files that you will be submitting as the copies of the photographs. A single uploaded file is limited to 500MB in size. A single compressed folder is also subject to this limitation. Alternatively, upload single files of each image instead of the recommended folder compression method.

The Copyright Office has not provided guidance on naming the compressed folder, but after you begin the online application an automated case number will be assigned. At that point you can add the case number (as well as the group title) to the folder's file name.

Compression Generally

Apple/Mac:	Highlight the folder, go to the Finder menu and select "Compress." A new compressed file will be created with the .zip extension.
Windows:	Press and hold (or right-click) the folder, select Send to, select Compressed (zipped) folder. A new zipped file with the same name is created.
IOS:	Press and hold the folder and select Compress from the contextual menu. A new compressed file with the .zip extension is created.

Different operating systems may have variations on the methods for creating a compressed or zipped file.

Step E: **Create the list.** Using a spreadsheet, text edit program, or word processing application, create a list of the photographs in this group with the information described in the steps following.

- Enter the **title for the entire group** at the top of the page AND incorporate the group title into the file name for the list document.

Optional Pre-Formatted Excel Templates are available.

Published photos: www.copyright.gov/eco/help/group/grpph-title-list-template.xlsx

Unpublished photos: www.copyright.gov/eco/help/group/gruph-title-list-template.xlsx

Enter data about the photographs in the registration group.

- For a group of **unpublished** photographs, the list must contain this data for *each* photo:
    - A **number** for the photograph on the list (1–750).

  - The **title** of each photograph.
  - The **file name** of the digital copy of the photograph. (This digital file will be later submitted with the deposit).

OR

- For a group of **published** photographs, the list must contain this data for *each* photo:
  - A **number** for the photograph on the list (1–750)
  - The **title** of each photograph
  - The **file name** of the digital copy of each photograph in the group. (This digital file will be later submitted with the deposit).
  - **Date of first publication** (month & four-digit year).
  - **Nation** of first publication.

Enter the photos and their titles in the order of their publication dates to facilitate the entry of titles later in the application process.

- **Save** the list document. The case number, once it is generated by the application system, will need to be added to the file name of the document and within the list document itself. If you are planning on submitting the list as a PDF, do not save a finalized version of the list until this information can be incorporated.

▸ Optional: Create a block entry of all titles separated by commas (1,995 character limit). This will be useful later in the application process.

Sample List Form for a Group of **Unpublished** Photographs

Group Title ______________________

Complete List of Photographs for **Case #** __-__________

Photo no.	Title of Photo	File Name	All Titles (optional)
1	*Image One*	*imageone.jpg*	*Image One, Portrait A, Image Three, Image Four... ... Image More*
2	*Portrait A*	*PortraitA.jpg*	
3	*Image Three*	*imagethree.jpg*	
...			
750	*Image More*	*imagemore.jpg*	

Sample List Form for a Group of Published Photographs

Group Title ______________________

Complete List of Photographs for **Case #** __-__________

Photo no.	Title of Photo	File Name	Month/ Year of Publication	Nation of Publication	All Titles (optional)
1	*Image One*	*imageone.jpg*	*1/2019*	*U.S.A.*	*Image One, Portrait A, Image 3, Image Four, ... Image More*
2	*Portrait A*	*portraitA.jpg*	*2/2019*	*U.S.A.*	
3	*Image 3*	*image3.jpg*	*3/2019*	*U.S.A.*	
...					
750	*Image More*	*imagemore.jpg*	*9/2019*	*U.S.A.*	

Completing the Group of Photographs Application

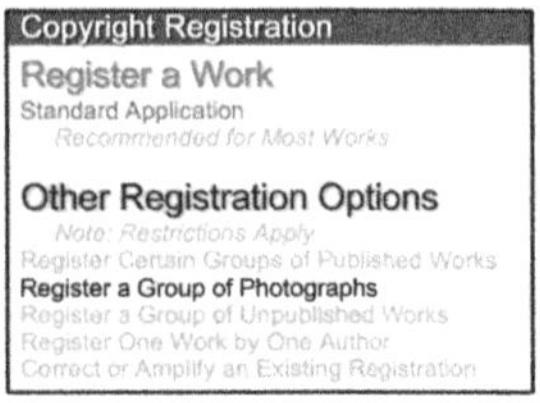

This section covers the steps for completing the Group of Photographs application. The Group Registration of Published Photographs (GRPPH) and the Group Registration for Unpublished Photographs (GRUPH) are accessed through the same link on the main registration page.

START ▶ On Copyright.gov, go to the Registration menu. Select Register Your Work or Register a Copyright. Login to the eCO system. Under Other Registration Options, select **Register a Group of Photographs**

- **Review** the text on the overview screen, which shows eligibility requirements for the application. Confirm that the group of photographs to be registered meets the criteria for this application.

  If all of the eligibility requirements are *not* met, the registration will need to be completed using a different application form. Or, if only some of the works do not meet the criteria, those works can be removed from the group and from the list, and the application can be continued. Otherwise, if all of the requirements are met, continue with the application.

1 Select **Start Registration**.
This will take you to the next screen.

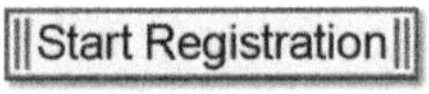

↓

Select the **Type of Group** from the drop-down list:

○ **Unpublished** Photographs

OR

○ **Published** Photographs

When you make a selection, contextual information about the requirements will appear.

- **Review** the text that appears on the page for your type of group. To confirm that the work meets all of the requirements for the group registration, **click the box** at the bottom of the page.

> Once you click Continue, the type of group **cannot be changed**. If there is a mistake, select the Save For Later button, return to the registration home page, delete the application, and start over.

- Select **Continue**.

2-A Finalize the List

A case number should now be visible in the upper area of the screen, just above the Titles heading.

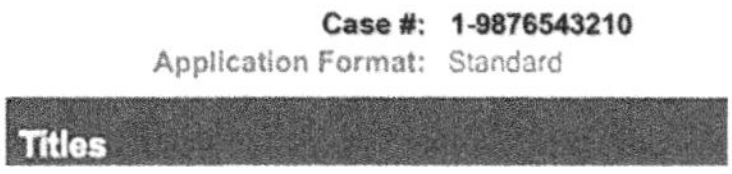

- Open the list document that you made earlier.

- **Copy the full case number** onto the document so that it is shown at the top of the list along with the group title. (Include the number 1, the dash and all numbers that follow). Or, if you are using the Copyright Office's Excel template, enter the case number and group title into the template.

- Adjust the **list's file name** so that it includes (1) the title of the group and (2) the full case number, in 200 characters or less. Example: *Project Photos 1-9876543210.xls*

- **Save the list** document. If the list is not an Excel (.xls or .xlsx) document, it should be saved as or exported as a PDF document. Most word processing programs, such as Word, can create a PDF file through the Print menu function.

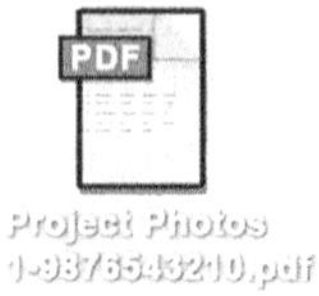

- If you will be uploading the deposit copies of your photos, save the finalized list in the same folder with the digital files that will later be submitted.

▸ If you are planning on uploading all image files in the electronic system, at this point you can (optionally) **compress** the folder containing all images and the list into one file, so long as they total 500 MB or less. Do not compress the list file with the image files if you plan to use the mail-in option—the list document must still be uploaded. In any case, the list document can be uploaded as a standalone file.

2-B TITLES

Entering the titles of the photographs

Enter the title for the group and, optionally, enter titles for individual photographs in this section. A title must be entered for the group as a whole, but the individual titles are optional. However, the Copyright Office strongly encourages entering a title for each photo, and if applicable, the corresponding publication information. If individual titles are submitted in the application they will be included on the copyright registration certificate and will be listed in the searchable public record. If you choose to enter individual titles, a title must be entered for every photograph in the group. The steps described below reflect entering all titles.

- Select **New** on the Title Screen. A new screen will open.

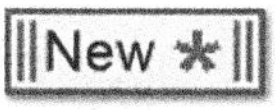

From this point on, **<u>follow the set of steps that matches your group</u>**, either published (page 143) or unpublished (directly below), and enter the titles.

To Enter Titles for a Group of <u>Unpublished</u> Photographs

- On the new screen, **enter**:

  1) The **title of the group** of unpublished photographs (1995 maximum characters).

  2) The four-digit **year of completion**. This is the calendar year in which the most recent photograph in the group was shot.

  3) From the pull-down list, select the **total** number of photos that are being registered with this application.

  4) Select **Save**. You will be returned to the main title page. The title of the group will be shown on the page as the title of the work being registered, along with the date entered.

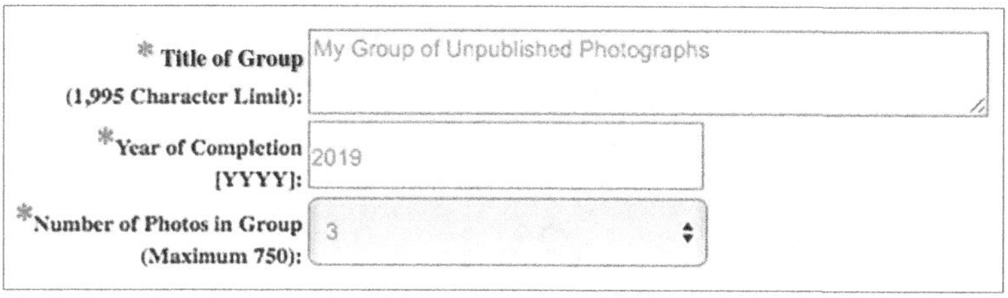

The Copyright Office recommends entering a title for each of the individual photographs in the group. These titles will then appear on the registration certificate.

▶ To enter individual titles (optional), select **New** again.

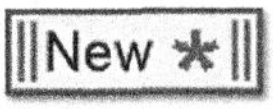

Choose one of the **methods** for entering the titles.

Method 1: **One Title**, one photo at a time.

- Select **1** in the pull-down list.
- **Enter a title** for a single photograph in the box, then select **Save**.

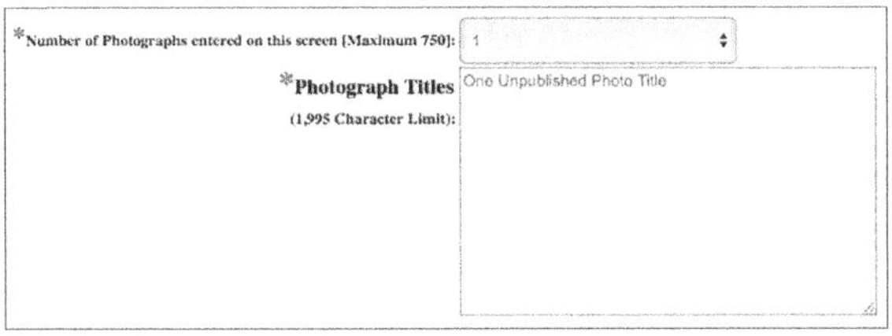

▶ **Repeat** this title entry process until all titles of individual photographs are entered in order from the list. Start by selecting **New** again, enter the information on each screen, and **Save**.

- When all titles are entered, on the main Title screen, select **Continue** to move on to the next step in the application.

OR

Method 2: **All Titles** entered at once.

- Select the number in the pull-down list that corresponds to the **total number** of photographs being registered with this application.
- Enter all titles of the individual works in the box, separated by commas. The optional **All Titles** section of the list can be copied and pasted here.
- Select **Save** when complete.
- When all titles are entered, on the main Title screen, select **Continue** to move on to the next step in the application.

> If the list of titles exceeds the 1995 character limit, use Method 1 or 3.

OR

Method 3: **Sub-Groups of Titles**.

This method can be used if the characters for All Titles exceed the maximum of 1995. Titles are entered in batches.

- Select the number in the pull-down list that corresponds to the **number of titles** to be entered in this **batch** only.

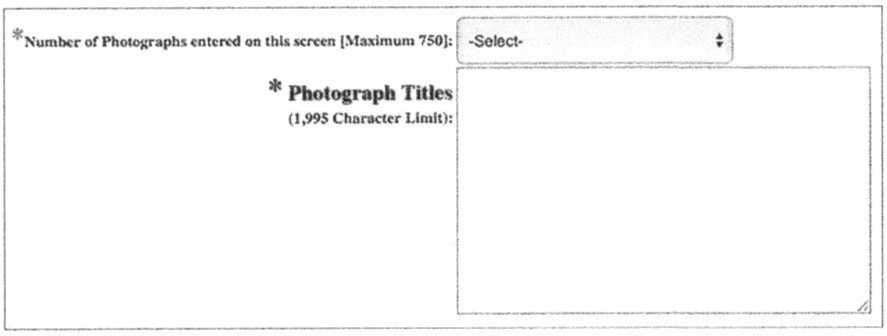

- **Enter** a selection of titles in the box, separated by commas. Confirm that the number of photographs entered in the pull-down list earlier reflects the appropriate number of titles entered on this particular batch only.

- **Save** the entry.

▶ **Repeat** this title entry process until all titles of individual photographs are entered in logical batches. Start by selecting **New** again, enter the information on each screen, and **Save**.

When all titles are entered and appear on the main Title screen, this concludes the title entries for a group of unpublished photographs.

- Select **Continue** to go on to the next step in the application.

All Titles

Title	Type	Number of Photos	Year of Completion
My Group of Unpublished Photographs	Title of work being registered	3	2019
One Unpublished Photo Title	Contents Title	1	
Another Unpublished Photo Title	Contents Title	1	
And Another Unpublished Photo Title	Contents Title	1	

▶ Now, **skip** over the instructions for published works and move on to **Step 3** on page 148 to begin the process entering the Author information.

To Enter Titles for a Group of Published Photographs

If you have completed each the steps for the application so far, you have already selected "published" photographs as the type of work, finalized the list, and selected the **New** button on the main Title screen.

- On the main Title screen, **enter** the following:

1) The **title of the group** of published photographs (1995 maximum characters).

2) The **total number** of photos that are being registered in this application. Select the number from the pull-down list.

3) Enter the four-digit **year of completion**. This is the calendar year in which the most recent photograph in the group was shot.

4) The date of the first publication in the group.

   Enter the **earliest date** in the calendar year that one of the photographs was first published (MM/DD/YYYY).

5) The latest date for a first publication in the group.

   Enter the **most recent** date in the calendar year that one of the photographs was **first published** (MM/DD/YYYY).

   Note: These entries reflect the parameters of the first-time publications within the group. Individual publication dates for each of the photos should have been entered in the list of photos created earlier.

6) Select the **nation of the first publication** from the pull-down list. This is the country where the

photographs were *first* published. If you are unsure, select "Not Known." If the photos were first published in multiple countries, include that information in the comments box later at Step 9.

- Select **Save**. You will be returned to the main title page. The title of the group will be shown on the page as the title of the work being registered, along with the date entered.

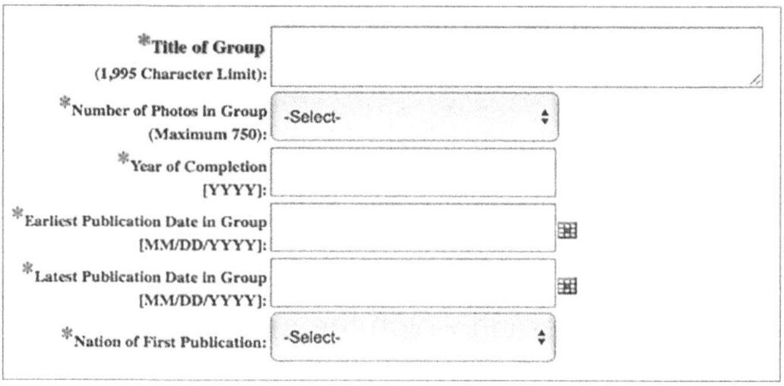

The Copyright Office recommends entering individual titles for each of the photographs in the group. These titles will then appear on the registration certificate.

- ▶ To enter individual titles (optional), select **New**.

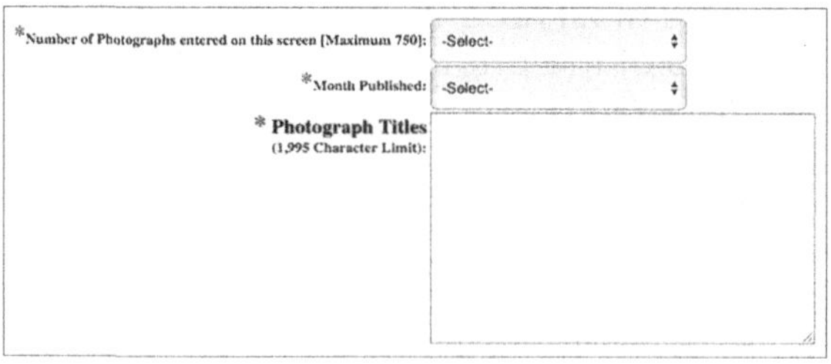

Choose one of the **methods** for entering the titles.

Method 1: **One Title**, enter one photograph at a time.

- Select the number **1** from the first pull-down list.
- Enter a title for a single photograph, beginning with the first one on the list you created earlier.

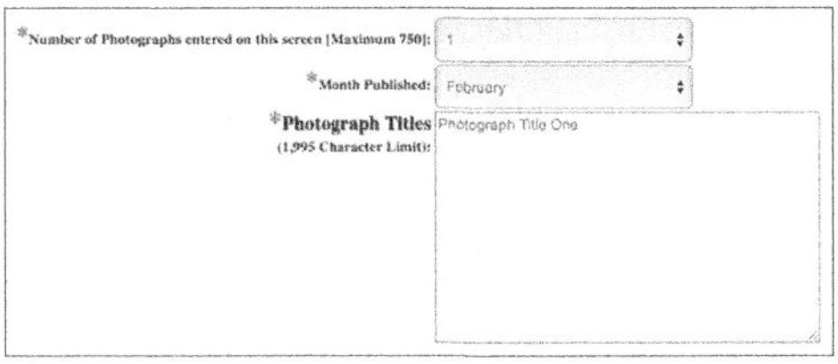

- On the second pull-down list, select the calendar **month** in which the photograph was published.
- Select **Save** when complete. This will return you to the main Titles screen.

▶ **Repeat** this title entry process until all titles of individual photographs are entered in order from the list. Start by selecting **New** again, enter the information on each screen, and **Save**.

OR

Method 2: **All Titles**, enter all of the titles in the entire group at once.

- On the first pull-down list, select the number that corresponds to the **total number** of photographs being registered in this application.

> If the list of titles exceeds the 1995 character limit, use Method 1 or 3.

- Enter all titles of the individual works in the box, separated by commas. Characters are limited to 1995. The optional All Titles section of the list of photos can be copied and pasted here. (To use this method, all of the photographs in the registration group must have been published in the same month and year. If not, use method 3 instead).

- From the pull-down list, select the calendar **month** in which all of the photographs were published.

- Select **Save** when complete. This will return you to the main Titles screen.

OR

Method 3: **Sub-Groups of Titles** are entered in batches. This method can be used if the characters for All Titles exceed the maximum of 1995 or when photos were published in different months or simply to enter titles in logical groupings.

- Select the number in the first pull-down list that corresponds to the **number of titles** to be entered in this **batch** only.

- **Enter titles** for a portion of the photographs in the group, separated by commas, in a batch that has a common month of publication.

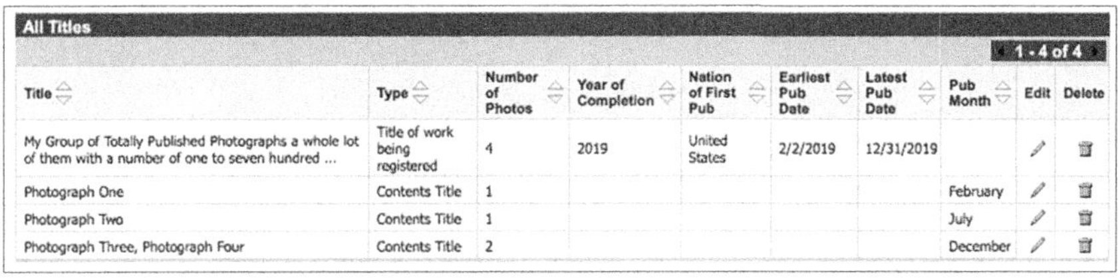

All Titles

1 - 4 of 4

Title	Type	Number of Photos	Year of Completion	Nation of First Pub	Earliest Pub Date	Latest Pub Date	Pub Month	Edit	Delete
My Group of Totally Published Photographs a whole lot of them with a number of one to seven hundred ...	Title of work being registered	4	2019	United States	2/2/2019	12/31/2019			
Photograph One	Contents Title	1					February		
Photograph Two	Contents Title	1					July		
Photograph Three, Photograph Four	Contents Title	2					December		

- On the second pull-down list, select the calendar **month** in which all of the photographs in this batch were published.

- Select **Save** when complete. This will return you to the main Titles screen.

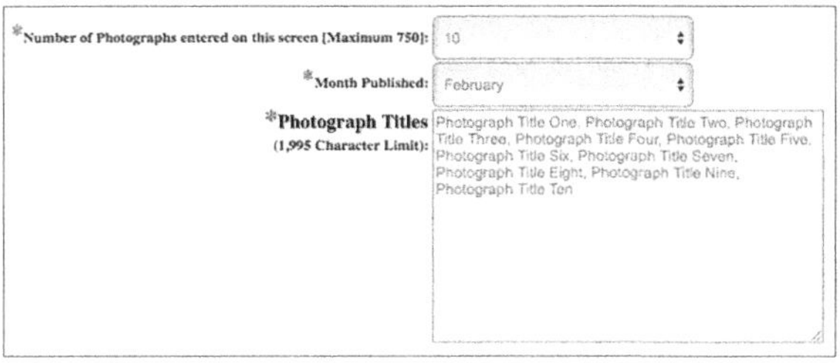

▶ **Repeat** this title entry process, until all titles of individual photographs are entered in logical batches. Start by selecting **New** again, enter the information on each screen, and **Save**.

If you have entered multiple screens of titles, in batches or as individual titles, confirm that the number of titles entered by you includes at least one title for every photograph you are registering.

- When all titles are complete, select **Continue** on the main Titles page to move on to the Author information in the next section.

3 AUTHOR

Entering Author/Artist/Photographer Information

The author is the photographer or the artist that created the photographs in the group.

- Select the **Add Me** button to automatically enter yourself and the information from your eCO login account.

OR

- Select **New**.
  Enter the **name of the photographer/artist** (author).
  Or, if the author is an organization, such as in a work made for hire situation, enter the organization's name here.

Next, enter additional information about this author:

- The author's **citizenship country** or **domicile** (country of permanent residence).

- The **author's year of birth** (optional). Note that if entered, this will be become public information.

- Is this an **anonymous** or **pseudonymous** work? If yes, check the appropriate box. Enter the pseudonym in the box.

- Indicate if the author's contribution is ***work made for hire***. Enter yes or no.

  Refer to pages 44-48 to determine if the photographs constitute work made for hire in this context.

- Select **Continue** when complete.

4 CLAIMANTS

Entering information about the copyright claimant(s)

The claimant is the person who owns the copyrights that are being registered. The claimant is usually the person who made the photographs, or it can be another person or organization that owns all of the rights in the photographs that initially belonged to the creator. If you made the photographs and you own the copyrights, you are the claimant.

First, review the text on the Claimants screen. Then enter the individual claimant information:

- Select the **Add Me** button to automatically enter yourself and the information from your eCO login account.

OR

- Select **New**. Enter the name of the claimant and the address information.
  A single claimant entered here must be either an individual or an organization, but cannot be both. Additional claimants can be added later.

> Transfer Statement
>
> If actual ownership of the copyright has been transferred from the author (photographer) to someone else, enter a transfer statement on this screen. Select how the copyright was obtained by the claimant: By written agreement, Inheritance, or Other. If Other is selected, enter a description of the transfer. If you created the photographs and own the copyrights, skip the transfer statement section.

- Select **Save**. This will return you to the main Claimants page.

  - ➤ If there are **additional Claimants** repeat the steps above to enter their information and select Save.

- Back on the main Claimants page, when all claimants are entered, select **Continue**.

5 RIGHTS & PERMISSIONS

This section is for entering contact information related to the **management** of the copyrights you are registering. Enter yourself as the contact person. Or, identify another person or organization that should be contacted for copyright management issues, such as a request for permission to use the works. Information entered here will be publically viewable in the Copyright Office's online catalog. If you do not want this information to be public, do not complete this section and select Continue to skip to the next screen.

- ○ Select **Add Me** to automatically enter yourself and your login account information.

OR

- ○ Select **New** and enter contact information manually or for another person or organization.

OR

- ○ Skip this section and do not enter any information.

- Select **Continue** when done.

6 CORRESPONDENT

Contact information for a person that can communicate with the Copyright Office if there are any questions about the registration is required. Enter your own information here or that of someone else of your choosing.

- ○ Select **Add Me** to automatically enter yourself and the login account information.

OR

- ○ Select **New** and enter contact information manually or for another person or organization.

- Select **Continue** when done.

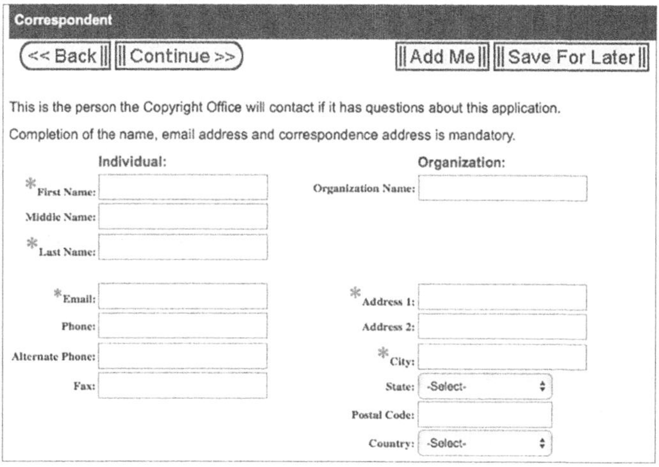

7 MAIL CERTIFICATE

The **mailing** information for the copyright registration certificate is entered in this screen. Enter your own name and mailing address information here. Or, enter information for another person to whom you want the copyright registration certificate to be delivered.

If lost, a replacement certificate has an additional fee. If you change addresses in the interim period be sure to set up mail forwarding for a sufficient period of time or contact the Copyright Office for more information.

- Select **Add Me** to automatically enter yourself and the login account information.

OR

- Select **New** and enter contact information manually or for another person or organization.

- Select **Continue** when done.

8 SPECIAL HANDLING

This section of the application concerns expedited processing. The service is **restricted** to expected or pending litigation, customs issues, and publication deadlines. There is a **significant additional fee** and a request for expedited handling may be rejected by the Copyright Office–without a refund–if the criteria is not satisfied. The special handling surcharge is a minimum of $800 per claim at publication time, and additional fees may also apply. If you believe you want and qualify for expedited handling, review the requirements on the screen carefully.

- If you are **not** seeking special handling, do not enter anything and **skip this section** entirely by clicking **Continue**.

OR

- If you want and qualify for special handling, then you must indicate the **compelling reason** for the request: (1) Pending or prospective litigation, (2) customs matters, or (3) contract or publication deadlines that necessitate the expedited issuance of a certificate.

  - A certification is required, indicating that you are the author, claimant, or authorized agent. If this is the correct, **check** the appropriate box.
  - Enter an **explanation** for the Special Handling request in the text box as indicated.
  - Select **continue** when complete

9 CERTIFICATION

The required certification statement affirms that the application information is true and correct to the best of your knowledge and that the person making the registration is the proper person to do it. The text refers to penalties for improper representations. Review the text on this screen carefully before proceeding.

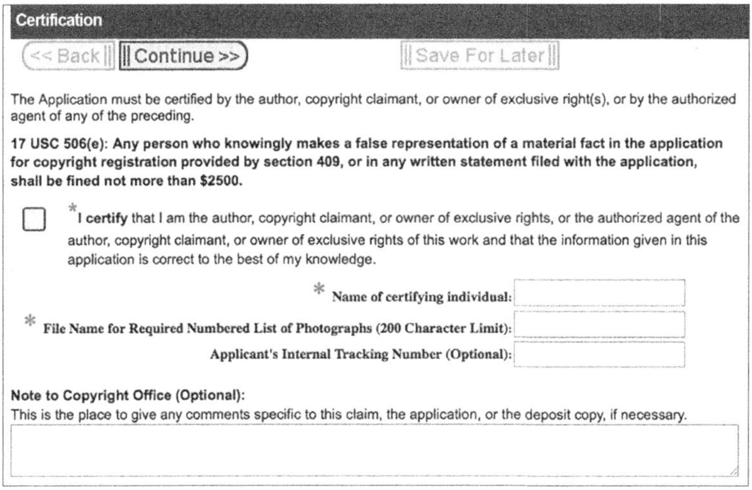

Certification

<< Back | Continue >> | Save For Later

The Application must be certified by the author, copyright claimant, or owner of exclusive right(s), or by the authorized agent of any of the preceding.

17 USC 506(e): Any person who knowingly makes a false representation of a material fact in the application for copyright registration provided by section 409, or in any written statement filed with the application, shall be fined not more than $2500.

* **I certify** that I am the author, copyright claimant, or owner of exclusive rights, or the authorized agent of the author, copyright claimant, or owner of exclusive rights of this work and that the information given in this application is correct to the best of my knowledge.

* **Name of certifying individual:**

* **File Name for Required Numbered List of Photographs (200 Character Limit):**

Applicant's Internal Tracking Number (Optional):

Note to Copyright Office (Optional):
This is the place to give any comments specific to this claim, the application, or the deposit copy, if necessary.

- To certify the application, **check the box**. When doing so, you are affirming facts, as shown on the screen:

> **I certify** that I am the author, copyright claimant, or owner of exclusive rights, or the authorized agent of the author, copyright claimant, or owner of exclusive rights and that the information given in this application is correct to the best of my knowledge.

- To complete the certification, **enter your name** in the box provided and, if desired, a personal tracking number can be entered as well. (The tracking number will appear on the registration certificate).

- Enter the **file name for the numbered list** of photographs that you made earlier (200 character maximum).

  The list's file name should now include the case number and the title of the group (Step 2-A) and it should be either a PDF or Excel document. The list document itself will be submitted later.

- ▶ **Optional**: Enter a **personal tracking number**. This number will appear on the registration certificate.

- ▶ **Optional**: **Add a comment** for the Copyright Office. At the bottom of the screen is a box for providing further information concerning the registration. Enter any pertinent comments concerning the claim, the application, the deposit copies, or other related issues, such as clarifying publication details.

- Select **Continue**.

10 Review Submission

This screen shows the entries that you have made in the application. This point in the application is the last opportunity to make changes to the information that you entered. Review your entries carefully and correct any errors or omissions.

► **To make any changes** use the links on the left side of the screen to navigate to the section that you want to change. Save the entries on each screen that you change.

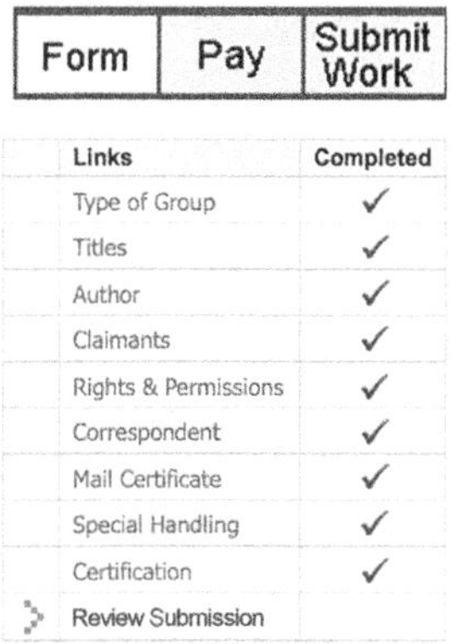

- **Return** to the Review Submission screen by clicking the link. All sections of the application should have a checkmark by their link, showing that they have been completed. If not, return to that section and complete any missing information required, saving the changes by selecting either the save or continue button, as necessary. Return to the Review Submission screen.

- Review the final application entries.

The process is not yet complete. Continue with the steps below to complete the application submission and payment processes, and to deposit a copy of the work.

11 Submit the Application & Pay the Fee

- On the Review Submission screen, select **Add to Cart.**

  Note: Changes cannot be made to the application once it is added to the cart.

On the **My Cart** screen, you should see your application in the **Cases in Cart** list with the **Fee Due** indicated.

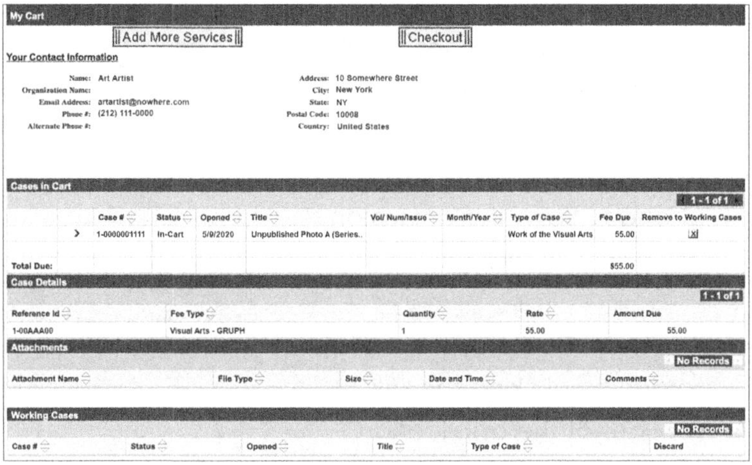

- Select the **Checkout** button.
  (Alternatively, the Add More Services button takes you out of the pay system to add more items from the registration home page).

To enter payment information:

- Select **Pay - Credit Card/ACH** to pay with a credit or debit card, or to pay from a checking or savings account. Those users with a pre-paid Copyright Office account, you can select the Pay-Deposit Account option instead.

Do you wish to proceed with the payment?

- Select **OK.** (Alternatively, Cancel to discontinue, but note that the registration is not complete without payment).

↓

The system will automatically redirect you to a Pay.gov screen for **Copyright Fee Services**.

Choose your method of payment:

○ A withdrawal from a checking or savings account (ACH)

OR

○ A debit or credit card. Accepted types are shown on the screen.

> Registrations filed fully via the eCO system become effective for the date the application is submitted online (along with the fee and uploaded deposit copies).

- Select **Continue**.

- Enter your payment details and review the information.

- To submit the payment, select **Continue**. This will return you to the eCO application system. (To discontinue the payment process at this stage, select Cancel or Previous instead).

- When you see the **payment successful** screen, select **Continue.** This will take you to the deposit section of the registration process.

12 Submit Deposit Copies of the Photographs

The final step is uploading copies of the photographs. This is called the deposit and to use the online system, the copies must be in digital form. Each digital file uploaded is limited to 500 MB and must be in .jpg (.jpeg), .tif (.tiff) or .gif format. Once uploaded, the digital files cannot be deleted or changed. Alternatively, the deposit can be made by mailing digital files of the images on a device to the Copyright Office. The claim processing time is typically shortest when the upload deposit method is used. Be advised that the Copyright Office has said that there is a "significant delay" in processing mailed-in deposits. **Choose either the upload or mail-in method, but not both.**

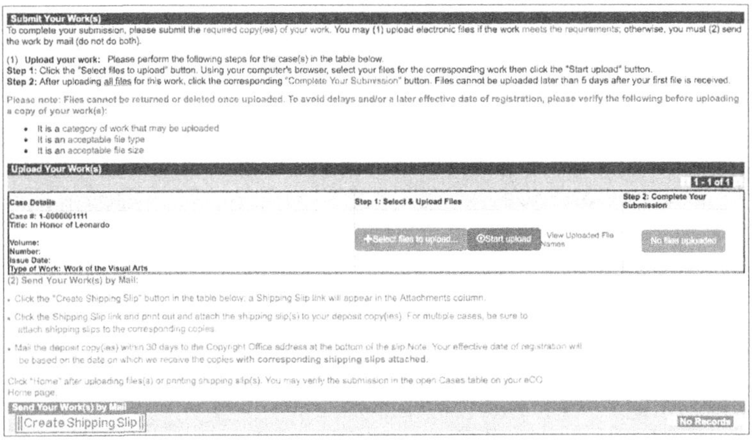

To Upload the Deposit:

- **Review** the text on the page and confirm that your files match the requirements, the **file types** are acceptable, and each file to be uploaded is 500 MB or less. If you opt to upload a single compressed file, it must be 500 MB or smaller.

- Select the **+Files to Upload** button. A new screen will open.

- Navigate to the files on your computer. **Select each file** to be uploaded. Select all files to be uploaded, whether you are submitting a single compressed folder file or individual files, including the photos and the list document.

- Click **Open**. You will be returned to the main Submit Your Works screen. The files you selected will be listed on the screen.

  - ▶ Confirm that you have also selected the **list document** for uploading.

- Select the **Start Upload** button. When each file is successfully uploaded, "*Successfully Uploaded*" will be automatically added to its file name. (Repeat this process if necessary).

> → Confirm that you have selected the correct image file or files for uploading. To delete a file, select the ⊘ Remove button shown to the right of the item listing.
>
> → Do not leave the page or close the application until all of the files have been successfully uploaded.
>
> → No more files may be uploaded after the "Click Here to Complete Your Submission After Uploading All Files" link has been activated.

- When ALL files are successfully uploaded, click the green **Complete Your Submission After Uploading All Files** link.

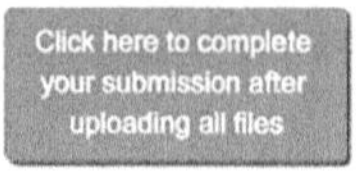

The screen should now display a message stating that the **Claim Submission Complete, No Further Action Required**. You should receive an e-mail from the Copyright Office confirming the receipt of your files. Do not print a shipping slip and do not mail physical copies.

At this point, **logout** of eCO. Or, select **Home** from the upper right menu on the screen to return to the main Registration page where you can confirm that the application you just completed is shown as an Open Case or continue with other services.

To Mail-In the Deposit Materials:

As an alternative to the upload method, the Group of Photographs application permits the submission of your deposit copies in a digital form by mail.

The mail-in option may be used when files exceed the current maximum of 500 MB. Do not mail your deposit copies if you have already submitted them through the upload process. However, the numbered list of photographs (with titles, file names, etc.) must be submitted in all cases by uploading it as part of the online application process.

The mail-in process begins on the **Submit Your Works** screen that appears after the fee payment has been completed.

- Select the **+Files to Upload** Button. A new screen will open.

- Navigate to the list document on your computer and **select** it to be uploaded.

- Click **Open**. You will be returned to the main Submit Your Works screen. The file you selected will be listed on the screen.

- Select the **Start Upload** button. When the list document is successfully uploaded, the phrase *Successfully Uploaded* will be automatically added to its file name.

> → Confirm that you have selected the correct file for uploading. To delete a file, select the ⊘ Remove button shown to the right of the item listing.
>
> → Do not leave the page or close the application until the list's document file has been successfully uploaded.
>
> → No more files may be uploaded after the "Click Here to Complete Your Submission After Uploading All Files" link has been activated.

- When the list document has been successfully uploaded, click the green **Complete Your Submission After Uploading All Files** link.

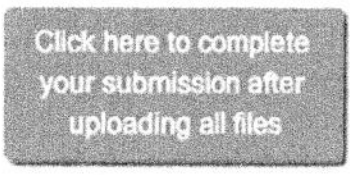

A message will appear, indicting that the process is complete, and you will receive a confirmation e-mail from the Copyright Office. The confirmation pertains only to the uploading of the list document in this case, and the copies of the photographs will be submitted by mail on a device or disk.

- Select the **Create Shipping Slip** button on the lower part of the Submit Your Works screen. Within a few seconds, an attachment link will appear on the lower area of the screen. Click the link to open the document and select **OK** in the pop-up window. When the document opens, print a copy of it.

  At this point you may **logout** of eCO. Or, select **Home** from the upper right menu on the screen to return to the main Registration page where you can confirm that the application you just completed is shown as an Open Case.

- **Attach** the shipping slip to the device that contains the files to be submitted–a CD/DVD type disk, a flash drive, or other storage device. Refer to page 218 in Chapter 5 for important considerations when mailing an electronic device to the Copyright Office.

- Mail the materials to the address shown on the shipping slip **within 30 days**. Because the registration is not effective until the materials are received by the Copyright Office, prompt mailing is important. This completes the registration and deposit process.

Form VA: The Paper Application For A Single Work of Visual Art

As an alternative to the electronic applications for single works, paper-based forms are available. To use this method of copyright registration, download the appropriate form from the Copyright Office website, complete it, and mail the completed application, the appropriate fee, and the deposit copy of the artwork to the Copyright Office.

Form VA can be used to register a single work of visual art that is pictorial, graphic or sculptural, such as 2-D and 3-D works, including, for example, a photograph, a painting, a drawing, a print, an art reproduction, a map, a globe, a chart, a technical drawing, a model, or a sculpture. The work can be either published or unpublished.

Form VA has limitations that may make it unsuitable for certain types of artwork, and particularly multi-media artworks that contains copyrightable non-visual media (such as a sound recording) in addition to the traditional visual media (painting, drawing, sculpture, photography, etc.). Form VA provides no means of indicating the inclusion of some other types of media in the copyright claim. For this reason, it may be preferable to register a multi-media or other complex work using one of the online options. (Alternatively, some other types of works may be registered on Form PA, such as video or films). For reference, a sample of Form VA and select other paper forms are included in Appendix D. Further instructions and information are included with the downloaded form. The following section illustrates the basic steps for completing Form VA.

Completing Form VA

START ▶ **Download the application form.**

On Copyright.gov, select, download, and print an application form. The paper forms are not clearly advertised and can be difficult to find on the website. Here are three potential methods for locating a paper registration form on the website:

- ▶ A link to all **Forms** can found under the Helpful Links heading on the lower part of the Registration Portal page. Following that link, the Visual Art registration form is listed under the Basic Registration heading.

  Copyright.gov > Registration menu > Register York Work
  > scroll to Helpful Links > **Forms** > (Basic Registration)
  Visual Form VA or Form VA

- ▶ Go to **https://www.copyright.gov/forms/** (active 2021).

- ▶ Or, on the home page, perform a search for *Form VA*.

Complete the application in black ink.

1 **Title(s)** and Type of Work.

- Enter the **title** of the work being registered.
  Optionally, also enter previous or alternative titles.

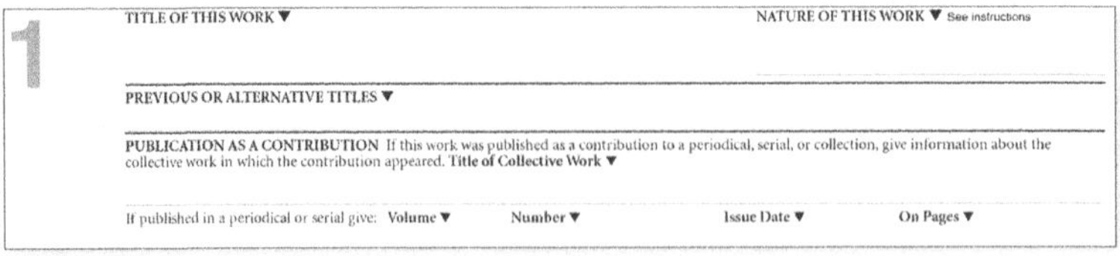
1
TITLE OF THIS WORK ▼ NATURE OF THIS WORK ▼ See instructions
PREVIOUS OR ALTERNATIVE TITLES ▼
PUBLICATION AS A CONTRIBUTION If this work was published as a contribution to a periodical, serial, or collection, give information about the collective work in which the contribution appeared. Title of Collective Work ▼
If published in a periodical or serial give: Volume ▼ Number ▼ Issue Date ▼ On Pages ▼

- Enter **publication** information, if applicable. For a work published in a periodical, serial, or collection, enter the title of the collective work (such as the title of the magazine or published collection). Enter, as applicable, the volume, number, the issue date, and identify the page number the work appears on. More publication information will be entered in Step 3.

- In the **Nature of this Work** space (upper right area of Section 1), enter the appropriate type. Some examples are: oil painting, charcoal drawing, etching, lithographic print, scale model, map, photograph, jewelry design, fabric design, sculpture.

2 **Artist/ Author** Information.

- In Section 2-A, enter the **name** of the author (artist) on the appropriate line, unless this is an anonymous or pseudonymous work.

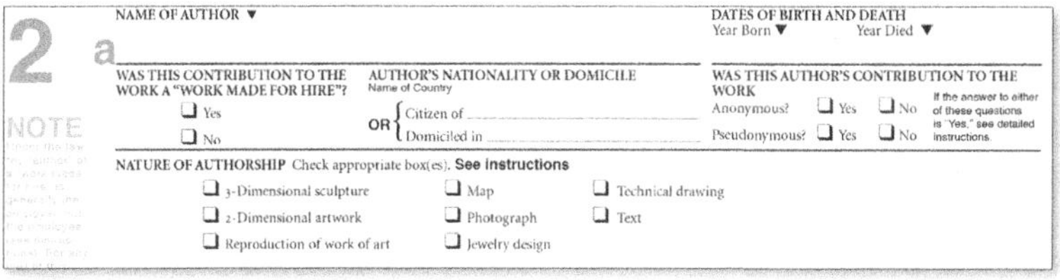
2 a
NAME OF AUTHOR ▼
DATES OF BIRTH AND DEATH
Year Born ▼ Year Died ▼
WAS THIS CONTRIBUTION TO THE WORK A "WORK MADE FOR HIRE"?
☐ Yes
☐ No
AUTHOR'S NATIONALITY OR DOMICILE
Name of Country
OR { Citizen of ______
Domiciled in ______
WAS THIS AUTHOR'S CONTRIBUTION TO THE WORK
Anonymous? ☐ Yes ☐ No
Pseudonymous? ☐ Yes ☐ No
If the answer to either of these questions is "Yes," see detailed instructions.
NOTE
NATURE OF AUTHORSHIP Check appropriate box(es). See instructions
☐ 3-Dimensional sculpture ☐ Map ☐ Technical drawing
☐ 2-Dimensional artwork ☐ Photograph ☐ Text
☐ Reproduction of work of art ☐ Jewelry design

- Check ***yes*** or ***no*** to indicate whether the **work was made for hire**.

- Identify the **country** of the artist's nationality or the artist's domicile (permanent residence). Enter the country name either for the artist's citizenship *or* domicile. This information is mandatory.

- Enter the **year of this artist's birth**. (Optional, but recommended). If the work was made for hire, do not enter a birthdate.

- If the artist is no longer living, enter the **year of death**. If the work was made for hire, leave the death date blank.

- Check ***yes*** or ***no*** to indicate if the work was made **anonymously**. If yes, you may either leave the author's name line blank or write in "anonymous." Or, you can enter the artist's name if you choose to do so.

- Check ***yes*** or ***no*** to indicate if the work was made under a **pseudonym** (fictitious name).

  - **If yes**, do one of the following:

    1) Leave the author's name line blank, *or*
    2) Enter the pseudonym (such as "Rrose Sélavy, pseudonym"), *or*
    3) Reveal the author's real name and clearly state the pseudonym (for example, "Marcel DuChamp whose pseudonym is Rrose Sélavy").

- **Nature of Authorship**: Check the box to indicate the type of creative contribution (original authorship) that the above artist made to the work. Multiple boxes can be selected. Choices are: 3-Dimensional sculpture, 2-Dimensional artwork, Reproduction of work of art, Map, Photograph, Jewelry design, Technical drawing, Text.

Additional Authors:

- If there is a **second artist** that contributed to the work, complete Section 2b in the same manner as for section 2a.

  If only one artist made the work, do not complete Section 2B or the Continuation Form. Skip to step 3.

- If there are **more than two artists** that contributed, use the paper Continuation Form (Form CON) to add those additional artists. Do not use Form CON if there are only 1 or 2 artists that contributed to the work. A copy of Form CON can be downloaded from the Copyright Office website through one of these methods:

  1) A link to all **Forms** can found under the Helpful Links heading on the lower part of the Registration Portal page. Following that link, the Form CON is listed under the Supplementary & Renewal Registration heading.

     Copyright.gov > Registration > Register York Work > scroll to Helpful Links > **Forms** > (Supplementary & Renewal Registration) **Form Con**

  2) Go to https://www.copyright.gov/forms/

  3) Or, on the home page, perform a search for *Form CON*, download a copy.

  - If you are using Form VA, enter or write "VA" in the upper left corner of Form CON.

  - Section A of Form CON: Enter the same title for

the work that is indicated in Section 1 of Form VA. Enter the name(s) and addresses of the claimants, as it is shown in Section 4 of Form VA.

- Section B of Form CON: Enter the information for additional artists that contributed to the work, in the same manner as Section 2a of Form VA

- Section C: Enter additional information on titles, claimants, or derivative works as needed.

- Section D of Form CON: Enter the same certificate mailing information that appears in Section 9 of Form VA.

3 **Completion Date** and **Publication** information.

- In Section 3a of Form VA, enter the **year** that the work was **completed**.

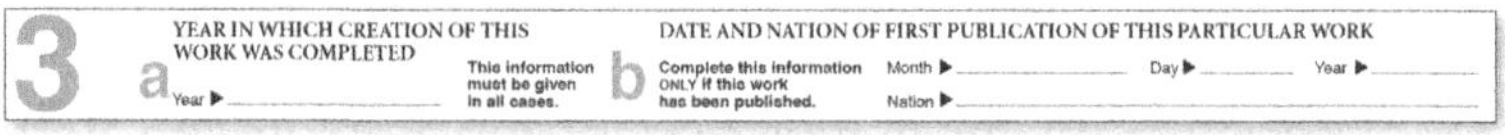
3
a YEAR IN WHICH CREATION OF THIS WORK WAS COMPLETED
Year ▶
This information must be given in all cases.
b DATE AND NATION OF FIRST PUBLICATION OF THIS PARTICULAR WORK
Complete this information ONLY if this work has been published.
Month ▶ Day ▶ Year ▶
Nation ▶

▶ If the work was **published**, also complete Section 3b:

- Enter the date (month, day, and year) of the **first publication** of the work.

- Enter the name of the **nation** where the first publication occurred.

4 **Claimant** Information.

- Enter the name and address of the **claimant**(s). If you are an artist registering your own independently made artwork, enter your name and address in the space.

4

COPYRIGHT CLAIMANT(S) Name and address must be given even if the claimant is the same as the author given in space 2. ▼

See instructions before completing this space

TRANSFER If the claimant(s) named here in space 4 is (are) different from the author(s) named in space 2, give a brief statement of how the claimant(s) obtained ownership of the copyright. ▼

- Transfer of Copyright Ownership: If the author(s) indicated in Section 2 are different than the claimant, make a brief statement on how the claimant(s) obtained ownership of the copyright in the work. By written agreement, by inheritance, or by another means.

  If you are the artist and you continue to own the copyright in the work, leave the transfer area blank and do not enter a statement here.

5 Prior Registration.

PREVIOUS REGISTRATION Has registration for this work, or for an earlier version of this work, already been made in the Copyright Office?
❑ **Yes** ❑ **No** If your answer is "Yes," why is another registration being sought? (Check appropriate box.) ▼
a. ❑ This is the first published edition of a work previously registered in unpublished form.
b. ❑ This is the first application submitted by this author as copyright claimant.
c. ❑ This is a changed version of the work, as shown by space 6 on this application.
If your answer is "Yes," give: **Previous Registration Number** ▼ **Year of Registration** ▼

5

- Check yes or no to indicate whether this work was previously registered.

▶ If **no**, the work has not been previously registered, leave the rest of the section 5 blank and **go on to Step 6**.

▶ If **yes**, the work has been previously registered:
(1) check the appropriate box (a, b, or c) to describe

the situation, and (2) **enter the previous registration** number issued and the year of the prior registration in the spaces provided.

6 **Derivative Works, Changed Works**, and **Compilations**

If the artwork consists entirely of (new) original authorship and does not contain any preexisting material, **leave Section 6 blank** and go on to Step 7.

For a **derivative work**, complete both section 6a and 6b on Form VA. For a work that is a **compilation**, only complete 6b in this section.

> A derivative work is based on or incorporates one or more preexisting works.
>
> A compilation is a work that has been formed by the collection and assembly of preexisting material that has been selected, coordinated, or arranged so as to create a new work of authorship.

Section 6a: This section asks you to identify any preexisting work or works that the artwork is based on or incorporates. This includes public domain matter, or a prior work by the artist that was previously registered or published and which is incorporated into the new work, or other preexisting material. Material that is identified in section 6a will be excluded from your copyright claim.

- Enter a brief description of any such **pre-existing material** contained in the work.

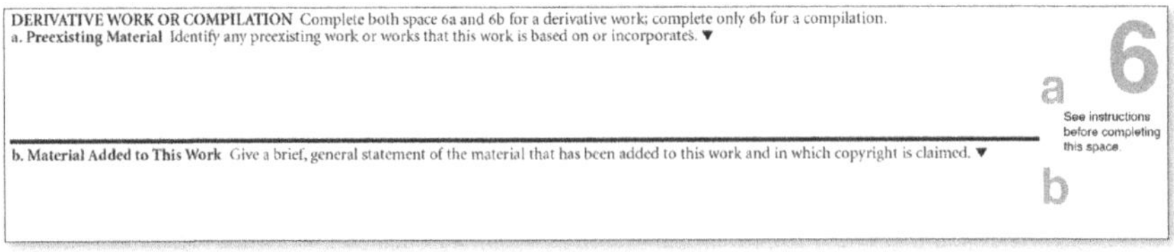
DERIVATIVE WORK OR COMPILATION Complete both space 6a and 6b for a derivative work; complete only 6b for a compilation.
a. Preexisting Material Identify any preexisting work or works that this work is based on or incorporates. ▼

6 a

See instructions before completing this space.

b. Material Added to This Work Give a brief, general statement of the material that has been added to this work and in which copyright is claimed. ▼

b

Section 6b: This section asks you to identify the new original aspect of the artwork that is now being registered. The material identified in 6b will be included in your copyright claim.

- For derivative works, enter a brief general description of the **new** material that has been added to create the work that is being registered.
- For compilations, enter a brief general statement that describes the nature of the material compiled and the compilation itself. For example, a "compilation of 19th century photographs."

7 **Contact** Information and Preexisting Payment Accounts.

Section 7a: Leave Section 7a blank if you do not have a pre-existing Copyright Office deposit account. If you have previously established a Copyright Office (financial) deposit account to pay fees, enter the name and account number.

DEPOSIT ACCOUNT If the registration fee is to be charged to a Deposit Account established in the Copyright Office, give name and number of Account.
Name ▼ **Account Number ▼**

a 7

CORRESPONDENCE Give name and address to which correspondence about this application should be sent. Name/Address/Apt/City/State/Zip ▼

b

Area code and daytime telephone number ( ) Fax number ( )

Email

Section 7b: Enter contact information. Identify who should be contacted if the Copyright Office has questions about this application. Identify yourself here or someone else of your choosing.

- Enter the name, address, telephone number, fax number (if applicable), and an email address for the person that should be contacted.

8 Certification

The purpose of this section is to certify that the application is correct to the best of your knowledge and that you have the authority to register the copyright in the artwork.

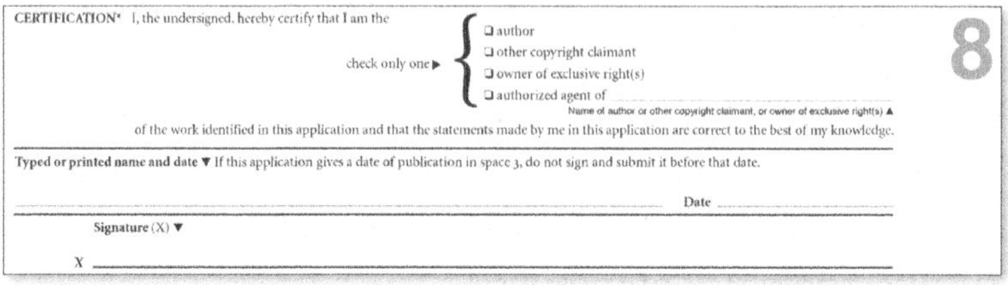
CERTIFICATION* I, the undersigned, hereby certify that I am the

check only one ▶
❑ author
❑ other copyright claimant
❑ owner of exclusive right(s)
❑ authorized agent of ______
Name of author or other copyright claimant, or owner of exclusive right(s) ▲

of the work identified in this application and that the statements made by me in this application are correct to the best of my knowledge.

8

Typed or printed name and date ▼ If this application gives a date of publication in space 3, do not sign and submit it before that date.

Date ______

Signature (X) ▼

X ______

- Identify your status. The choices are: (1) **author** (artist that created the work), (2) other copyright claimant (not the author/artist), (3) owner of exclusive right(s) or (4) the owner's authorized agent (agents should also enter whom is represented on the line provided).

  If you are an artist registering your own work, check the author box.

- Print your name and the date in the space provided.

- Read all of the text in Section 8. If you agree, you are certifying that you are the person indicated and "the work identified in this application and the statements made by me in this application are correct to the best of my knowledge." To indicate your agreement, **sign** at the X.

9 Certification Mailing Information

- Enter the name of the person and the address where the copyright certificate should be mailed. Enter your own information here or that of another person that should receive the certificate.

10 The Fee

- **Confirm the current filing fee** for **Form VA**. Go to the Copyright Office website and locate the filing fee information for **paper** filing Form VA. As of January 2021, the fee for Form VA is $125, but this is subject to change at any time. Confirm the correct filing fee each and every time you submit a paper based registration form.

Copyright.gov > Research > Fees
Go to Registration heading > Paper filing forms

OR

https://www.copyright.gov/about/fees.html
Go to Registration heading > Paper filing forms

OR

Call to request the current fee for paper Form VA at 1-877-476-0778 or (202) 707-3000.

- ▶ Acceptable payment forms are personal check or money order made payable to the *U.S. Copyright Office*. Filing fees are non-refundable.

11 Deposit Copies of the Artwork

A copy of the work must be mailed along with the fee and the application.

- Assemble the copy or copies of the work that you will submit to the Copyright Office. Do not send original work. The copies will not be returned.

  The form of the deposit copy depends upon whether the work was published and where.

  - **Unpublished work**: If the work has not been published, deposit **one complete copy** of the work.

  - **Published work**: If the work has been published, then submit the deposit according to the following condition that best applies.

    - For works that were first published in the **United States**, deposit **two complete copies** of the best edition.

      OR

    - If the work was *first* published outside the United States deposit **one complete copy** of the **first foreign edition**.

      OR

    - If the work is a contribution to **a collective work**, deposit one complete copy of the best edition of the collective work.

For more information on complete copies, identifying material, and best editions refer to Chapter 5.

12 Submit All Materials

- **Assemble** all of the elements together in one package:

    1. Completed and signed Form VA. If you used Form CON include it also.
    2. The correct filing fee.
    3. The deposit materials (copy or copies of the artwork).

- Address and **promptly mail** the package to the address on Form VA: Library of Congress, U.S. Copyright Office-VA, 101 Independence Avenue SE, Washington, DC 20559-6000.

For more information on mailing materials to the Copyright Office, refer to the section on *Mailing Deposits to the Copyright Office* in Chapter 5.

CHAPTER FIVE

REGISTRATION CONCEPTS & REQUIREMENTS

The registration of a copyright is essentially an official claim of rights in a specific work. Perhaps most significantly, the process can serve to define the scope of the copyright itself. By entering information about the original elements of the work in an application, or by stating a limitation, an assertion is made about the extent of the copyright in the work. The completed application is a statement of the parameters of the copyright that is claimed. Because the copyright covers only the original aspects of the work, it may encompass a part or parts of the work, or the entire work.

This chapter covers the topics of publication status, the fee, the deposit copies of the work, and determining the extent of the copyright claim in more detail. Essential concepts for copyrights and registration are further built upon.

The topics can be read from the beginning or reviewed as needed, depending upon how you decide to approach the registration process. This chapter further discusses the terminology of the application and the technical information or materials that are required in some cases.

Determining if the Work Has Been Published

Has the artwork been published? Before registering your copyright you will need to make a determination of whether the work has been published or not. *Publication* in the context of copyrights, sometimes has a different meaning than every day language. In many cases the question of whether a work has been published is straightforward—such as in the case of artworks physically printed in books or magazines—but in some cases more thought as to how the work has been used or distributed may be needed to make that determination.

When you complete a registration application, you will make the determination as to whether the work was published or not. The Copyright Office will accept this assertion unless it is implausible or conflicts with information stated elsewhere in the application materials or with other sources.

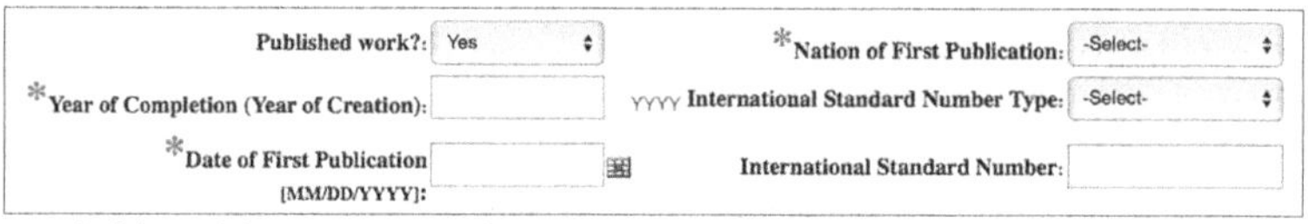
Published work?: Yes
*Nation of First Publication: -Select-
*Year of Completion (Year of Creation): YYYY
International Standard Number Type: -Select-
*Date of First Publication (MM/DD/YYYY):
International Standard Number:

Detail of the Publication section of the Standard Application.

Timing is also significant. The publication determination should be based on the facts that exist at the time the registration application is filed with the Copyright Office. If the publication is prospective or has otherwise not occurred at the time the application is filed, the work is considered unpublished. If a publication is planned or potential, but has not yet occurred, identify the work as unpublished in the application.

The word "publication" has some different meanings in the context of copyright registration. Along with the typical forms of print-based publishing, it also encompasses other acts that do not involve physical printing.

> "Publication" is the distribution of copies or phonorecords of a work to the public by sale or other transfer of ownership, or by rental, lease, or lending. The offering to distribute copies...to a group of persons for purposes of further distribution, public performance, or public display, constitutes publication. A public performance or display of a work does not of itself constitute publication.
>
> (U.S. Copyright Law, 17 USC § 101, excerpt)

Factors to consider are distribution, offers to sell or transfer, renting out or leasing the work to another. These acts may constitute publication in some instances. For instance, if you offer a photograph for licensing through a stock photography company, or if you offer licenses directly, these scenarios each likely constitute a publication of that photograph.

On the other hand, **simply displaying an artwork in public does not constitute publication**, no matter how many people view or experience the work.

- Displaying an artwork in a **museum, gallery, or in a space** like the lobby of a building alone does not constitute a publication.
- Displaying a work in a storefront alone does not constitute a publication.

> **A public performance or display of a work does not of itself constitute publication.**
>
> "To perform or display a work "publicly" means– (1) to perform or display it at a place open to the public or at any place where a substantial number of persons outside of a normal circle of a family and its social acquaintances is gathered; or (2) to transmit or otherwise communicate a performance or display of the work to a place specified by clause (1) or to the public, by means of any device or process, whether the members of the public capable of receiving the performance or display receive it in the same place or in separate places and at the same time or at different times."
>
> (U.S. Copyright Law, 17 USC § 101, excerpt)

To be considered as a *published* work in the context of copyrights, something more than a display or performance is required. The additional act that transforms it into a published work can be a voluntary distribution, a sale, or certain offers intended to cause a public distribution or sale of copies–such as the licensing example above or by authorizing the reproduction of the work in a book or magazine that will be distributed or sold.

Internet / Online

The copyright meaning of *publication* can be narrower than the way the term is used in ordinary speech. We may casually say that a text or an image has been *published* on the internet, but that may or may not mean publication in the copyright sense of the word. The distinction is partly due to the legal definitions in the Copyright Law itself, which pre-date the existence of the public internet.

The Copyright Office has stated that it does not generally consider a work to be published if it is merely displayed online. This does not mean that publication does not happen online—it can—but it reflects the persistent ambiguity of works displayed online. To date, the Copyright Office has not established a bright line for determining instances where online display is absolutely a publication.

Publication in a copyright context means an act that is more than simple display or exhibition. If an artist-copyright owner placed a copy of an artwork online and expressly authorized others to reproduce it or distribute it publically, perhaps with text stating the image could be freely downloaded or shared, then that work could be considered to be published. Or, a web button with the word *download, save, or email* on it, would tend to imply an authorization to distribute a particular image. By extension, the existence of a download button or link implies that the image has been distributed or was offered for distribution, and was thus published.

On the other hand, if some act that could constitute publication occurs without authorization of the copyright owner, this would not be considered to be a publication. Again, the Copyright Office has not established a bright line rule, but it would seem that if an artist took steps to prevent unauthorized downloads or sharing, that would imply that the work was not published.

Publication status does not usually affect whether or not the work can be registered or protected by copyright, but there are some other important limitations. For example, a group of photographs application does not permit mixing published and unpublished works on the same application—they must be registered on separate forms. The copies of the published work submitted as the deposit may have different requirements depending upon the publication status. A "best edition" of the actual publication may be required (but in many cases a digital reproduction may be acceptable).

More significantly, when registration is made after the publication has occurred, the duration of the copyright can be shorter or different in certain instances. This apparent unfairness does not affect most artists directly, but it happens in some cases where the calculation of the copyright term is based upon the date of the first publication rather than the date of completion or the life of the artist. For certain anonymous works, works made for hire, and for works made under a pseudonym, the duration of the copyright can potentially be shorter than the standard, depending on the circumstances.

The Scope of the Claim: Excluded and Included Material

Each application requires defining the copyright that is being claimed. In the electronic applications this part of the application is titled the Limitation of Claim. The parallel section in paper Form VA is part 6. Defining–or limiting–the copyright is arguably the most important part of registration. It is not a complicated process, but the terminology used by the Copyright Office can be confusing.

At its essence, the limitation of the claim is simply identifying what in the artwork is original (and therefore copyrightable) and what parts are not original (and not copyrightable).

The "claim" you make when you register a copyright in your work is an assertion of the existence of the copyright in the original aspects of the artwork. By extension, you are also asserting ownership of that property right.

The original authorship—the creative contribution of the artist— is the material that is copyright protected. To state the claim, typically, the original authorship is identified. This could be the entire work, or it could be parts of the work. The original authorship is essentially the source of the copyright in the work. However, some applications have an inverted process, where you identify the unprotected aspects of the work and all the rest is assumed to be the claim. Most of the application forms refer to this process as *limiting* the claim, irrespective of which method is used.

There are two essential concepts to defining the copyright, the material that is ***excluded*** from the claim and the material that is ***included*** in the claim.

The part or parts of the artwork that are copyrightable are said to be *included* in the claim. The *included* material is the original authorship—the aspect of the work that is purely the artist's original creation. The material that is *excluded* from the claim are elements that were preexisting, not copyrightable, or otherwise not original to the work. Material that is *excluded* from a claim typically includes public domain matter that was incorporated in the work or other elements that were not the result of the artist's creativity.

> Copyright protection subsists...in **original works of authorship** fixed in any tangible medium of expression, now known or later developed, from which they can be perceived, reproduced, or otherwise communicated, either directly or with the aid of a machine or device...
>
> U.S. Copyright Law, 17 USC § 102 (a) (excerpt)

Determining what part, if not the entire work, is the original authorship is the key to correctly identifying a copyright claim for the purpose of registration.

Artist's Creativity → Original Authorship → Included Material = Copyright Claim

For many artworks there may be **no excluded material** at all because the entire work is the artist's creativity–it completely consist of original authorship. For example a painting, a photograph, an illustration, or a sculpture that is not a copy itself, and which is completely original to the artist, would likely not have any material excluded from the claim. A few examples of the many, many possibilities are a painting of a landscape, a photograph of a street scene, or a ceramic sculpture depicting a human model. These works do not include any externally sourced elements; they are entirely the product of the artist's creativity.

It is also common for artworks to include elements that were not the products of the artist's creativity. Whether those elements are from public domain sources or some other form preexisting material, they should be identified as excluded from the claim.

It is also possible for a work of visual art to be composed of entirely preexisting elements (excluded material), but still be the product of the artist's creativity (included material). For instance, sometimes the *arrangement* of the elements—even when those elements are not original—is a product of the artist's original authorship in the work as a whole. There are innumerable ways that this can occur. An example could be a sculpture composed entirely of preexisting mass-produced objects. Or, perhaps a collage of antique advertisements with an original drawing superimposed on the surface. In the later example, when new work (original drawing, arrangement) is added to pre-existing material (the old ads) these types of works may be referred to as derivative works. Marcel Duchamp's L.H.O.O.Q. is another example that was discussed in Chapter 2.

Excluded	Included
Pre-existing material; each element that is not original to this work	All original authorship; the creative contribution of the artist
Each element not made by the artist, material from any source	Original, new element(s) made by the artist in this work (as part of a derivative work)
Public domain material	May include the selection or arrangement of elements in the work, as a creative contribution, such as in a derivative work or compilation
Works previously made by the same artist incorporated into the new work, generally need not be identified as excluded matter so long as the prior work was not previously registered or published.	*Included elements must have more than de minimus creativity and qualify as copyrightable matter.*

Different Application, Different Terminology

The older and the newer applications take different approaches to defining the claim. This can be confusing when looking at the forms, but the goal of defining the claim is the same.

For instance, paper-based Form VA does not request identification of excluded or included material. Rather, Form VA refers to new artwork that incorporates pre-existing material as a derivative work. Paper Form VA's request for identification of pre-existing material (step 6a) is equivalent to the excluded material in the newer online forms. Form VA's *Material Added* part (step 6b) is equivalent to the included material section in some of the online application forms.

A Hypothetical Case

This work is a composite of Leonardo da Vinci's *Mona Lisa* and a new original illustration of the New York City skyline. The image of Mona Lisa is obviously a (digital) copy and since the painting was

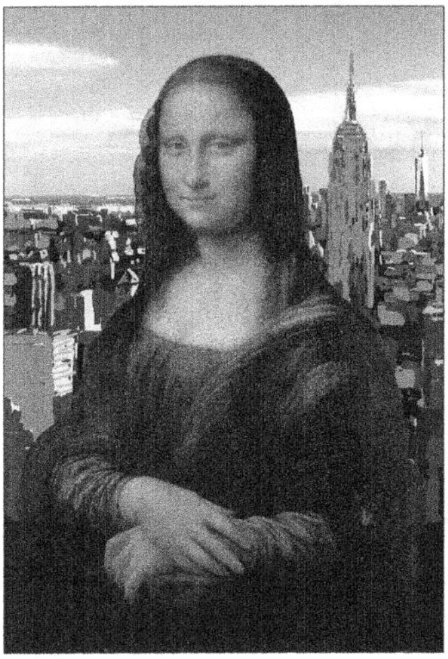

made hundreds of years ago, there is clearly no copyright protection. *Mona Lisa* is not my original work. It is a copy and it is in the public domain. For these reasons, Leonardo's Mona Lisa is excluded from a new copyright claim that incorporates it.

On the other hand, the illustration in the background is an original work that was created in 2020, and it is copyrightable as an original pictorial work. It should be included in the claim.

	Material Excluded	Material Included
Description:	Copy of painting, Leonardo Vinci's Mona Lisa, circa 1503-1517	Illustration of New York skyline, 2020
Type of work:	2-D artwork	2-D artwork
Reason:	Public domain (Also, non-original copy; material not created by artist of the new work).	Original authorship

The included material is the essence of the work that is original; it is equivalent to my copyright in the work. The excluded column is not covered by the claim, but must be declared in the registration.

Material Excluded	Material Included
☑ 2-D artwork *(Leonardo's Mona Lisa)*	☑ 2-D artwork *(Original illustration)*

If I registered this work on the **Standard** Application, I would identify Leonardo's Mona Lisa as excluded material and my own illustration as included material. In this example, both are forms of 2-D artwork.

The **One Work By One Author (Single)** application only requires identifying excluded material. Included material is not listed. Registering the work on the Single application, I would only identify Leonardo's Mona Lisa as material excluded form the claim. As you can see from the applications themselves (Chapter 3), these indications are fairly general and typically only require a check in a box. If you choose to, you can provide a different very brief description in the *Other* box on the Limitation of Claim screen for each of these applications.

Or, if I register the work on paper **Form VA** I would list Leonardo's Mona Lisa in the *Preexisting Material* area of step 6 and identify the new illustration (2-D artwork) in the area for *Material Added to This Work*. In essence, Form VA construes my new work, *Mona Lisa NYC*, as a derivative work of Leonardo's *Mona Lisa*. This is just a different practical approach to limiting the claim in comparison to the other applications. It does not change the scope of my copyright in the work; the claim is really the same regardless of which application is used for the registration.

If I register the copyright in *Mona Lisa NYC*, I would not include any digitizing process or other manner of reproducing Leonardo's *Mona Lisa*. Digitizing a public domain image does not convert it into copyrightable matter, and as a process, digitization is not copyrightable. (Refer to Chapter 2 for more on copyrightability).

For some works that include multiple pre-existing elements, it may be appropriate to claim the *arrangement* of the elements in the composition as a whole, or possibly even the *selection* of such elements—so long as the arrangement or selection is sufficiently creative. I have not changed the position of the Mona Lisa figure in the frame to an appreciable degree and I would not claim any original authorship in regard to a new arrangement of elements in this particular case.

Strategies For Determining A Claim in a Derivative Work

The hypothetical case is one simple example of a claim in a derivative work, one that combines both older preexisting material and newer original creative elements. There are so many different ways that artists construct works out of old and new material. If the claim is not quite clear, there are strategies for looking at a work, even a complex one, and sorting out the claim.

Focus on the excluded material first. When the *excluded* material is subtracted, the remainder should consist of the *included* material for the claim. Some application forms, including the Single Application and the unpublished group application take this approach. Whatever isn't excluded is assumed to be included in the claim and there is no separate identification of included material.

Does the work contain any element that is **not original** to this work or was not created by the artist?

No → There is no material excluded from the claim.

Yes → The material should be excluded from the claim.

Does the work incorporate any public domain material? Or is based upon public domain material?

Yes → The public domain material should be excluded from the claim.

Does the work contain any pre-existing material in the work, from any source?

Yes → The specific material should be excluded from the claim–**unless** this is a derivative of unpublished, unregistered, copyright material that is owned by a claimant-artist. (Generally, when a derivative work involves the artist's own prior work, and it has not been published or registered before, it need not be excluded from the new claim).

Does the work contain any previously registered material?

Yes → The specific material should be excluded from the claim.

Does the work contain any copyrightable material owned by a third party (a person or organization that is not a claimant)?

Yes → The specific material must be excluded from the claim.

The claim can be conceptualized by a method of subtraction—when the excluded elements are taken out, the included material remains. The remainder should be the original authorship; the artist's contribution. For applications that require a specific identification of the included material, such as the Standard Application or Form VA, this contribution should be identified as included, new, or added material in the pertinent application. At this time only the Standard Application and Form VA still require an express identification of the included material.

> Does the work incorporate original creativity (original authorship) to at least a minimal degree?
>
> Yes → This is the artist's contribution. **The material should be included in the claim.**
>
> Did the artist use creativity in composing (unoriginal) elements, including the composition of actual excluded material?
>
> Yes → If applicable to the work, the arrangement or selection of elements, so long as it contains *de minimus* creativity, may be categorized as included material.

For the applications that require identifying the included material specifically, such as the online Standard Application and the paper-based Form VA, the claim stated in the application should include all of your original authorship. You want your claim to be as broad as possible, but any element that is not properly part of the copyright should also be identified. Material that is not original to the work must be indicated as excluded from the claim.

Describing the Included or Excluded Material

As you can see in the application details covered in Chapter 4, there is usually only a general description of included or excluded material. The applications require only a check in a box or a brief description. For visual art, a description of material can be as simple as "2-D artwork" or "sculpture" or "photograph."

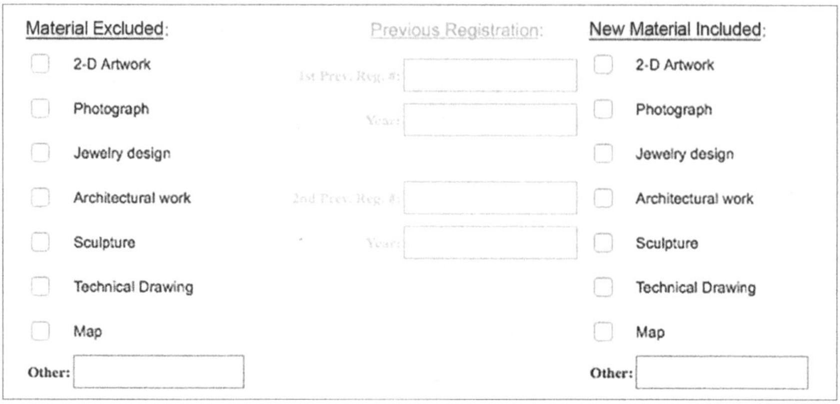

Detail of the Standard Application's Limitation of Claim screen.

For a work of visual art the main options for describing included or excluded material are: **2-D Artwork, Photograph, Jewelry design, Architectural work, Sculpture, Technical Drawing** and **Map**. To complete the Limitation of Claim section, simply check the box that describes the authorship. If there are multiple forms of authorship, check all boxes that apply to the work. In the Standard Application, you will do this for both included and for excluded material. Other online applications only require identification of the material that is excluded from the claim.

The pre-established authorship categories are fairly broad and it may not be immediately obvious that they encompass the type of element that you need to identify. If one or more of the options describes the work in accurate general terms, then the checkbox categories are usually the best way to describe the material.

As a general rule, the Copyright Office prefers a description of the authorship in pictorial, graphic, or sculptural works as "2-D Artwork" or "sculpture" respectively, so long as the selected term accurately identifies the element or the work. For example, 2-D artwork includes not only traditional fine art forms (drawing, painting, collage, prints, posters, etc.), but also labels, greeting cards, stencils, posters, calendars, and more.

"2-D artwork" can also be used to describe drawings or graphics that appear on a website or which are displayed on a computer screen (but images that are animated are best described as *audio-visual work*). 2-D artwork can be used to describe pictorial images that are applied to a utilitarian object, provided that the artwork is separable (distinctly identifiable) from the functional object.

Similarly, in a copyright context, the word "sculpture" encompasses more than 3-D fine art works. *Sculpture* can potentially describe objects like globes and models, as well as some artistically crafted works such as jewelry, vases, and toys. Sculpture also includes 3-D artwork that is incorporated into a useful or functional article, but as discussed in the Useful Article section of Chapter 2, the utilitarian aspect of the object is not covered.

Describing Other Types of Work

If the standard visual art options can accurately describe the claim material, it is preferable to use them. But, if the work includes or incorporates something different than those categories describe, you should enter your own description of the element.

In the application form depicted on the previous page, there is an option to describe the material when it does not fit into the preexisting categories: **Other**.

When the work incorporates non-visual art material, the Copyright Office's terminology for other types of work may be adapted to describe it. For reference, the chart below shows some selected types of authorship, including visual art, but also other categories of work. These terms may be useful for describing other types of material that are incorporated in your claim. Descriptions of materials are not limited to these terms, but the list may be a useful starting point when the standard terminology for visual art does not appear to adequately describe the material at issue.

Visual Art	Motion Picture/ AV Works	Literary Work
Photograph 2-D artwork	Entire Motion Picture (can include video, film, etc.)	Text (including literary work or writing)
Jewelry design	Production	Computer program
Sculpture	Cinematography	
Map	Direction	
Architectural Work	Editing	
Technical Drawing	Script/Screenplay	
Other (enter a description)	Other MP/AV authorship.	
	Example: Audiovisual material (such as animated 2-D artwork)	

Sound Recording	Work of Performing Arts	Single Serial Issue (periodical)
Sound Recording (performance/ production)	Music Lyrics Other text (including script, screenplay, dramatic work) Musical Arrangement	Collective Work authorship (for the issue as a whole, including selection, coordination, arrangement of independent works)

All of the work, or all of the elements that you are claiming (included) or disclaiming (excluded) should be identified if the application requires it. Presumably, if you are using an online application you have selected work of visual art as the work being registered. The

Other box can be used to identify types of material that do not meet the description of visual artwork, but are incorporated in that work.

For example, when registering a work composed of multiple media that incorporates a non-pictorial element, such as a sound recording, the description of "sound recording" could be entered in the *Other* box. Alternatively, if you are using paper Form VA, this would be entered in the appropriate area of step 6. The primary work is registered as visual art (2-D artwork, photo, sculpture, etc.).

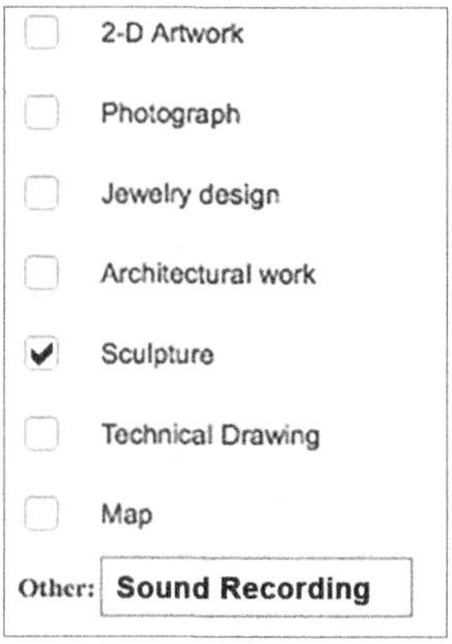

If the other material does not fit any of the established descriptions for any type of work, then create your own brief description of the material. Enter this in the *Other* box in the Limitation of Claim section in the electronic application (or if you are using Form VA, the appropriate area of step 6). If you feel that more information is needed, the comment box in the Certification section of the online applications can be used for further clarification.

When crafting your own description of any material, try to keep it brief and clear. Avoid using phrases like the "entire work," which the Copyright Offices considers to be too vague. (Motion picture works are an exception in some cases). Try to specify the (physical) type of work in the description.

To prevent confusion about your claim, avoid using words that seem to refer to a process. Rather, choose words that describe the tangible, physical product. (Remember that ideas, concepts, and methods are not copyrightable).

Instead of a word like "concept," choose a word or phrase that describes the finished, physically tangible element of work. It may be that your artistic concept resulted in a 3-D (sculptural) work, for example. In that case, you could simply check the corresponding box on the application rather than developing a brand new description for the type of work.

When the Copyright Office reviews your application the agent will compare the claim stated (excluded and/or included material) with the deposit copy of the work you submitted. If there is something unclear, the agent may contact you for a correction or clarification, which can cause some delay in processing the registration.

> There are words and phrases that should **not** be used to describe material that is excluded or material that is included in the claim, if it is possible. Words or phrases to avoid include those that the Copyright Office has specifically deemed as unclear, and also those that suggest an idea, procedure, process, system, method, concept, principle, discovery, fact, or other uncopyrightable matter in some contexts.
>
> Some words and phrases to generally avoid:
> *Character, design, game, packaging*, a term that describes the artist or author's profession, *story, storyline, plot, idea*, **concept**, *conceived, conception, research, song, ballad, cancion, vocals, musical instruments, equalization, remastering, reverberation*, **reprocessing**, *re-engineering, rap, hip hop, beats, loops, transcription, narration, spoken words, sound effects, entire work*, **everything**, and *entire project*.

Fee Payment Options & Issues

Once you complete the informational portion of an online registration application you must pay the filing fee. After the fee is paid the deposit materials can be uploaded and then the process should be complete in most cases.

For **online applications**, payment is currently accepted only by a debit or credit card or electronic check (ACH debit), which is processed through a redirection to Pay.gov. When the payment process is completed you will be automatically directed back to the Copyright Office's website. The details are described in Chapter 4 for each respective application.

If you expect to be making a large number of registrations, you can consider establishing a **deposit account** with the Copyright Office in advance and then pay each application fee with the deposit account funds. (A minimum initial deposit is usually several hundred dollars). Information on opening a deposit account can be found on the Copyright Office's website.

For applications filed in paper form, such as **Form VA**, payment can be made only by a personal check or money order made payable to the *U.S. Copyright Office*. Paper based filing is more expensive than electronic filing—be sure you are paying the current correct fee for the form you are submitting. An incorrect fee can cause a delay or rejection of the application. **It is important to confirm the current fee on the Copyright.gov website before mailing in any paper-based application**.

All fees are subject to change. Fee changes that took effect in 2020 are shown in **Appendix B**.

The Copyright Office typically reviews its fees every three to five years. At the time of publication, there were recent increases to some fees, but the group of photographs registration fee was held at a lower rate. However, be aware that any fee may change in coming years, and there could be interim changes as well. If you are registering online, you will be advised of the proper fee for the type of registration application, but if you are filing a paper application, confirm that you have a current application form and the proper filing fee to avoid delays and fines.

If an application fee is made with an uncollectable check or insufficient deposit account, the application will be delayed until a proper fee is received—along with a hefty service charge. In some instances a registration may be cancelled entirely if the payment is uncollectable. Especially when using paper application forms, make sure your fee is correct and do not mail cash.

Accuracy is important. There can be additional fees or service charges levied for errors. The fees for correcting unidentified deposits, extra certificate copies, and to appeal a denied claim, although not usual, reflect the importance of preparation and review. Plan your application accordingly, complete it correctly, and save your records.

Submitting A Copy of the Artwork: The Deposit Requirement

To complete the registration process, a copy of the artwork must be submitted to the Copyright Office. This copy is referred to as the **Deposit.** Depending upon the type of work and the application form used for the registration, there are two forms of deposits:

- **Electronic copies** submitted by upload (digital images files, such as **JPG, GIF, TIFF**, or other formats for different types of works).

OR

- **Hard copies** submitted by mail (such as prints, printed materials, film copies, photographic prints, and also DVDs, CDs, and storage devices containing electronic files).

The submission of digital files by the upload process is the simplest means of fulfilling the deposit requirement, and it most cases, it is preferred by the Copyright Office. The deposit requirement for an unpublished 2-D work of visual art, registered via one of the online applications, can be fulfilled by uploading a digital file of the work. Similarly, for an (unpublished) 3-D artwork, digital photographic images of the work will suffice and can be uploaded during the online application process. Other types of work, and some work that has been published, has other technical considerations discussed later in this section.

Most artists are able to submit their deposit by uploading the digital file at the end of the online registration application process. Otherwise either a digital file or a physical copy of the work is submitted by regular mail to the Copyright Office. These materials can be hard copies, like prints or photographs, or they can be digital files stored on a device like a flash drive, CD or DVD.

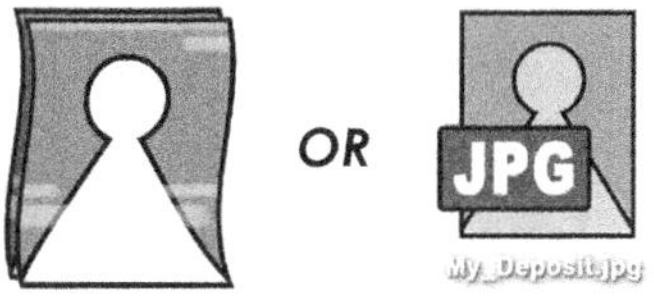

Whichever means is used for the deposit, the copyright registration application is only considered to be complete when the material is received by the Copyright Office (along with the proper fee and application). When the electronic upload method is used, the Copyright Office receives the deposit immediately, and you can confirm this through the eCO system. A mail-in deposit will delay the effective date of the registration and have a longer processing time.

Do not send originals. The deposit material will not be returned. Once submitted, the deposit materials cannot be copied or otherwise reproduced without the permission of the copyright owner for the full period that the work is protected. Of course, you can create derivative works, make reproductions, and otherwise still use your copyright in its entirety. The copy of the work on file with the Copyright Office will be safe; no one will be permitted to reproduce it without your permission.

For the majority of works, uploading or mailing a digital copy will be the appropriate method of fulfilling the deposit requirement. That is fairly straightforward. However, the following sections discuss the form of copies that must be submitted in more detail. Some of the nuances in terminology are also covered for those who may want more information about the process. Again, for *most* works, a simple, accurate digital copy of the work should be sufficient to fulfill the deposit requirement.

•

The form or content of the deposit is based upon the publication status and the type of work that you are registering. You may see certain technical terms, such as: *identifying material* (ID material), a *complete copy*, or a copy of a *best edition*.

Identifying Material – or ID material– is a two-dimensional reproduction or rendering of a work, such as a photograph, photocopy, transparency (photo slide), or drawing that shows the complete content of the work that is being registered. A *best edition* is a copy of the work in a preferred form, such as one that is reproduced on archival paper. A *complete copy* contains all of the authorship—original creative elements—in the work that is being registered. These technical terms are covered in more detail further on in the chapter.

Visual Art Media Deposits

This section is an overview of deposit requirements for art media, traditional, and some non-traditional media examples. Most deposits for visual art works can be submitted in electronic form with an online application, or digital files or hard copy material, can be sent by mail to the Copyright Office. However, note that the Group of Unpublished Works application only permits deposits that are uploaded through the online application and paper Form VA requires mail-in deposits only.

2-D Visual Art Works and Single Photographs

Unpublished work: One complete copy, or one identifying material (such as a photograph of the work).

Published work, U.S. publication: Two complete copies of the "best edition" (for a work first published on January 1, 1978 or later). However, the Copyright Office has said that in this type of case, a single digital file may be uploaded when an electronic application is used to register the work.

Published work, first publication in a foreign country (outside the U.S.) March 1, 1989 or later: One complete copy of either the first published edition or the best edition of the work. When the work was subsequently published in the United States, submit either one complete copy of the first foreign publication or a complete copy of the best edition of the U.S. publication so long as the content is identical.

Certain Published Limited Editions of Pictorial or Graphic Work

When the artist/author is the copyright owner, and 300 or fewer copies were published, submit one complete copy of the best edition or, alternatively, ID material may be submitted (such as a photograph of the work). If less than 5 copies of the work have been published, irrespective of the identity of the copyright owner, submit one complete copy or one ID material.

3-D Visual Art

Published and unpublished 3-D works: Deposit ID material, such as photographs, of the work.

Multiple Photos Registered as a Group of Photographs

(online application only)

For a group of photographs the submission of a digital copy is required for each item in the group along with a numbered list containing certain information.

Only digital files are accepted for the group deposit, regardless of whether the original photos are digital or print media. The digital copies should be in JPEG (.jpg), GIF or TIFF (.tif) format. Individual files must be 500MB or less in size. Or, you may elect to upload the required list of photographs and the image deposit files together as a compressed zip file, so long as the individual image files are also compressed. The final compressed file may not exceed 500 MB.

Alternatively, the deposit can be made by submitting the photo files on a device, such as a flash drive or a DVD and delivering them to the Copyright Office by mail. This is a useful option, for instance, when individual files exceed 500MB or when the upload process may be overly burdensome due to the number of works. If you elect to submit the deposit by mail this will delay the effective date of the copyright registration until the time the Copyright Office receives the works and processing time will be substantially longer. The device or disk will not be returned.

The required list of photographs must be uploaded in the later part of the online application process. This process is covered in Chapter 4 in the section on completing the Group of Photographs Application. If you elect to mail in the digital files on a device, be sure to comply with the requirements and properly attach the shipping slip. (Fees may result if the Copyright Office has difficulty matching the mailed materials with the corresponding application).

If you choose to submit the digital files by mail, the list must still be submitted via the online process. The numbered list must be in either .xls/.xlsx (Excel) or .pdf format only. The file name of the list must contain: (1) the title of the group and (2) the registration case number that is assigned during the online application process. (See examples at page 135).

For a group of unpublished photographs, the numbered list should contain the case number, the title of each photograph, the name of the digital file being submitted for deposit (file name), the year the work was completed, and (optionally) a combined list of all of the individual photo titles in the group.

For a group of published photographs, the numbered list should contain the case number, the title of each photograph, the name of the digital file being submitted for deposit, month and year of (first) publication, nation of publication, and (optionally) a combined listing of all photo titles in the group.

For artworks that are not 2-D, 3-D, or are not photographs, see the Other Work Types and Multi-Media Deposit Issues section later in this chapter for general deposit information.

Complete Copies, Identifying Material, and Best Editions

There are three main technical terms used by the Copyright Office to describe the form of a deposit: complete copy, the best edition, and identifying material. For those using the online registration system and submitting digital files for the deposit, the process is largely straight forward—you simply upload a digital image file of the work. The deposit copy should always be a *complete* one; it should contain all of the original creative authorship that you are registering.

In some cases, or if you are delving into the nuances of deposit terminology, you may see references to the three terms. Or, if you communicate with a Copyright Office agent directly, you may hear these terms. In the context of copyright registration, the terms have distinct meanings, which are discussed further in this section.

If you think there may be a distinct deposit form required for your work, perhaps the work is unusual in some way, or if the deposit is just unclear, you can contact the Copyright Office directly, through the website or by phone. Contact information is shown in **Appendix A**. To get the most accurate response to your inquiry, include information about whether or not the work was published, the manner in which it was published, when and where it was published, and the type of work that is involved (2-D, 3-D artwork, motion picture work, sound recording, or something else).

A Complete Copy

The deposit requirement for most types of work specifies a ***complete copy*** of the work, or in some cases, a complete copy of the best edition.

A copy is considered to be complete when it contains all of the copyrightable authorship claimed in the application. In other words, the deposit copy should include the entire work or at least all of the original creative elements included in the copyright claim you are registering. For instance, if you are registering a 2-D work, you should not submit a cropped copy of the work and if the work is in color, you should submit a color copy, not a black and white copy.

A complete copy of a *published* work has different requirements, though in many cases it is acceptable to submit a complete copy of the artwork alone, rather than the entire publication. Some deposit requirements specify the submission of *a complete copy of the best edition*. Best Edition requirements are discussed later in this chapter.

For *published* works, the copy is considered complete when it includes the entire publication, including those parts that are not necessarily copyrightable. For instance, consider an art book that reproduces a number of artworks by several different artists, including a single artwork that is the subject of the copyright registration. The copyright claim involves some of the artworks published in the book, but not the book itself. One deposit option is to submit a complete copy of the book in which the work was published. This is perfectly acceptable, but there can be some practical issues—the book contains numerous other works that are not being registered, the book may be expensive, and the deposited book will not be returned to you.

Fortunately, exceptions to the completeness requirement can lessen the burden of submitting an entire print publication. The exception to the rule says that a publication copy should be considered to be complete for registration purposes even when there are physical elements missing from the material, so long as:

- The deposit copy contains all of the parts of the work claimed in the registration application, and
- the missing elements do not physically damage the copy of the work being registered, and
- the missing element consists only of a container for the work, such as an envelope, box, slipcase or similar (if applicable); and
- the work is not subject to the mandatory deposit rule (see page 232 on this topic).

In the example of the art book, the Copyright Office has stated that **a copy of the pertinent artwork alone is sufficient** for the deposit in these types of situations. The artwork is the only item(s) being registered, the deposit copy contains all elements claimed in the registration application, and there is no loss or damage to the artwork by submitting a copy of the artwork alone. (The last point in the bulleted list above does not apply in this case).

Alternatively, if you choose, a complete copy of the physical book could be submitted through the mail-in deposit process. In my experience it is easier and more economical to simply submit the digital file copy of the specific artwork in an online application as usual. This option should normally comply with the exceptions (or it may constitute ID material in those instances where it may be accepted) so long as the copy is otherwise complete and meets those four points listed above.

Electronic copies of non-digital works present slightly different issues. As for other *unpublished* works, electronic (digital) copies of unpublished works are considered complete so long as they contain all of the copyrightable authorship claimed in the registration. The digital copy should be in color if the original work is, it should not be cropped, and should otherwise reflect all original aspects of the work.

However, the Copyright Office has said that electronic copies of works that were *published solely* in electronic form should include the metadata as well as the other content (authorship) contained in the publication—even when copyright registration is not being sought for those other elements. The digital file must be in the exact same form and with the same content as the first publication of that work.

ID Material

Identifying Material—or ID material—is a two-dimensional reproduction or rendering of a work, such as a photograph, photocopy, transparency (slide), or drawing that shows the complete content of the work that is being registered. The simplest form of ID material is often a photograph of the work that is being registered.

Sometimes the words copy and identifying material are used interchangeably, but strictly speaking, ID material is not a pure copy of the work, but a reproduction that shows the content of the work.

ID material is required for the deposit of 3-D artworks. Submitting objects is not permitted, so the deposit copy must be representative of the object instead. A photograph or photographs of the 3-D work is the simplest form of deposit in most cases. If you are registering a sculptural work, for instance, you can upload digital images of the work for your deposit.

ID material is also required for oversized 2-D artworks. For instance, hardcopy deposits over 96 inches (243.8 cm) are not permitted. The solution is to submit a deposit that is ID material, usually a photograph, or a digital image file of the work.

Many visual art registrations permit the submission of either ID material or a true copy of the work. For 2-D digital native works, these may be the same, a digital file of the work. A true copy would be the native file form, but if the deposit is in a different file format than the original, that would be considered to be ID material. Similarly, when a deposit for a film-based photograph is submitted in a digital file format (JPEG or TIFF), this is technically ID material.

Identifying material is **required** for:

- Sculptures and other 3-D objects.
- Artwork and illustrations that are upon 3-D objects, and other works that are incorporated, applied to, or embodied in 3-D objects.
- Works that are larger than 96 inches (243.8 cm) in any dimension. (Also, hardcopies over 96 inches are not accepted).
- Published pictorial or graphic works that are fixed only in a machine-readable form.
- Certain textile products (such as a heat transfer image applied to a t-shirt, artwork for home products) when the material cannot be folded into 4 inches or less.
- Published holograms if the image is not visible without the aid of a machine (2 copies of the identifying material and instructions are required in that case).
- Computer programs (ID material is a document version of the source code).
- Certain audiovisual works that are fixed in a media other than a CD-ROM.

For works of visual art, identifying material is **permitted**, but *not* required when the work consists of:

- Unpublished 2-D artworks.
- Published limited edition posters, prints, or etchings– when less than 5 copies are published – or when less than 300 copies and the individual author (artist) is also the owner of the copyright.
- Unpublished greeting cards, postcards, calendars, stationery, business cards.
- Unpublished fabric emblems, patches, decals, (unapplied) heat transfers, bumper stickers.
- Certain textile products, e.g, a heat transfer image applied to a t-shirt, artwork for home products, linens, etc., when the material can be folded into 4" or less.
- Unpublished holograms (either a complete copy or identifying material is acceptable, with a copy of a CD-ROM if the work is fixed in that format).
- Jewelry works.

As you can see, many forms of visual art fall under the required or permitted provisions, and ID material, such as a photograph of the work, can be submitted as the deposit copy.

Submitting ID Material

ID material is submitted in the same manner as any other deposit copy; either by upload or by mailing it to the Copyright Office, in accordance with the requirements of the application form being used for the registration.

Normally there is no need to specify the submission of ID material in lieu of an identical copy of the work. However, if you wish to describe the deposit material, the comments field on the Certification screen of the online application can be used for this purpose.

Submit as many pieces of identifying material as necessary to show the entire copyrightable content of the work. For example, submit photographs of a sculpture that show multiple perspectives of the work. Generally, the ID material should clearly show the full extent of the work being registered. There should not be cropping or exclusion of any parts of the work covered by the registration. The ID material should reproduce the actual colors in the original work.

Include the title of the work on the identifying material when submitting a hard copy. If the artwork has been published, the location and content of the notice (such as a © mark) should be shown in the ID material. If there was no notice on the work, you can include other information that was published along with it, such as a label or packaging.

Only submit ID material for a deposit in place of a true copy when it is permitted for that type of work. Or, if you believe it is necessary to submit ID material in your case, but it is not normally accepted for that particular type of work, special permission can be requested in advance.

The Copyright Office has limited storage space for physical deposits and there may be other circumstances where ID material may be preferred. If you are unsure about the deposit, and whether it can or should be made by ID material instead of an actual copy, contact the Copyright Office about your particular situation.

Best Editions

Some categories of work require the submission of the *best edition* as the deposit. A best edition is typically required when the work has been published in some form. What constitutes a best edition varies by media and the type of publication involved. First, determine if your work is subject to the best edition rule. Generally, if a work was published in the United States in 1978 or later, the best edition of the work should be submitted as the deposit.

Unpublished works and works published solely outside of the United States are exempt from the best edition requirement. The requirement also does not apply to most editions that are published only online. Works that are published solely in editions or in formats that are not identified as a preferred best edition are usually also exempt. If the deposit requirement for your work does not specifically state that a *best edition* should be submitted, then you can disregard the subject, but you still must submit a copy of the work to fulfill the regular deposit requirement.

A *best edition* usually means the highest quality copy of the work. For example, a copy on acid-free paper would be preferred over one on inferior paper. A clean copy of a film is preferred over a copy that has damage or splices. As a registrant, it is your responsibility to select the best edition of the work that exists when this type of deposit is necessary.

For some published visual art works, the *best edition* is one of the options for the deposit. Most published 2-D artwork permits a deposit that is either one complete copy of the *best edition* or ID material.

For artworks published in books, for example, a copy of the artwork alone, such as a digital image file depicting only the artwork that is the subject of the registration, is usually sufficient for deposit purposes. Strictly speaking, when a digital image or print of the artwork reproduced in a publication is submitted instead of the publication itself, the deposit is considered to be ID material. (See the previous section on ID material).

However, in the example above, you could submit a copy of the actual hardcopy publication. What you choose to submit may depend upon your access to the material and whether you want to upload the deposit or mail it in. In my view, for artworks published within books and periodicals that contain numerous other works by other artists and writers, it may be preferable to go the route of submitting a digital image of the artwork alone through an online registration application. There are advantages, including an earlier registration date and the ability to confirm the receipt of the deposit.

Alternatively, a hard copy reproduction of the artwork could be deposited by using the mail-in procedures for the submission. In my view, either of these options are likely to represent a better reproduction of the artwork than a mass-market print, and for registration and archival purposes, that is preferable. To be clear, this example is for the case where an artwork alone is being registered, but the artwork happens to have been published in a book. Registering the copyright on an *entire* book would be a different matter, and that would necessitate depositing copies of the entire (book) work.

Some artworks are published in forms that are not contained in bound objects like books or periodicals. For works that are published in the form of print editions exceeding 300 in number, such as posters, two copies of the *best edition* must be submitted. In other words, two of the posters, in the highest quality existing.

Best Edition Preferences

The person making the deposit has the responsibility of determining what constitutes the best edition of the work. Generally, this determination will be accepted by the Copyright Office as correct, so long as there is not a contradiction in the application or in the deposit itself. You do not need to create a new edition of the work or a new form in order to satisfy the best edition requirement.

The Copyright Office's preferred forms for best editions are related to the goal of quality in the Library of Congress archive and for record maintenance purposes. It should be the best example of the material that is covered by the copyright claim. However, the best edition can also be one which fulfills some other purpose that the Copyright Office has determined is desirable, and it may not necessarily reflect the most archival output of the work. For instance, the most preferred edition for a published photograph is the one most widely distributed.

These preferences apply only when a best edition is required for the deposit, and generally, when hardcopies will be submitted for that purpose. If a certain edition exists or is already available in one of these forms, then it is simply preferred for deposit. The following chart contains representative examples of Copyright Office preferences that may be most pertinent to visual art works. For media issues or works that are not covered here, contact the Copyright Office for instructions. The preferences are subject to change.

Media Type / Preferred Forms of Best Edition
(listed in the order of preference)

Graphic material, including published 2-D artwork	
Paper & printed matter	• Archival preferred over lower quality or less permanent paper • Color preferred over black & white
Size and Content	• Larger preferred over smaller size (Maximum permitted is 96 inches or 243.84 cm) ▷ For maps (cartographic works), edition with greatest information & detail
Rarity	• For works published in only a limited numbered edition, 1 copy outside of the numbered series, but otherwise identical to the others is preferred. (Note: this could be an artist's proof, i.e., a/p, type of print so long as it is identical quality to the series). • Most widely distributed edition preferred over one of limited distribution

	▷ By special arrangement, a photographic reproduction of the original.
Text and other materials (as graphic matter)	• Primary preference is for edition with annotations, accompanying tabular or textual matter, or other interpretative aids, rather than those without them.
Binding & packaging	• Bound preferred over unbound; rolled rather than folded; with protective coatings rather than without.
Photographs (when submitted as prints)	1. Most widely distributed edition 2. 8 x 10 inch glossy print 3. Other size or finish • Unmounted preferred over mounted • Archival-quality preferred over less-permanent paper or printing stock
Motion Picture works	
Film formats	1. Preprint material, by special arrangement 2. 70mm positive print if original production negative greater than 35 mm. 3. 35mm positive prints 4. 16mm positive prints
Video Formats	1. Betacam SP 2. Digital Beta (Digibeta) 3. DVD 4. VHS Cassette
Phonorecords **(sound recordings;** excluding motion pictures and other audio visual works)	1. Compact digital disc (most preferred), 2. Vinyl disc, preferred over tape, 3. Open-reel preferred over cartridge, 4. Cassette over quadraphonic, 5. Stereophonic over monaural,

	6. Monaural over electronically rechanneled stereo ▷ Inclusion of any special enclosures is preferred
Electronic Works Available *only online* (published in U.S.; excluding serials)	Generally: • UTF-8 encoding, ASCII, other non UTF-8 encodings Online websites and material: 1. XHTML or HTML, as made available online, with presentation stylesheets rather than without 2. XML, with presentation stylesheets rather than without 3. Plain text 4. Other formats ▷ PDF/A format is preferred over PDF; searchable text is preferred over non-searchable
Works that exist in more than one medium (as applicable)	• Generally, 1. Printed matter, 2. microform, 3. phonorecord. • Newspapers and certain other works, are preferred in 1. microform, or 2. printed matter.
Works published in both digital and physical editions (through 2021)	• Physical edition is preferred over the digital version (for a best edition type of deposit)

If the work does not exist in any of the preferred formats, a copy can be submitted in an existing form—preferably the highest quality version. However, if a *best edition* deposit does not meet one of the criteria and consists of something entirely different, or if it consists of unreadable media for instance, it could be rejected. The chart is not an exclusive list of works and if the form of the deposit is not clear, it is worth an e-mail or call to the Copyright Office for instructions.

There are times when a best edition cannot be submitted or submitting a best edition is not feasible. In these cases you can request special relief from the requirement.

Special Relief for Unusual Media and Other Deposit Exceptions

When it is impossible or unusually difficult to comply with the deposit requirement for your work, you can make a written request for special relief from the normal deposit requirement.

In your request for relief you will need to explain why you are unable to provide the required copy form and describe the substitute copy that you propose for the deposit. State the reason or reasons that your request should be granted. There is no guarantee that the alternative deposit will be accepted, but if you genuinely cannot make the deposit in one of the ordinary forms, then you should request relief.

If you are using one of the electronic applications, you may submit a letter requesting relief as part of the application process. First, in the Note to the Copyright Office field, which is located on the Certification Screen near the end of the application, indicate that you are seeking special relief from the deposit requirement. Continue completing the application. After the fee is paid electronically you will reach a screen for uploading the deposit copy (the Submit Your Work screen). Upload the special request letter first, and then upload the deposit file(s) after that. The letter and the deposit should be separate files. If you are using the mail-in shipping slip option, the special relief request may be attached to the shipping slip (with the deposit). The Copyright Office will advise if it will accept the deposit form or not.

If you are using a paper-based form, such as Form VA, the request must be made in writing. The request should be signed by or on behalf of the person who signed the registration application. Mail the request letter with the application, the filing fee, and the deposit materials. The request will only be considered once the Copyright Office has received the completed registration application, a correct filing fee, and the deposit copy or copies.

Special relief may also be requested after an application has been filed in response to a communication from the Copyright Office. Alternatively, submit a request by mail to: Associate Register of Copyrights and Director of Registration Policy & Practice, U.S. Copyright Office, P.O. Box 70400, Washington, DC 20024-0400.

Electronic Deposits

For online registration applications, the deposit may be made by uploading digital files at the end of the process. The steps for uploading the copy are covered for each of application type in Chapter 4.

As an alternative to uploading copies, digital files may be mailed to the Copyright Office on a storage device (except for the Group of Unpublished Works application, which requires uploaded electronic deposits only).

Uploading deposit copies is often preferable when it is permitted. The receipt of the deposit by the Copyright Office can be confirmed immediately. This can be important because an application is not considered complete until all elements are received, including the application, the fee, and the deposit materials. When a copyright registration certificate is issued, it is backdated to the day on which all materials, including the deposit, were received. For uploaded deposits this means that the registration's effective date will usually be the same date that the copy was uploaded to the Copyright Office system. For mailed in deposits, the effective date of the registration will be later, after the materials are physically received by the Copyright Office.

Many works of visual art fit within the criteria permitting electronic deposit. Electronic deposits through the online registration system are permitted when the works meets one or more of the following requirements:

- The work is **unpublished**, or
- The work has been **published** in **digital format** only, or
- The work has been **published** and a deposit of ***identifying material*** is appropriate.

In the last case, you can usually submit an electronic file (as ID material), so long as it shows the whole authorship that is being registered, the copy is complete, and the representation of the work is undamaged in the copy submitted.

If your work does not seem to fit the criteria, but you want to upload an electronic file for as the deposit copy, you can request special permission in advance from the Copyright Office.

For many fine art works, ID material, such as a photograph of the work, is acceptable for the deposit. Review the deposit information starting on page 198. Some commercially oriented works may require a physical deposit submission. For works of visual art that are unpublished, a deposit made by uploading electronic files should be acceptable in most cases.

Acceptable File Forms For Deposit

The electronic deposit must be made in a form that is acceptable and readable by the Copyright Office. For electronic registrations, the Copyright Office has designated certain file types as acceptable for typical media types. The file types accepted for the online upload process are more limited out of concern for compatibility with the system, but this may change over time. Prepare your file(s) before you start the registration process and confirm that they conform with the type and size accepted by the system.

Electronic Deposit (Upload via eCO)

For works submitted electronically **online**, any of the following file formats are generally acceptable for registration: **PDF, TXT, WPD, DOC, TIF, SVG, JPG, XML, HTML, WAV,** and the **MPEG** family of formats, including **MP3**.

Groups of Photographs must be submitted in **JPG, TIF** or **GIF** format.

The numbered list for a Group of Photographs application must be submitted in **XLS** or **PDF** form.

Additional file formats are acceptable for deposits that are mailed in to the Copyright Office on a disc or device.

Electronic Deposit (Physical Mail-In Submission)

Images	.bmp, .dwg, .dwf, .gif, .giff, .jpg, .jpeg, .jfif, .pdf, .pic, .png, .psd, .pub, .tga, .tif, .tiff, .wmf
Photographs (Group Registrations of Photographs)	.jpg (.jpeg), .tif (.tiff), .gif
Video, Audio-visual, *sequential images*	.avi, .mov, .mpg, .mpeg, .rm, .rv, .swf, .wmv, .3gp, .3gpp, .mp4, .m4v, .4v, .flv

Audio	.aif, .aiff, .au, .mp3, .ra, .ram, .rmi, .wav, .wma, .mp4, .m4a, .m4p
Text	.doc, .docx, .htm, .html, .pdf, .rtf., .txt, .wps, .fdr
Presentation	.pps, .ppt

The list is not necessarily a limitation, but it contains the file formats that the Copyright Office has already deemed to be acceptable for deposits. Newer formats may be added and if they are, these changes should be noted on the Copyright.gov website. In any case, if you are planning to submit an atypical file type and are not sure if it is acceptable for a deposit, check with the Copyright Office first to avoid complications.

File Size Limits

The maximum size for an uploaded single file is **500 MB**. If a file exceeds 500 MB, the Copyright Office recommends using compression to reduce the size or, if appropriate, breaking the file into smaller files so that none exceed 500 MB. The last suggestion is not really feasible for most visual image files.

Compression is generally recommended for large files. When multiple files are to be uploaded for the deposit they may be compressed (zipped) into a single file. The ZIP file or folder cannot exceed the 500MB limitation.

Compression

When compressed files are permitted for the deposit submission, the compressed files must be in one of the following formats: **.cab**, **.rar**, or **.zip**.

The eCO file upload system has a 60 minute time out feature that will automatically terminate an upload if it takes longer to be completed. If the deposit cannot be uploaded within that time window, consider some of the measures discussed above or use the mail-in process instead which does not have those limitations.

Mailing Deposits to the Copyright Office

If you do not use the upload process for submitting your deposit copies, you will need to complete the registration process by mailing your deposit to the Copyright Office. Be aware that mail-in deposits, including electronic files on a device, are not permitted for the **Group of Unpublished Works** application–those deposits must be uploaded. By contrast, the **Group of Photographs** application does not permit the submission of hard copies (prints), but either the upload process or submission of digital files on a device by mail are accepted options at this time.

The mail-in process is covered for each of the applications in Chapter 4. It is generally the same for any electronic application. (For example, refer to the Standard Application at page 93). Be sure to include the shipping slip when you submit any mail-in deposit for an electronic application. If you are using a paper-based application, the deposit process for Form VA begins on page 174.

Mailing an Electronic Deposit on a Device

In most cases the digital file or files can be physically mailed to the Copyright Office to fulfill the deposit requirement as an alternative to uploading the files. The deposit can be submitted on a flash drive, CD, DVD, or other storage device. The storage media or device will not be returned to you.

Mailed deposits should be packaged securely. The Copyright Office recommends packaging CDs, DVDs, or other items that could be damaged in boxes rather than envelopes. CDs and DVDs should be sent in the stronger standard jewel boxes rather than slim-line cases or envelopes. All mailed-in deposits are subjected to a radiation process.

Mailing a Hard Copy Deposit

When physical (hard copy) materials are being used for the deposit, they must be mailed to the Copyright Office to fulfill the requirements. Hard copy deposits may consist of photographs, photocopies, prints, illustrations, DVDs, videotapes, best editions of a printed publication, or some other type of material, depending upon the work. Package them securely to avoid damage in the mail.

Send only copies, not any originals. The deposit materials will not be returned to you. Be aware that physical mail-in deposits are not permitted for the electronic Group of Unpublished Works application and hardcopy prints cannot be permitted for the Group of Photographs applications at this time.

Other Types of Work and Multi-Media Deposit Issues

This section discusses deposit requirements for some forms of art that are not 2-D or 3-D works and do not fit into the visual art category covered in the first part of this chapter. Because art can be anything, the information here is a representative sample of deposit forms that may be appropriate for some works. If your work is unusual or difficult to categorize, contact the Copyright Office for specific deposit requirements.

Generally, the deposit requirement for **motion picture** works, including some **video** artworks, has two parts: a *complete copy* of the work and a descriptive document.

For **unpublished motion picture works**, deposit *a copy* that contains all of the visual and aural elements that the registration is intended to cover and a separate written description of the work, such as a shooting script, synopsis, or press book. For **published motion picture** works, submit one *complete copy* of the work and a separate description of the nature and general content.

If the work was first published in the U.S., the complete copy submitted should be the *best edition* of the work. If the work was first published outside of the U.S., the complete copy should be of the first published edition or one copy of the best edition.

The copy of the work that is submitted should be clean and have no damage or defects that could interfere with the viewing of the work or cause distortion.

The motion picture category spans the range of fine art works to home movies to commercial enterprises, and there are additional complexities in registering some motion picture works that exceed the scope of this book. For instance, works predating 1978 may have different deposit requirements. Some motion picture works are subject to a separate deposit, known as mandatory deposit, discussed in Chapter 6.

Other **audiovisual works** that were published in electronic and hard copy formats, generally require a deposit of two complete copies of the best edition of the work in the hard copy format. If the work was published solely in electronic format, you may submit digital files containing a single complete copy of the work.

For audiovisual works in a CD-ROM form, deposit one complete copy of the entire CD-ROM package, including a complete copy of any accompanying software and instructional manuals. Submit ID material for AV works that are fixed in a machine-readable form that is not a CD. For example, ID material could be a videotape or a series of photographs depicting representative portions of the copyrightable content along with a separate (written) synopsis of the work. Packaging or other material that is a part of the claim should be submitted as well. Titles should be included on these items and if the work was published, any copyright notice on the materials should be shown.

Websites typically include multiple forms of content, photographs, 2-D illustrations, text, etc. There are some complexities to registering web-based content. Generally, each component work on a website would be registered with an individual application or, if they qualify, as works in one of the group applications. (A website as a whole is not currently recognized as copyrightable subject matter, but it could potentially be registered as a compilation). Copyright registrations in this area—websites, web based works, and other works only available online—appears to be evolving and it is possible that the Copyright Office may alter the deposit requirements in the future.

The general deposit requirement for **websites** and **web-based content** is a complete copy, whether it is unpublished or published solely online. For published website content, the deposit copy of the material placed online should match the date of publication specified in the registration application.

Submit a copy of each web page being registered. For an entire website, submit a copy of each page, including all of the pages in the website. The Copyright Office has a preference for PDF documents for this purpose. The Copyright Office has said that a PDF package can be used to *fix* an entire website in a sufficient (physical) form, and maintain the organization and navigation of the site, for the purposes of the deposit.

Keep in mind that the scope of the registration is limited to what is shown in the deposit materials. If you submit a PDF for an online video work, the registration would not include anything more than the 2-D image shown in it; it would not include the actual audiovisual work itself or any audio that may be embedded. You may want to consider a different form of deposit that will fully represent the work you are registering in this example.

If you are registering an individual work that appears on a website, the deposit is required to show the work in the context in which it appears. The deposit should show how a user of the site would perceive the work when it is accessed online.

Do not submit separate files or folders of content that is disassembled or disassociated from the web page or from website where it originally appeared. Do not submit a link to the website. If the deposit form is burdensome for you, consider requesting special relief to deposit another format.

It is usually unnecessary to include the underlying code of the website content. If HTML code is a part of the copyright claim, it is typically classified as a literary work; the code would need to meet the creative expression standards for copyrightability. A PDF file is the preferred format for that type of deposit.

Multimedia and Deposits for Works Made in Multiple Media

Multimedia is work that consists of more than one medium or combines more than one type of work within it. In the copyright context, a multimedia work combines authorship in two or more areas that may included artwork, photography, sculpture, cinematography, music, sounds, choreography, text (literary work), or any other copyrightable work.

The Copyright Office refers to works that are mixture of materials or a mixture of authorship (creative) elements as a multimedia kit. A multimedia kit may contain 2-D artwork, photography, sculpture, text, music, sound recordings, or cinematography. It could be in the physical form of printed matter, audiovisual material, or a computer readable disc, for example.

The copyright in a multimedia work is typically registered as the type of authorship that is most dominant in the work. This categorization is primarily for administrative purposes and does not have a particular bearing upon the scope of the copyright.

The deposit requirement for multimedia varies depending upon if it is published or unpublished and according to the type of work involved. There are sometimes additional requirements for the deposit, on top of the basic requirements discussed below. Generally, you submit the basic deposit materials plus those required for the type of work that forms the elements of the multimedia work. For complex multimedia works, it doesn't hurt to contact the Copyright Office in advance to confirm that you are correctly submitting all of the required deposit materials for the type of works involved. General guidelines for multimedia deposits follow.

First, for **unpublished** multimedia, submit one complete copy of the multimedia kit, containing all of the elements covered by the registration. If the work contains color, the copy should also be in color. The title of the work should be shown on all elements.

For a multimedia work that was *first* **published** in the U.S. on or after 1978, submit one complete copy of the best published edition. It should include all of the copyright elements in the published work (the unit of publication). If it was first published outside of the United States, submit one complete copy of the first publication *or* one complete copy of the best edition.

In addition to those basic deposit requirements above, multimedia works tend to have additional requirements for the elements contained in the work. For instance, in addition to the basic deposit (above), the deposit requirements for motion pictures would apply to multimedia that contains a motion picture element. See the earlier section on motion pictures for those details.

Multimedia works embodied in a machine-readable form, such as a disc, or those which require equipment to view or perceive, typically require the deposit of ID material. The ID material should be appropriate for the type of work and be a form which best represents the copyrightable content. All items submitted should have the title of the work and any copyright notice that was present on published works.

If the multimedia work produces pictorial images (such as a video game would do), submit the regular deposit for the work (above), plus a synopsis or outline; a reproduction of the AV elements in video, illustrative, or photographic form; and any container and guide included in the package.

As you can see, multimedia works can be somewhat detailed in their deposit requirements. If the deposit for your multimedia work is not clear to you, it is beneficial to contact the Copyright Office in advance for clarity.

Privacy Concerns

The electronic files submitted for the deposit are not available to the public over the internet. The deposit and the registration record can be viewed by authorized users at the Library of Congress physical premises in Washington D.C. Because the registration is a public record, it is possible that someone seeking permission to reproduce or use the work could contact you. This rarely happens, but it is a possibility, especially as the existence of the archive and the records becomes more widely known.

Library staff may also access the electronic content off-site via a secure connection as part of their duties. If for some reason the Library of Congress is interested in making an electronic work publically viewable over the internet, it is required to obtain permission from the rights holder. (If you are the artist and you own your copyright in the work, then you are the rights holder). The deposit you submit will not be displayed online by the Copyright Office unless it is specifically requested and unless you give permission for that to happen.

CHAPTER SIX

POST-FILING & NON-REGISTRATION ISSUES

The first part of this chapter covers further details in the process of registration, including receiving your certificate of copyright registration and the (relatively uncommon) need for correcting a registration after it has been issued. The later part of this chapter covers some topics that apply only to a limited number of registrations, and may not be applicable to most claims filed by artists, but they are here for reference, such as the mandatory deposit rule.

Pending Review of Your Application

At the end of the eCO process online applicants should be notified by email that the application was received. After submitting an application, you can check the status of your application online by logging in to the Registration Portal. Applications that are awaiting review or in the process of review are listed in the Open Cases link on the left menu of the main registration screen. When the application has been fully processed it will be shown as a Closed case in the All Cases listing.

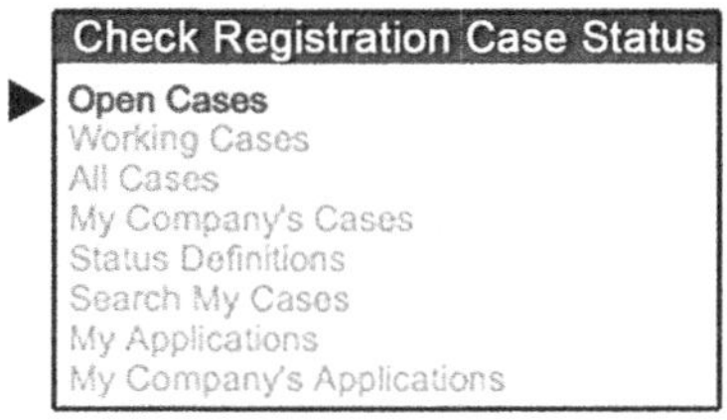

The Copyright Office does not have an acknowledgement system for the receipt of materials sent by regular mail. For general information on your pending claim, you can reach out to the Public Information Office at (202) 707-3000 or 1-877-476-0778 (toll-free) or by web form at https://www.copyright.gov/help/.

After all materials have been received by the Copyright Office, the application, the correct fee, and the deposit, the claim review process will begin. When the review is completed and the registration is approved, a certificate will be mailed.

The Copyright Office has a broad timeline for processing registration applications, normally 1 to 7 months for those filed online, with an average wait time of 4 months. Exigent or unusual circumstances may extend the processing time or delay the issuance of certificates.

The Copyright Office says that the average time for processing a registration claim is 2.2 months when there are no issues causing a delay. An error in an application or other such issue may delay the claim for up to 15 months. For paper-based applications, the average processing time is at least 8 months.

An agent of the Copyright Office may contact you (or whomever is listed as the correspondent in the application) if there is a question about your application or the deposit materials. It is important to be reachable within a reasonable time frame. If your email address or phone number changes, send a message through the Contact Us link on the Copyright.gov website or call the Office and inquire about updating the contact information on your pending registration application.

It is important to respond promptly to any request for information from the Copyright Office. The Copyright Office's email communications are primarily from cop-ad@copyright.gov or cop-ad@loc.gov and responses to questions submitted through the web portal are currently sent from copyinfo@copyright.gov. Consider adding these email addresses to your email safe list and keep an eye on your spam or junk folders for any misdirected messages. It is best to respond ASAP to any inquires. In any case, do respond to emails and letters within 45 days after they were sent in order to prevent a potential closure of your registration case. If you are unable to respond with requested information within the appropriate time you can request an extension by email. Also respond to any telephone calls from the Copyright Office promptly.

Receiving Your Copyright Registration Certificate

Assuming all has gone well, a copyright registration certificate will be issued to you by the Copyright Office—typically within a few months of submitting a fully electronic application and deposit. Again, paper-based applications and mailed-in deposits take longer. Also, exigent circumstances may cause delays in mailing certificates. In the meanwhile, the status of electronically filed cases can be determined through your eCO account.

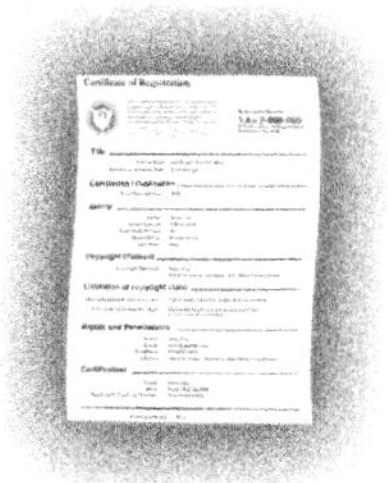

The certificate will be mailed to the person and address entered in the application for that purpose. If you move while the application is pending, contact the Copyright Office and update the information promptly—otherwise there may be an additional fee to replace a missing or misdirected certificate.

The certificate is documentary proof of the registration. It contains the information about work that you entered into the application and the copyright registration number. Confirm that the information is correct. Keep the certificate in a safe place.

The certification should be post-dated to the day on which the Copyright Office received all of the required elements, the complete application, the fee, and the deposit, all in proper form. So long as an electronic application, fee, and deposit were submitted correctly, the registration date should match that of the submission.

Waiting for the certificate does not prevent you from using your copyright in the interim; you can license a use of the work, display the work, create a derivative work, or make any other use of the copyright while the application is being processed. The one thing you cannot do before the certificate is issued is to commence certain lawsuits for infringement. A copyright registration or registration refusal is a prerequisite to filing a lawsuit for copyright infringement involving a U.S. work. Otherwise, because the copyright itself is automatic, you are free to exercise your rights as usual.

If you have registered multiple works or if you plan to register more works in the future, a spreadsheet, list, or database containing an inventory of your registered artworks along with their registration numbers, the year of the copyright, the date of registration, and any other important details can be useful. This is a simple start to organizing and accessing records of your registered intellectual property.

Making Corrections or Amplifying a Claim Through Supplementary Registration

If you find a significant error in your application after the certificate has been issued, or the public record of the claim should be changed, you may be able to correct the record by filing a supplementary registration. This process can only be done after the claim is processed and a certificate has been issued.

Supplementary registration involves a substantial additional fee that is not refundable irrespective of the outcome. The process is subject to a review and the Copyright Office may or may not permit the supplementation requested.

An *error* in this context is information that was incorrect *at the time* the registration was made. If the facts changed after the registration was submitted–for example, the work was registered as unpublished, but was published sometime after the registration application was submitted–this is not error. However, if the work was unpublished at the time of the registration, but the application stated that it was published, a correction would be appropriate. Supplemental registration can be used to correct misspellings, but it is usually unnecessary for correcting simple typographical errors.

Supplementary registration may also be used to amplify or expand upon information given in the original registration application. This could include information that was correct at the time of the registration, but was later altered. For example, the title of the work changed. It could also be used to clarify information.

A supplementary registration may be appropriate to update the author's **address**, to add an **omitted author** or correct an author's **name**, to correct or add an author's **citizenship** or domicile at the time of the original registration, to clarify that a work identified as **published** was actually unpublished at the time of the original registration or vice verse, to correct the **spelling** of a name or title, to **change a name** or address, to add other **titles** for the work or reflect a change in a title, to add a **real name** to a registration for pseudonymous or anonymous work, to add the name of a co-claimant that should have been identified in the original application, to complete or correct **work made for hire** information, to correct a **year of completion or publication** (so long as the date is not later than the effective date of the original registration), to exclude works incorrectly included in a group application and remove them from that registration, or to **clarify** the scope of the claim described in the nature of authorship or limitation claim sections of the original application.

The process should not be used to correct errors or omissions in the deposit copy, or to make any changes to the deposit. It cannot be used to reflect a change in ownership that occurred *after* the certificate was issued. The process cannot be used to register a new version of an existing registration.

Supplementary registration can only be used for registrations that have been actually issued (a certificate has been sent to you). It cannot be used when the claim is still pending. It cannot be used for applications that have been refused.

As a general rule, the online electronic form for supplemental registration must be used for most works, irrespective of how the work was originally registered. This applies to virtually all current art-related copyright registrations. Paper-based supplement registration is very limited and generally only for pre-1978 works. In exceptional cases only, special exceptions to the online filing requirement can be requested in writing.

Only the author, claimant, owner or partial-owner of the copyright involved, or an agent for those persons, can file a supplementary registration. This person will be required to certify the correctness of the information as part of the application.

Before going through this process, consider contacting the Copyright Office about your situation. The agent will not be able to provide legal advice, but may be able to give practical guidance to the process. Some rules are evolving. Contact the Copyright Office before submitting an application for correcting or amplifying a group registration.

Effect of Supplemental Registration

Supplementary registration does not cancel or replace the existing registration or alter the information already contained in the original registration. Rather, it adds information to the public record of the registration. If it is accepted, a new certificate and registration number will be issued and will be linked to the original in the public record. A supplemental registration may have legal implications in some cases.

Overview of eCO Supplementary Registration:

- Log in to your eCO account (or create an account if you do not yet have one).
- Go to the "Correct or Amplify an Existing Registration"

link under Other Registration Options on the main registration home page.

- Read the eligibility requirements on the screen and enter the requested information. You will need the original registration number and the effective year of the registration. You can refer to the registration certificate for this information.

- In the drop-down list, select the category that best describes the type of work covered by the registration. When complete, select Start Registration.

- Complete each screen. Provide all of the information that should have been included in the original basic registration application. You may refer to records of your original registration as an aid.

- Provide a brief statement identifying and explaining the reason(s) for the correction or amplification.

- Confirm that the application is correct, make any necessary corrections to the information entered in the application.

- The form must be certified by the author, claimant, owner, or agent.

- Complete the payment process.

The Copyright Office may request additional documentation, particularly if copyright eligibility, authorship, or ownership issues are involved. You may also be asked to provide a copy of the original certificate of registration.

A Refused Claim

Sometimes copyright registration claims are rejected by the Copyright Office. If a registration is refused, a notification will be sent to the person listed as the correspondent in the application. The notification should state why the registration was refused. Common reasons for claim rejection are an incomplete application, a missing or incorrect filing fee, deposit copies that were not submitted or were insufficient, the review found that the work lacked a minimum level of creative authorship (originality), the work was not authored by a human, or the work was not fixed in a tangible medium of expression. It may be that the registration was refused because the work did not meet the copyrightability requirements for some reason, or other essential information was missing or obviously incorrect, or perhaps there is a conflict evident in the registration.

If you believe a decision rejecting a registration was wrong, you can file for a reconsideration—with an additional fee. The reconsideration request must be made within three months of the date the refusal that was *issued* (which may be before you received it). For more information about requesting reconsideration of a refusal to register, you can review Circular 20 on the Copyright.gov website, which can be accessed through the Law & Policy pull-down menu on the home page.

The Mandatory Deposit Program for Certain Published Works

For some types of published works there is a required submission called a *Mandatory Deposit*. This is *distinct* from a deposit that is made for the purpose of registration. **If you have already registered the copyright in your work, you have already satisfied the Mandatory Deposit rule by registering the work, and you can disregard the information in this section.**

You may see references to the Mandatory Deposit rule on the Copyright Office's website. This process should not be confused with the deposit that is a part of the copyright registration application process. *Mandatory Deposit* in itself is not a copyright registration and it does not fulfill those distinct deposit requirements.

Mandatory Deposit is a Copyright Office program that is designed to create a cultural archive in the Library of Congress for certain types of work, essentially, works that have not been registered.

If you have not registered the copyright in the work, you can satisfy the mandatory deposit requirement in one of three ways: (1) register the work; submit an application to register the copyright in your work, with the fee and normal deposit required, or (2) you can elect to not register the work, but send in the Mandatory Deposit copies within 3 months of publication, or (3) if you receive a written demand from the Copyright Office, respond to it appropriately.

Technically, the Mandatory Deposit rule applies to **all works published in the United States**, unless there is an exemption. This includes many forms of published works of art.

The following categories of artworks and some other types of work are **exempt** from the Mandatory Deposit program requirement at this time:

- 3-D sculptural works
- ALL *unpublished works*
- Works published solely in an electronic format that are available only online
- Literary, dramatic, and musical works that are embodied in a sound recording published only in phonorecords (a physical recording) form; a soundtrack that is integral to a motion picture
- Certain motion pictures that consist of television

transmission programs in connection with a nonprofit institution

- Greeting cards, picture postcards, and stationery works
- Prints, labels, and other advertising materials
- An individual contribution to a collective work that was first published in the U.S. (although the collective work may be subject to the rule)
- Works only published outside of the United States

For a complete list of exempt categories, including those that are not visual art related, refer to Circular 7D in the Law & Policy section of the Copyright Office website.

If you find that your work is subject to the mandatory deposit rule, you can send in the copies as indicated—or alternatively, for most works it is acceptable to instead file a copyright registration application and include two complete copies of the best edition as the regular deposit. The copyright registration application should be submitted promptly, usually within three months of the publication of the work. In my view, this is the most effective means of fulfilling the requirement mandatory deposit rule when it applies; just **register the copyright**.

Otherwise, **to submit a mandatory deposit**, mail the appropriate form and number of copies to the Library of Congress, U.S. Copyright Office, Attn: 407 Deposits, 101 Independence Avenue SE Washington, D.C. 20559-6600. Deliveries to the Library of Congress for mandatory deposit are subject to screening and should be packaged well to avoid damage.

There is a small concession for visual arts works published in a limited edition, instead of two copies of the best edition for a Mandatory Deposit, you may submit one complete copy of the work. Or, if fewer than five copies of the work have been published, or if the work has been published and sold or offered for sale in a limited edition consisting of 300 or fewer numbered copies, then you can submit identifying material (such as a photograph of the work). To be clear again, if you have registered the copyright of the work already, then you should not submit another deposit for this program.

If the work is not exempt from this rule, you have not registered the copyright, and the *Mandatory Deposit* is a burden, you may write and request special relief from it. Address requests for special relief to Associate Register of Copyrights and Director of Registration Policy and Practice, U.S. Copyright Office, P.O. Box 70400, Washington, DC 20024-0440.

In the event you receive a notice from the Copyright Office demanding a Mandatory Deposit, follow the directions on the notice and promptly send the materials, along with any fee indicated, to the address identified in the notice. There is a possibility of fines for noncompliance with the mandatory deposit rules.

If you have questions about the application of the program, or the form of a deposit, or you need more information about an exemption, you can contact the Copyright Office. Specifically refer to the Mandatory Deposit requirement when you call, describe the work involved, and its publication status.

A Note on the Visual Artist's Rights Act

The Visual Artists Rights Act (VARA) is a Federal statute that provides additional, though limited, rights to the creators of certain artworks. The VARA provisions are incorporated into the text of Section 106A of the U.S. Copyright Law. VARA does not affect copyrights, but it specifies others that are sometimes referred to as moral rights or natural rights of the artist.

The central provision of VARA provides for rights of attribution and integrity, meaning that the artist has a right to be known in connection with the work they created and a right to prevent certain damage to the work. The rights have some significant limitations in the United States and the definition of visual art itself is fairly narrow in the VARA context. Still, VARA does recognize some basic rights for artists, including attribution and integrity.

- The artist has a right to claim that they made a particular work (to "claim authorship") and also the right to prevent association with a work that they did not create.
- Prevent someone else from wrongfully claiming that they made the artwork that was made by the artist.
- Disclaim association with artwork that the artist did not make.
- If a work has been distorted, mutilated, or modified to the extent that it could damage the artist's reputation, the artist can prevent the use of his or her name as the author of the work.
- Prevent intentional distortion, mutilation or modification of the artwork in limited situations.
- Prevent intentional distortion, mutilation or modification of the artwork that would tend to damage the artist's reputation.
- Prevent destruction of a work that is deemed to be of recognized stature (generally, a work that is well-known or widely recognized as important).
- Prevent destruction, whether intentional or the result of gross negligence, of a work that is deemed to be of recognized stature.

It is important, but VARA is imperfect and reflects a minimum of rights for artists. For instance, a significant caveat is the limitation of these rights to certain media and conditions. VARA protects only paintings, drawings, prints, sculptures and photographs with specific criteria:

- Paintings, drawings, prints, sculpture that exist in a single copy or in a limited edition of 200 or less that are signed and consecutively numbered by the author/artist. For sculpture another identifying mark can suffice for the signature requirement.

- Photographs that were made for exhibition purposes only, and which exist in a single signed copy or a signed limited edition of 200 copies or less that are consecutively numbered.

The criteria for protection under the VARA provision was derived from its definition of a work of visual art, which was designed to excluded commercial work. Posters, maps, globes, charts, technical drawings, diagrams, models, applied art, motion pictures and other audiovisual works are among those that are specifically excluded from VARA coverage. The result is a narrow view of art, one that is, in my view, far too confined for contemporary work. Along with media exclusions, such as video, literary works, and sound recordings, some commissioned works may be excluded from VARA coverage.

In contrast, copyright protects a much broader category of works and includes those that are beyond traditional 2-D and 3-D media and does not have restrictive limitations, signature, or edition requirements. This does not mean that VARA rights should not be exercised, they should. Rather, be mindful that in their present form, the rights are not as broad as they could be.

A second caveat is the limitation placed upon the right to prevent destruction, mutilation and modification of a work. This right is less about protecting the physical integrity of the artwork. Rather, it is concerned with injury to the artist's honor or reputation that might be caused by the destruction or involuntary alteration of a work. The right is only predicated on an injury to the artwork when it is deemed to be of "recognized stature." What does that mean? Generally, that the work has been publically recognized as important, perhaps articles have been written about it, or it has become renown in some way. Works that are determined (typically by a court in the context of a lawsuit) to not meet that level of recognition may not be protected from destruction, mutilation, or modification. There have been successful applications of the law though, notably in the recognition of the unlawful destruction of the 5Pointz complex in New York City.

There are other caveats. The provisions against destruction may not apply to works made before 1990 and there are limited practical options for an artist when an owner seeks to remove a work that is embedded in a part of a building. If a building owner wants to remove a work that is attached to the building, including works made after 1990, and this removal can be done without damage, then the owner is suppose to make a diligent and good faith effort to contact the artist. In theory, the artist can potentially preserve the work without damage, or pay for its removal, though cost could be prohibitive in some cases.

VARA is not an ideal solution for preserving art and the artist's interests, but it shows another good reason for keeping the artist's copyright contact information up to date. (See the earlier section on supplemental registration). Alternatively, the artist's information and address can be recorded with the Copyright Office for this purpose.

VARA rights are personal to the artist, meaning that only the artist can exercise them. An artist can elect to waive the rights as well, and permit the modification or destruction of a work. The rights cannot be enforced by any other person or organization. There are other exceptions to rights, specifically with regard to modifications made to the work. For example, natural processes due to time or degradation of the materials are excluded and not considered to be a destruction.

These rights are separate from copyrights and the artist's VARA rights exist even if the artist does not own the copyright to the work. VARA rights cease to exist when the artist does.

There is no registration process for VARA rights, they technically exist automatically to the extent that they apply to a given artwork or situation. These are really barebones rights for artists, and the limitations of VARA reflect a continuing need for the development of rights and a reasonable, affordable mechanism for enforcement. VARA is an important step for artist rights in the United States, but the limitations and the absence of a Federal art resale royalty law show that full artist rights have not yet been realized in the United States. Nonetheless, together with copyrights, the VARA provisions do provide the critical ability for artists to control their works, both in economic and moral rights contexts.

(a) Rights of **Attribution and Integrity**...the author of a work of visual art–

(1) shall have the right– (A) to claim authorship of that work, and (B) to prevent the use of his or her name as the author of any work of visual art which he or she did not create;

(2) shall have the right to prevent the use of his or her name as the author of the work of visual art in the event of a distortion, mutilation, or other modification of the work which would be prejudicial to his or her honor or reputation; and

(3) subject to the limitations...

(A) to prevent any intentional distortion, mutilation, or other modification of that work which would be prejudicial to his or her honor or reputation, and any intentional distortion, mutilation, or modification of that work is a violation of that right, and (B) to prevent any destruction of a work of recognized stature, and any intentional or grossly negligent destruction of that work is a violation of that right.

17 U.S.C. § 106A (excerpt)

APPENDIX

Resource & Contact Information

The United States Copyright Office
Library of Congress

www.copyright.gov

General Information

Telephone: **(202) 707-3000** or 1 **(877) 476-0778** (toll free)

8:30 am to 5:00 pm, Eastern Standard Time, Monday through Friday, except Federal holidays. Wait times may be significant during busy hours.

General Communications Address (not for service requests):

Library of Congress
Copyright Office
101 Independence Avenue, SE
Washington, DC 20559-6000

Questions about procedures, form selection, general copyright, eCO technical issues, and other matters via web form:

https://www.copyright.gov/help/

General information via email: copyinfo@loc.gov

For information by mail write to:

Library of Congress
U.S. Copyright Office
Publications Section
101 Independence Avenue, SE #6304
Washington, DC 20559-6304

Registration

Registration Portal: www.copyright.gov/registration

Electronic Copyright Office (eCO) registration system:

https://eservice.eco.loc.gov

or

www.copyright.gov > Registration (menu) > Register Your Work Registration Portal (link) > Log in to eCO (button link)

General mailing addresses for applications filed on paper and for hard-copy deposits (active 2021):

> Library of Congress
> U.S. Copyright Office
> 101 Independence Avenue SE
> Washington, DC 20559

Application Status Request:

> **https://www.copyright.gov/forms/status_form.html**
>
> Note: General status for eCO filed applications can be checked on your main registration page.

Registrations of Visual Art Works:

> Library of Congress
> Copyright Office-VA
> 101 Independence Avenue, SE
> Washington, DC 20559-6000

Registrations of Motion Pictures and Audiovisual Works:

> Library of Congress
> Copyright Office-MP
> 101 Independence Avenue, SE
> Washington, DC 20559-6000

Registrations of Performing Arts Works:

> Library of Congress
> Copyright Office-PA
> 101 Independence Avenue, SE
> Washington, DC 20559-6000

Registration of Sound Recordings:

> Library of Congress
> Copyright Office-SR
> 101 Independence Avenue, SE
> Washington, DC 20559-6000

Paper-based registration forms can be obtained online at:

> **https://www.copyright.gov/forms/**

Available forms include: Visual Art - Form VA, Performing Arts - Form PA, Literary Works - Form TX, Sound Recording - Form SR, Single Serials - Form SE, Serials Form SE/Group, Form CON

(continuation sheet for paper forms), Supplemental Copyright Registration Form CA, Forms for renewals (typically pre-1978 works), Special Handling Form

To request paper registration applications and circulars (guides on specific copyright topics), go to www.copyright.gov or call (202) 707-9100 or 1 (877) 476-0778 and leave a recorded message.

General mailing addresses for applications filed on paper:

Library of Congress
U.S. Copyright Office
101 Independence Avenue SE
Washington, DC 20559
(Active 2021; confirm the current address on your form and on www.copyright.gov)

Current fee information:

https://www.copyright.gov/about/fees.html

Deposit Issues

General mailing addresses for hard-copy deposits:

Library of Congress
U.S. Copyright Office
101 Independence Avenue SE
Washington, DC 20559
(Active 2021; confirm the current address on your shipping slip and on www.copyright.gov)

Alternative address for requesting special relief:

Associate Register of Copyrights and Director
of Registration Policy & Practice
U.S. Copyright Office
P.O. Box 70400
Washington, DC 20024-0400

To request an alterative form of deposit or other issues involving the registration of *a motion picture* only, call to inquire about the provisions of the Motion Picture Agreement procedures at (202) 707-8572 or write to:

Library of Congress
Motion Picture, Broadcasting, and Recorded Sound Division
Attn: Reference Assistant
101 Independence Avenue SE
Washington, D.C. 20540

Requests for Reconsideration

The envelope containing the materials should indicate whether it is a first or second appeal of a refusal to register.

[FIRST/SECOND] REQUEST FOR RECONSIDERATION
U.S. Copyright Office
RAC Division
P.O. Box 71380
Washington, DC 20024-1380

Note: In 2020, in response to the national emergency, the Copyright Office established an alternative procedure whereby a request for reconsideration may be emailed to copreviewboard@copyright.gov. Contact the Copyright Office to confirm if this process continues to be available and for further instructions.

Mandatory Deposit Program (not for copyright registration):

Submit mandatory deposit materials to:

Library of Congress
U.S. Copyright Office
Attn: 407 Deposits
101 Independence Avenue, SE
Washington, D.C. 20559

Replies to demands for a deposit (excluding serials) are addressed to:

Library of Congress
Copyright Office-CAD/AD
101 Independence Avenue, SE
Washington, DC 20559-6601

To request special relief from the mandatory deposit rule, write to:

Associate Register of Copyrights and
Director of Registration Policy and Practice
U.S. Copyright Office
P.O. Box 70400
Washington, DC 20024-0440

Inquiries may also be made through the general information numbers. State that you have a question specifically about "mandatory deposit."

Technical Issues

Telephone (877) 476-0778 toll free or (202) 707-3002
(Monday through Friday from 8:00 AM to 8:00 EST)

Email: ctoinfo@loc.gov.

Note: The contacts above are designated for technical issues only.

Other Services

Deposit Account information: How to Open and Maintain a Copyright Office Deposit Account for payment of fees (Circular 5), available at https://www.copyright.gov/circs/circ05.pdf

Licensing Division inquiries:

> Library of Congress
> Copyright Office-LD
> 101 Independence Avenue, SE
> Washington, DC 20559-6000

Freedom of Information Act (FOIA) requests: Copyright Office, P.O. Box 70400, Washington, DC 20024. FOIA appeals (refused requests): General Counsel of the United States, Copyright Office, Copyright GC/I&R, P.O. Box 70400, Washington, DC 20024.

Special Handling (expedited processing matters):

> Copyright Office
> RAC Division
> P.O. Box 71380
> Washington, DC 20024-1380

Time Sensitive Requests (certain requests for expedited services due to lawsuits, customs matters, publishing deadlines, etc.):

> Copyright Office
> P.O. Box 70400
> Washington, DC 20024-0400

Visiting the Library of Congress

Information: (202) 707-8000 or email veo@loc.gov

Library of Congress
James Madison Memorial Building
101 Independence Avenue, SE
Washington, D.C. 20540

James Madison Building: Prints & Photographs Reading Room, Motion Picture & Television reading Room, Performing Arts reading room, Copyright Public Records Reading Room, Copyright Information room

Library of Congress
Thomas Jefferson Building
10 First Street SE
Washington, DC 20540

Thomas Jefferson Building: Graphic Arts Galleries, American Folklife Center Reading Room, Asian Reading Room, African & Middle Eastern Reading room, Hispanic Reading Room, European Reading Room, Rare Books, Microform & Electronic Resource Center

Library of Congress
John Adams Building
2nd Street SE
Washington, DC 20540

Registration Fees & Other Service Charges

Electronic Copyright Claim Registration (Current January 2021)	
Standard Application	$65
Single Application, *One Work By One Author*	$45
Group registration applications	
Group of *unpublished* works (2 to 10 works per application)	$85
Group of *unpublished* photographs (2 to 750 per application)	$55
Group of *published* photographs (2 to 750 per application)	$55
Group of serials (certain publications), per issue, with minimum of 2 issues filed	$35
Group of newspapers or newsletter issues	$95
Group of contributions to periodicals	$85
Group of short online literary works	$65
Paper Based Registration Applications *Fees are subject to change; confirm the correct current fee at Copyright.gov or by calling the Copyright Office before mailing your registration materials.*	
Applications filed on Form VA, Form PA, Form TX, Form SE, or Form SR (one work, one claim per form)	$125

Other Registration Related Fees

Supplementary registration to correct or amplify a completed registration (electronic filing only)	$100
Preregistration of certain unpublished works	$200

Other Fees

Special handling fee, per claim, to expedite processing of qualified claims	$800
Additional fee for each non-special-handling claim using the same deposit as the expedited claim	$50
Additional copy of certificate of copyright registration (licensing division service)	$55
Appeals for denied claims, *first* request per claim (request for reconsideration after refusal to register claim)	$350
Second appeal, per claim	$700
Handling fee for extra deposit copy for certification	$50
Charge for **overdraft** of (financial) deposit account; charge for dishonored deposit account replenishment check	$285; $500
Uncollectible personal check or other non-negotiable payment	$115
Voluntary cancellation of registration	$150
Copying of Copyright Office records by staff	$12
Service charge for delivery of documents via **fax**, per page, 7 page max	$1
Service charge for Federal Express mailing	$45

The fees listed here are current as of January 2021, but be advised that Copyright Office fees are subject to change. The submission of an incorrect fee may cause a delay or additional expense and may be not be refunded. Always confirm the correct current fee on the Copyright.gov website or contact the Copyright Office directly, especially for the non-electronic processes. Information on current fees and for other fees not listed here can be found on the Copyright Office website at https://www.copyright.gov/about/fees.html.

Overview of Registration Application Options

This chart shows an overview of the main application choices for works of visual art and some related types of work, organized according to the type of work or media to be registered. Each application for has requirements or restrictions for use.

Type of Work	Paper application form	Online application (eCO) options
Visual Art A single 2-D or 3-D artwork (pictorial, graphic, or sculptural works)	Form VA	Standard Application One Work By One Author/Single Application (with eligibility requirements)
One photograph	Form VA	Standard Application One Work By One Author/Single Application (with eligibility requirements)
Multiple photographs, up to 750	Not available	Group of Photographs application (with eligibility requirements; all photographs in one registration group must be published, or all must be unpublished).
Group of unpublished works, up to 10 of the same type, including **Visual Art** or other works	Not available	Group of Unpublished Works application (GRUW) (with eligibility requirements)
One motion picture, audio-visual work, video, film, animation, video games, etc.	Form PA (performing arts) or Form SR (sound recordings)	Standard Application One Work By One Author/Single Application (with eligibility requirements)

A group of ***unpublished* motion pictures**, audiovisual works, videos, films, animation works, video games, etc., up to 10 works of the same type.	Not available	Group of Unpublished Works application (eligibility requirements)
A literary work, such as a writing, fiction, non-fiction, poem, article, and some types of online text content	Form TX (literary work) or Form SE (serial publications)	Standard Application One Work By One Author/Single Application (with eligibility requirements) *Also see short online published literary works option*
Multiple **unpublished literary works**, such as writings, fiction, non-fiction, poetry, articles, periodicals, up to 10 works of the same type.	Not available.	Group of Unpublished Works application (eligibility requirements) *Also see short online published literary works option below*
One computer based work, or an audio-visual type work or other related type of work	Form TX (textual works, e.g., computer programs, original source code, data-bases, blog writing), or Form PA (banner advertisements, video games, videos, audiovisual works)	Standard Application or One Work By One Author / Single application (eligibility requirements)

Multiple unpublished computer based, or an audio-visual type work or other related type of work, up to 10 of the same type	Not available	Group of Unpublished Works application (eligibility requirements)
One multimedia work; a work that is composed of multiple media forms	*Refer to the category of the dominant media*	*Registration form selection is primarily based upon the dominant authorship of the work. Refer to the category of the dominant media.*
A Sound/Audio recording	Form SR	Standard Application or One Work By One Author / Single application (eligibility requirements)
Multiple **unpublished Sound/Audio recordings**, up to 10 of the same type	Not available	Group of Unpublished Works application (eligibility requirements)
One work of Performing Arts (musical works, lyrics, a song, scripts, stage plays, dramatic work, choreographic works, interviews, spoken word/vocal performance, sound effects, teleplays, broadcasts, etc.)	Form PA	Standard Application or One Work By One Author / Single application (eligibility requirements)
Multiple **unpublished performing arts works**, up to 10 of the same type	Not available	Group of Unpublished Works application (with eligibility requirements)

Contribution to a **periodical**; an individual issue of a serial	Form SE (for a serial public-cation only–*do not* use for individual contributions)	"Certain Groups of Published Works" online option (with eligibility requirements)
Short online published literary works, text only, (blog entries, social media postings, and short online articles) up to 50 works of the same type. *No visual works, photos or illustrations are covered by this form. Emails, podcasts, audiobooks, computer programs are not eligible.*	Not available	"Certain Groups of Published Works" option with Group Registration for Short Online Literary Works (GRTX) as the type of work (eligibility requirements)
Continuation Paper (when additional space is needed on a paper form)	Form Con	Not applicable

2021

The chart above shows selected types of work related to visual art, or those that may serve as comparisons. Other types of work not listed here may also qualify for copyright registration.

Form VA, Form PA, and Form TX

Copies of the paper forms illustrated here and other registration forms, along with instructions for each form, can be accessed at https://www.copyright.gov/forms/.

Form VA for registering a single work of visual art

Copyright Office fees are subject to change. For current fees, check the Copyright Office website at *www.copyright.gov*, write the Copyright Office, or call (202) 707-3000 or 1-877-476-0778 (toll free).

Form VA
For a Work of the Visual Arts
UNITED STATES COPYRIGHT OFFICE

REGISTRATION NUMBER

VA VAU

EFFECTIVE DATE OF REGISTRATION

Month Day Year

Privacy Act Notice: Sections 408-410 of title 17 of the *United States Code* authorize the Copyright Office to collect the personally identifying information requested on this form in order to process the application for copyright registration. By providing this information you are agreeing to routine uses of the information that include publication to give legal notice of your copyright claim as required by 17 U.S.C. §705. It will appear in the Office's online catalog. If you do not provide the information requested, registration may be refused or delayed, and you may not be entitled to certain relief, remedies, and benefits under the copyright law.

DO NOT WRITE ABOVE THIS LINE. IF YOU NEED MORE SPACE, USE A SEPARATE CONTINUATION SHEET.

1

TITLE OF THIS WORK ▼

NATURE OF THIS WORK ▼ See instructions

PREVIOUS OR ALTERNATIVE TITLES ▼

PUBLICATION AS A CONTRIBUTION If this work was published as a contribution to a periodical, serial, or collection, give information about the collective work in which the contribution appeared. **Title of Collective Work** ▼

If published in a periodical or serial give: **Volume** ▼ **Number** ▼ **Issue Date** ▼ **On Pages** ▼

2 a

NAME OF AUTHOR ▼

DATES OF BIRTH AND DEATH
Year Born ▼ Year Died ▼

WAS THIS CONTRIBUTION TO THE WORK A "WORK MADE FOR HIRE"?
☐ Yes
☐ No

AUTHOR'S NATIONALITY OR DOMICILE
Name of Country
OR { Citizen of ______
Domiciled in ______

WAS THIS AUTHOR'S CONTRIBUTION TO THE WORK
Anonymous? ☐ Yes ☐ No
Pseudonymous? ☐ Yes ☐ No
If the answer to either of these questions is "Yes," see detailed instructions.

NATURE OF AUTHORSHIP Check appropriate box(es). **See instructions**
☐ 3-Dimensional sculpture ☐ Map ☐ Technical drawing
☐ 2-Dimensional artwork ☐ Photograph ☐ Text
☐ Reproduction of work of art ☐ Jewelry design

NOTE
Under the law, the "author" of a "work made for hire" is generally the employer, not the employee (see instructions). For any part of this work that was "made for hire," check "Yes" in the space provided, give the employer (or other person for whom the work was prepared) as "Author" of that part, and leave the space for dates of birth and death blank.

b

NAME OF AUTHOR ▼

DATES OF BIRTH AND DEATH
Year Born ▼ Year Died ▼

WAS THIS CONTRIBUTION TO THE WORK A "WORK MADE FOR HIRE"?
☐ Yes
☐ No

AUTHOR'S NATIONALITY OR DOMICILE
Name of Country
OR { Citizen of ______
Domiciled in ______

WAS THIS AUTHOR'S CONTRIBUTION TO THE WORK
Anonymous? ☐ Yes ☐ No
Pseudonymous? ☐ Yes ☐ No
If the answer to either of these questions is "Yes," see detailed instructions.

NATURE OF AUTHORSHIP Check appropriate box(es). **See instructions**
☐ 3-Dimensional sculpture ☐ Map ☐ Technical drawing
☐ 2-Dimensional artwork ☐ Photograph ☐ Text
☐ Reproduction of work of art ☐ Jewelry design

3 a

YEAR IN WHICH CREATION OF THIS WORK WAS COMPLETED
Year ▶ ______
This information must be given in all cases.

b

DATE AND NATION OF FIRST PUBLICATION OF THIS PARTICULAR WORK
Complete this information ONLY if this work has been published.
Month ▶ ______ Day ▶ ______ Year ▶ ______
Nation ▶ ______

4

COPYRIGHT CLAIMANT(S) Name and address must be given even if the claimant is the same as the author given in space 2. ▼

See instructions before completing this space.

TRANSFER If the claimant(s) named here in space 4 is (are) different from the author(s) named in space 2, give a brief statement of how the claimant(s) obtained ownership of the copyright. ▼

DO NOT WRITE HERE
OFFICE USE ONLY

APPLICATION RECEIVED

ONE DEPOSIT RECEIVED

TWO DEPOSITS RECEIVED

FUNDS RECEIVED

MORE ON BACK ▶
• Complete all applicable spaces (numbers 5-9) on the reverse side of this page.
• See detailed instructions.
• Sign the form at line 8.

DO NOT WRITE HERE

Page 1 of ______ pages

Form VA page 2

EXAMINED BY

FORM VA

CHECKED BY

CORRESPONDENCE

❑ Yes

FOR COPYRIGHT OFFICE USE ONLY

DO NOT WRITE ABOVE THIS LINE. IF YOU NEED MORE SPACE, USE A SEPARATE CONTINUATION SHEET.

5

PREVIOUS REGISTRATION Has registration for this work, or for an earlier version of this work, already been made in the Copyright Office?

❑ **Yes** ❑ **No** If your answer is "Yes," why is another registration being sought? (Check appropriate box.) ▼

a. ❑ This is the first published edition of a work previously registered in unpublished form.

b. ❑ This is the first application submitted by this author as copyright claimant.

c. ❑ This is a changed version of the work, as shown by space 6 on this application.

If your answer is "Yes," give: **Previous Registration Number ▼** **Year of Registration ▼**

6

DERIVATIVE WORK OR COMPILATION Complete both space 6a and 6b for a derivative work; complete only 6b for a compilation.

a. Preexisting Material Identify any preexisting work or works that this work is based on or incorporates. ▼

a

See instructions before completing this space

b. Material Added to This Work Give a brief, general statement of the material that has been added to this work and in which copyright is claimed. ▼

b

7

DEPOSIT ACCOUNT If the registration fee is to be charged to a Deposit Account established in the Copyright Office, give name and number of Account.

Name ▼ **Account Number ▼**

a

CORRESPONDENCE Give name and address to which correspondence about this application should be sent. Name/Address/Apt/City/State/Zip ▼

b

Area code and daytime telephone number ( ) Fax number ( )

Email

8

CERTIFICATION* I, the undersigned, hereby certify that I am the

check only one ▶

❑ author

❑ other copyright claimant

❑ owner of exclusive right(s)

❑ authorized agent of ______________

Name of author or other copyright claimant, or owner of exclusive right(s) ▲

of the work identified in this application and that the statements made by me in this application are correct to the best of my knowledge.

Typed or printed name and date ▼ If this application gives a date of publication in space 3, do not sign and submit it before that date.

Date ______________

Signature (X) ▼

X ______________

9

Certificate will be mailed in window envelope to this address:

Name ▼

Number/Street/Apt ▼

City/State/Zip ▼

YOU MUST:

- Complete all necessary spaces
- Sign your application in space 8

SEND ALL 3 ELEMENTS IN THE SAME PACKAGE:

1. Application form
2. Nonrefundable filing fee in check or money order payable to *U.S. Copyright Office*
3. Deposit material

MAIL TO:

Library of Congress
U.S. Copyright Office-VA
101 Independence Avenue SE
Washington, DC 20559-6000

*17 U.S.C. §506(e): Any person who knowingly makes a false representation of a material fact in the application for copyright registration provided for by section 409, or in any written statement filed in connection with the application, shall be fined not more than $2,500.

Form VA- Full Rev: 05/2019 Printed on recycled paper

Form PA for registering a work of performing arts, including a motion picture or other audiovisual work.

Copyright Office fees are subject to change. For current fees, check the Copyright Office website at www.copyright.gov, write the Copyright Office, or call (202) 707-3000 or 1-877-476-0778 (toll free).

Form PA
For a Work of Performing Arts
UNITED STATES COPYRIGHT OFFICE

REGISTRATION NUMBER

PA PAU

EFFECTIVE DATE OF REGISTRATION

Month Day Year

Privacy Act Notice: Sections 408-410 of title 17 of the *United States Code* authorize the Copyright Office to collect the personally identifying information requested on this form in order to process the application for copyright registration. By providing this information you are agreeing to routine uses of the information that include publication to give legal notice of your copyright claim as required by 17 U.S.C. §705. It will appear in the Office's online catalog. If you do not provide the information requested, registration may be refused or delayed, and you may not be entitled to certain relief, remedies, and benefits under the copyright law.

DO NOT WRITE ABOVE THIS LINE. IF YOU NEED MORE SPACE, USE A SEPARATE CONTINUATION SHEET.

1

TITLE OF THIS WORK ▼

PREVIOUS OR ALTERNATIVE TITLES ▼

NATURE OF THIS WORK ▼ See instructions

2

a NAME OF AUTHOR ▼

DATES OF BIRTH AND DEATH
Year Born ▼ Year Died ▼

Was this contribution to the work a "work made for hire"?
❑ Yes
❑ No

AUTHOR'S NATIONALITY OR DOMICILE
Name of Country
OR { Citizen of ________ / Domiciled in ________

WAS THIS AUTHOR'S CONTRIBUTION TO THE WORK
Anonymous? ❑ Yes ❑ No
Pseudonymous? ❑ Yes ❑ No
If the answer to either of these questions is "Yes," see detailed instructions.

NATURE OF AUTHORSHIP Briefly describe nature of material created by this author in which copyright is claimed. ▼

NOTE
Under the law, the "author" of a "work made for hire" is generally the employer, not the employee (see instructions). For any part of this work that was "made for hire" check "Yes" in the space provided, give the employer (or other person for whom the work was prepared) as "Author" of that part, and leave the space for dates of birth and death blank.

b NAME OF AUTHOR ▼

DATES OF BIRTH AND DEATH
Year Born ▼ Year Died ▼

Was this contribution to the work a "work made for hire"?
❑ Yes
❑ No

AUTHOR'S NATIONALITY OR DOMICILE
Name of Country
OR { Citizen of ________ / Domiciled in ________

WAS THIS AUTHOR'S CONTRIBUTION TO THE WORK
Anonymous? ❑ Yes ❑ No
Pseudonymous? ❑ Yes ❑ No
If the answer to either of these questions is "Yes," see detailed instructions.

NATURE OF AUTHORSHIP Briefly describe nature of material created by this author in which copyright is claimed. ▼

c NAME OF AUTHOR ▼

DATES OF BIRTH AND DEATH
Year Born ▼ Year Died ▼

Was this contribution to the work a "work made for hire"?
❑ Yes
❑ No

AUTHOR'S NATIONALITY OR DOMICILE
Name of Country
OR { Citizen of ________ / Domiciled in ________

WAS THIS AUTHOR'S CONTRIBUTION TO THE WORK
Anonymous? ❑ Yes ❑ No
Pseudonymous? ❑ Yes ❑ No
If the answer to either of these questions is "Yes," see detailed instructions.

NATURE OF AUTHORSHIP Briefly describe nature of material created by this author in which copyright is claimed. ▼

3

a YEAR IN WHICH CREATION OF THIS WORK WAS COMPLETED **This information must be given in all cases.** ________ Year

b DATE AND NATION OF FIRST PUBLICATION OF THIS PARTICULAR WORK **Complete this information ONLY if this work has been published.** Month ________ Day ________ Year ________ ________ Nation

4

See instructions before completing this space

COPYRIGHT CLAIMANT(S) Name and address must be given even if the claimant is the same as the author given in space 2. ▼

TRANSFER If the claimant(s) named here in space 4 is (are) different from the author(s) named in space 2, give a brief statement of how the claimant(s) obtained ownership of the copyright. ▼

DO NOT WRITE HERE
OFFICE USE ONLY

APPLICATION RECEIVED

ONE DEPOSIT RECEIVED

TWO DEPOSITS RECEIVED

FUNDS RECEIVED

MORE ON BACK ▶
• Complete all applicable spaces (numbers 5-9) on the reverse side of this page.
• See detailed instructions.
• Sign the form at line 8.

DO NOT WRITE HERE

Page 1 of ________ pages

Form PA, page 2

EXAMINED BY

FORM PA

CHECKED BY

CORRESPONDENCE

☐ Yes

FOR COPYRIGHT OFFICE USE ONLY

DO NOT WRITE ABOVE THIS LINE. IF YOU NEED MORE SPACE, USE A SEPARATE CONTINUATION SHEET.

5

PREVIOUS REGISTRATION Has registration for this work, or for an earlier version of this work, already been made in the Copyright Office?

☐ **Yes** ☐ **No** If your answer is "Yes," why is another registration being sought? (Check appropriate box.) ▼ If your answer is No, do **not** check box A, B, or C.

a. ☐ This is the first published edition of a work previously registered in unpublished form.

b. ☐ This is the first application submitted by this author as copyright claimant.

c. ☐ This is a changed version of the work, as shown by space 6 on this application.

If your answer is "Yes," give **Previous Registration Number** ▼ **Year of Registration** ▼

6

DERIVATIVE WORK OR COMPILATION Complete both space 6a and 6b for a derivative work; complete only 6b for a compilation.

a **Preexisting Material** Identify any preexisting work or works that this work is based on or incorporates. ▼

See instructions before completing this space

b **Material Added to This Work** Give a brief, general statement of the material that has been added to this work and in which copyright is claimed. ▼

7

a **DEPOSIT ACCOUNT** If the registration fee is to be charged to a Deposit Account established in the Copyright Office, give name and number of Account.

Name ▼ **Account Number** ▼

b **CORRESPONDENCE** Give name and address to which correspondence about this application should be sent. Name / Address / Apt / City / State / Zip ▼

Area code and daytime telephone number ( ) Fax number ( )

Email

8

CERTIFICATION* I, the undersigned, hereby certify that I am the

Check only one ▶

- ☐ author
- ☐ other copyright claimant
- ☐ owner of exclusive right(s)
- ☐ authorized agent of ______

Name of author or other copyright claimant, or owner of exclusive right(s) ▲

of the work identified in this application and that the statements made by me in this application are correct to the best of my knowledge.

Typed or printed name and date ▼ If this application gives a date of publication in space 3, do not sign and submit it before that date.

Date ______

Signature (X) ▼

X ______

9

Certificate will be mailed in window envelope to this address:

Name ▼

Number/Street/Apt ▼

City/State/Zip ▼

YOU MUST:
- Complete all necessary spaces
- Sign your application in space 8

SEND ALL 3 ELEMENTS IN THE SAME PACKAGE:
1. Application form
2. Nonrefundable filing fee in check or money order payable to *U.S. Copyright Office*
3. Deposit material

MAIL TO:
Library of Congress
Copyright Office-PA
101 Independence Avenue SE
Washington, DC 20559-6000

*17 U.S.C. §506(e): Any person who knowingly makes a false representation of a material fact in the application for copyright registration provided for by section 409, or in any written statement filed in connection with the application, shall be fined not more than $2,500

Form PA—Full Printed: 05/2019 Printed on recycled paper

Form TX for registering a textual work.

Copyright Office fees are subject to change. For current fees, check the Copyright Office website at *www.copyright.gov*, write the Copyright Office, or call (202) 707-3000.

Form TX
For a Nondramatic Literary Work
UNITED STATES COPYRIGHT OFFICE

REGISTRATION NUMBER

TX TXU

EFFECTIVE DATE OF REGISTRATION

Month Day Year

Privacy Act Notice: Sections 408-410 of title 17 of the *United States Code* authorize the Copyright Office to collect the personally identifying information requested on this form in order to process the application for copyright registration. By providing this information you are agreeing to routine uses of the information that include publication to give legal notice of your copyright claim as required by 17 U.S.C. §705. It will appear in the Office's online catalog. If you do not provide the information requested, registration may be refused or delayed, and you may not be entitled to certain relief, remedies, and benefits under the copyright law.

DO NOT WRITE ABOVE THIS LINE. IF YOU NEED MORE SPACE, USE A SEPARATE CONTINUATION SHEET.

1

TITLE OF THIS WORK ▼

PREVIOUS OR ALTERNATIVE TITLES ▼

PUBLICATION AS A CONTRIBUTION If this work was published as a contribution to a periodical, serial, or collection, give information about the collective work in which the contribution appeared. **Title of Collective Work ▼**

If published in a periodical or serial give: **Volume ▼** **Number ▼** **Issue Date ▼** **On Pages ▼**

2 a

NAME OF AUTHOR ▼

DATES OF BIRTH AND DEATH
Year Born ▼ Year Died ▼

Was this contribution to the work a "work made for hire"?
❏ Yes
❏ No

AUTHOR'S NATIONALITY OR DOMICILE
Name of Country
OR { Citizen of ______ / Domiciled in ______

WAS THIS AUTHOR'S CONTRIBUTION TO THE WORK
Anonymous? ❏ Yes ❏ No
Pseudonymous? ❏ Yes ❏ No
If the answer to either of these questions is "Yes," see detailed instructions.

NATURE OF AUTHORSHIP Briefly describe nature of material created by this author in which copyright is claimed. ▼

NOTE
Under the law, the "author" of a "work made for hire" is generally the employer, not the employee (see instructions). For any part of this work that was "made for hire" check "Yes" in the space provided, give the employer (or other person for whom the work was prepared) as "Author" of that part, and leave the space for dates of birth and death blank.

b

NAME OF AUTHOR ▼

DATES OF BIRTH AND DEATH
Year Born ▼ Year Died ▼

Was this contribution to the work a "work made for hire"?
❏ Yes
❏ No

AUTHOR'S NATIONALITY OR DOMICILE
Name of Country
OR { Citizen of ______ / Domiciled in ______

WAS THIS AUTHOR'S CONTRIBUTION TO THE WORK
Anonymous? ❏ Yes ❏ No
Pseudonymous? ❏ Yes ❏ No
If the answer to either of these questions is "Yes," see detailed instructions.

NATURE OF AUTHORSHIP Briefly describe nature of material created by this author in which copyright is claimed. ▼

c

NAME OF AUTHOR ▼

DATES OF BIRTH AND DEATH
Year Born ▼ Year Died ▼

Was this contribution to the work a "work made for hire"?
❏ Yes
❏ No

AUTHOR'S NATIONALITY OR DOMICILE
Name of Country
OR { Citizen of ______ / Domiciled in ______

WAS THIS AUTHOR'S CONTRIBUTION TO THE WORK
Anonymous? ❏ Yes ❏ No
Pseudonymous? ❏ Yes ❏ No
If the answer to either of these questions is "Yes," see detailed instructions.

NATURE OF AUTHORSHIP Briefly describe nature of material created by this author in which copyright is claimed. ▼

3 a

YEAR IN WHICH CREATION OF THIS WORK WAS COMPLETED **This information must be given in all cases.**
______ Year

b

DATE AND NATION OF FIRST PUBLICATION OF THIS PARTICULAR WORK
Complete this information ONLY if this work has been published.
Month ______ Day ______ Year ______
______ Nation

4

See instructions before completing this space.

COPYRIGHT CLAIMANT(S) Name and address must be given even if the claimant is the same as the author given in space 2. ▼

TRANSFER If the claimant(s) named here in space 4 is (are) different from the author(s) named in space 2, give a brief statement of how the claimant(s) obtained ownership of the copyright. ▼

DO NOT WRITE HERE
OFFICE USE ONLY

APPLICATION RECEIVED

ONE DEPOSIT RECEIVED

TWO DEPOSITS RECEIVED

FUNDS RECEIVED

MORE ON BACK ▶
- Complete all applicable spaces (numbers 5-9) on the reverse side of this page.
- See detailed instructions.
- Sign the form at line 8.

DO NOT WRITE HERE

Page 1 of ______ pages

Form TX, page 2

EXAMINED BY

FORM TX

CHECKED BY

☐ CORRESPONDENCE Yes

FOR COPYRIGHT OFFICE USE ONLY

DO NOT WRITE ABOVE THIS LINE. IF YOU NEED MORE SPACE, USE A SEPARATE CONTINUATION SHEET.

5

PREVIOUS REGISTRATION Has registration for this work, or for an earlier version of this work, already been made in the Copyright Office?

☐ **Yes** ☐ **No** If your answer is "Yes," why is another registration being sought? (Check appropriate box.) ▼

a. ☐ This is the first published edition of a work previously registered in unpublished form.

b. ☐ This is the first application submitted by this author as copyright claimant.

c. ☐ This is a changed version of the work, as shown by space 6 on this application.

If your answer is "Yes," give: **Previous Registration Number** ▶ **Year of Registration** ▶

6

DERIVATIVE WORK OR COMPILATION

a **Preexisting Material** Identify any preexisting work or works that this work is based on or incorporates. ▼

See instructions before completing this space.

b **Material Added to This Work** Give a brief, general statement of the material that has been added to this work and in which copyright is claimed. ▼

7

a **DEPOSIT ACCOUNT** If the registration fee is to be charged to a deposit account established in the Copyright Office, give name and number of account.

Name ▼ **Account Number** ▼

b **CORRESPONDENCE** Give name and address to which correspondence about this application should be sent. Name / Address / Apt / City / State / Zip ▼

Area code and daytime telephone number ▶ Fax number ▶

Email ▶

8

CERTIFICATION* I, the undersigned, hereby certify that I am the

Check only one ▶

☐ author

☐ other copyright claimant

☐ owner of exclusive right(s)

☐ authorized agent of

Name of author or other copyright claimant, or owner of exclusive right(s) ▲

of the work identified in this application and that the statements made by me in this application are correct to the best of my knowledge.

Typed or printed name and date ▼ If this application gives a date of publication in space 3, do not sign and submit it before that date.

Date ▶

Signature ▼

9

Certificate will be mailed in window envelope to this address:

Name ▼

Number/Street/Apt ▼

City/State/Zip ▼

YOU MUST:

- Complete all necessary spaces
- Sign your application in space 8

SEND ALL 3 ELEMENTS IN THE SAME PACKAGE:

1. Application form
2. Nonrefundable filing fee in check or money order payable to *U.S. Copyright Office*
3. Deposit material

MAIL TO:

Library of Congress
Copyright Office-TX
101 Independence Avenue SE
Washington, DC 20559-6000

*17 U.S.C. §506(e): Any person who knowingly makes a false representation of a material fact in the application for copyright registration provided for by section 409, or in any written statement filed in connection with the application, shall be fined not more than $2,500.

Form TX - Full Reviewed: 05/2019 Printed on recycled paper

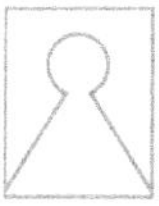

About the Author

Jennifer Unruh has extensive experience in the art world and firsthand knowledge of an artist's experience. As a lawyer and advocate she has worked directly with artists and related organizations. She supports the progress of artists' rights, the goal of genuine diversity, and the need for reliable economic aid for the arts. She lives in New York City.

Made in the USA
Monee, IL
04 November 2026

67384618R00154